Beyond Edge Computing

Ana Juan Ferrer

Beyond Edge Computing

Swarm Computing and Ad-Hoc Edge Clouds

 Springer

Ana Juan Ferrer
Barcelona, Spain

ISBN 978-3-031-23343-2   ISBN 978-3-031-23344-9   (eBook)
https://doi.org/10.1007/978-3-031-23344-9

This Springer imprint is published by the registered company Springer Nature Switzerland AG
The registered company address is: Gewerbestrasse 11, 6330 Cham, Switzerland

This book is dedicated to Jordi, whom I could never thank enough for his unconditional support, insuperable common sense, and constant encouragement.

Disclaimer

Opinions expressed in this book belong solely to the author and should not be considered as representative to the author's employer opinions, or opinions of other groups or individuals.

Contents

1   Introduction 1
   1.1   Motivation 1
   1.2   Swarm Computing and Ah-hoc Edge Clouds 3
   1.3   Book Organisation 5
   References.. 8

Part I   Current Status of Computing at the Cloud and Network Edges
   References.. 10

2   Setting the Scene: Cloud, Edge, Mobile and Ad-hoc Computing Context.. 13
   2.1   Cloud, Edge, Mobile and Ad-hoc Computing Relations 13
   2.2   Decentralisation of Cloud Computing.............................. 16
   2.3   Edge and Fog Computing Terminology 19
   References.. 19

3   Cloud Computing... 21
   3.1   Introduction to Cloud Computing 21
   3.2   Basic Definitions, Benefits and Drawbacks 22
   3.3   Cloud Foundations 25
         3.3.1   Virtualisation and Containerisation Technologies 25
         3.3.2   Cloud Native Software Architectures..................... 28
   3.4   Services in Public Clouds 29
         3.4.1   Infrastructure-as-a-Service (IaaS)........................ 29
         3.4.2   Platform-as-a-Service (PaaS) 31
   3.5   Hybrid and Multi-Cloud Management 37
   References.. 39

4   Mobile Cloud Computing.. 43
   4.1   Introduction to Mobile Cloud Computing 43
   4.2   MCC Challenges 44

4.2.1   Inherent Mobile Devices Challenges 44
4.2.2   Network Connectivity 45
4.2.3   Security 46
4.2.4   Off-Loading and Application Partitioning................. 46
4.3   MCC Models 47
4.4   Analysis of Existing Works in MCC 48
4.4.1   Approaches Based on Off-Loading to a Server 49
4.4.2   Approaches Based on Off-Loading to
          Public/Private Cloud Computing 50
4.4.3   Approaches Based on Off-Loading to Cloudlets.......... 52
4.4.4   Approaches Based on Off-Loading to Other
          Mobile Devices 54
4.4.5   Features Comparison 56
References... 58

5   Mobile Ad-hoc Cloud Computing 61
5.1   Introduction to Mobile Ad-hoc Cloud Computing (MAC)......... 61
5.2   MAC Challenges 62
5.3   MAC Models 64
5.4   Analysis of Existing Works in MAC 65
5.4.1   Dynamic Mobile Cloud Computing: Ad Hoc
          and Opportunistic Job Sharing 65
5.4.2   MoCCA, A Mobile Cellular Cloud Architecture 66
5.4.3   Ad-hoc Cloud as a Service 67
5.4.4   MobiCloud 67
5.4.5   mClouds... 68
5.4.6   Aura 68
5.5   Features Comparison... 69
References... 70

6   Edge and Fog Computing... 73
6.1   Computing Perspective, Edge and Cloud 73
6.1.1   Edge Computing Challenges 74
6.1.2   Edge Computing Models..................................... 78
6.1.3   Existing Works in Research 80
6.1.4   Existing Products in the Market 83
6.1.5   Existing Open-Source Initiatives 84
6.1.6   Features Comparison 88
6.2   Mobile Edge Computing and Networking Perspectives............ 90
6.2.1   ETSI Multi-Access Edge Computing Framework
          and Reference Architecture 92
6.2.2   Existing Products in the Market 93
6.2.3   Conclusions 95
References... 96

7   Additional Technologies for Swarm Development 101
   7.1   Security Requirements for Computing at the Edge 101
   7.2   The Role for P2P and Consensus Algorithms 102
   References 104

Part II   Computing Beyond the Edge: Swarm Computing and
**   Ad-hoc Edge Architectures**
   References 109

8   Computing Beyond Edge: The Swarm Computing Concept 111
   8.1   Overview 111
   8.2   Foreseen Evolution Towards Swarm Computing 112
   8.3   Definition of Ad-hoc Edge Clouds, the Swarm
       Computing Concept 114
   8.4   Swarm Computing Characteristics and Principles 116
       8.4.1   Swarm Characteristics 116
       8.4.2   Key Principles 117
   8.5   Ad-hoc Edge Cloud Resources Characteristics 119
   8.6   Lifecycle of a Swarm 122
   8.7   Swarm Computing Motivational Use Cases 125
   References 127

9   Building Blocks for Ad-hoc Edge Clouds 131
   9.1   Introduction 131
   9.2   Ad-hoc Edge Cloud Framework 132
       9.2.1   Edge Device Context 134
       9.2.2   Ad-hoc Edge Context 135
       9.2.3   Ad-hoc Edge Cloud Architecture Flow of Events 137
       9.2.4   Conclusions 138
   References 139

10   Cognitive Resource Management in Ad-hoc Edge Clouds 141
   10.1   Overview 141
   10.2   IoT Device Availability Protocol 142
       10.2.1   Publication 142
       10.2.2   Registration 144
       10.2.3   Select 145
       10.2.4   Use 145
       10.2.5   Release 145
       10.2.6   Un-register 146
   10.3   Ad-hoc Edge Cluster Instantiation and Management 146
       10.3.1   Ad-hoc Edge Cluster Instantiation 147
       10.3.2   Ad-hoc Edge Cluster Management 148

     10.4   Evaluation 152
           10.4.1   Lab Evaluation 152
           10.4.2   Large Scale Evaluation in AWS EC2 156
     10.5   Conclusions.. 159
     References... 161

11 **Service Placement and Management** 163
     11.1   Overview.. 163
           11.1.1   Admission Control in Service Lifecycle of
                     Ad-hoc Edge Infrastructure 164
     11.2   Ad-hoc Edge Service Model... 165
     11.3   Admission Control Mechanism Formulation 166
           11.3.1   Resource Availability Prediction........................... 169
     11.4   Evaluation 172
           11.4.1   Node Quality... 174
           11.4.2   Service Quality 178
     11.5   Related Works 180
     11.6   Conclusions.. 184
     References... 184

**Part III   Looking Ahead, Next Steps for Ad-hoc Edge Clouds and
             Swarm Computing Realization**

12 **Next Steps for Ad-hoc Edge Cloud and Swarm Computing
    Realization**... 189
     12.1   Edge Computing Research Areas.................................... 189
           12.1.1   Heterogeneity Exploitation and New Hardware
                     Architectures: Neuromorphic Edge Computing........... 189
           12.1.2   Energy Efficiency Optimisation........................... 189
           12.1.3   Multi-Level Edge 190
           12.1.4   Edge Intelligence 191
           12.1.5   Data Management 191
           12.1.6   Edge Management.. 191
           12.1.7   Computing Continuum Exploration 192
     12.2   Swarm Computing Research Areas 193
           12.2.1   Swarm Management Techniques 193
           12.2.2   Resource Discovery 193
           12.2.3   Self-management and Autonomic Systems 194
           12.2.4   Bio Inspired Optimisation Techniques 194
     References... 195

About the Author

Ana Juan Ferrer holds an international PhD in Network and Information Technologies from the Open University of Catalonia (UOC). Her thesis examined the ad-hoc formation of Edge infrastructures out of available IoT Edge devices. Before, she obtained a Master's Degree in Information and Communication Technology Security (2011–2013), a Bachelor's Degree in Computer Engineering (2004–2010), and a Technical Engineering Degree in Computer Management (1995–1998).

At a professional level, Ana currently works as Programme Officer for the European Commission Directorate-General for Communications Networks, Content and Technology, Future Networks, Cloud, and Software Unit. Prior to this position, she spent 15 years performing industrial research as Head of Edge Computing Unit at Atos, Research & Innovation department. During this period, she was an Atos Distinguished Expert in the Cloud Domain and an Atos Scientific Community founding member in charge of Edge and Swarm computing Track.

Ana's research focuses on Cloud and Edge Computing technologies, distributed systems, and service engineering. Contact Ana at anajuanferrer@gmail.com.

Chapter 1
Introduction

1.1 Motivation

Computing plays a crucial part in our everyday reality which is largely attributable to the development of microprocessor technologies during the last decades. This particularity has allowed us to have computation readily available on our smartphones and owing to its assistance we have discovered new ways to utilise applications and services.

The advances in Internet of Things (IoT) are simultaneously causing the global rise of the number of connected devices, from figures of billions of units estimated to exist today, to over tens of billions of units expected to be available in the near future. Challenges in the context do not only revolve around managing this massive number of connected devices, but also the mechanisms able to cope with data volumes generated by these devices. Reproducing today's IoT environments, created data from connected devices would have to be transmitted over the network and processed into centralised Cloud data centres. This results in significant latencies for IoT data processing. The expected rise of device connections together with the latency across IoT deployments locations and cloud environments, renders the existing IoT approach unsustainable over time. Therefore, the development of IoT heightens the need to process close to the data sources. Furthermore, the emergence of IoT favours the presence of computing on our smartphones as well as all kinds of connected devices.

The principal aim of Edge Computing is to tackle this issue by providing a novel paradigm which extends capacities of Cloud Computing to the edge of the network, avoiding present latency constraints.

Edge computing (referred to as Fog computing by various previous authors) has emerged so as to bring Cloud computing capacities at the Edge of the network to address latency issues present in IoT scenarios. Edge computing serves the purpose of providing a compute environment located in the vicinity of data generation sources able to prevent latency issues detected in accessing Cloud services. Edge Computing links networking with distinctive cloud principles to define distributed

A. Juan Ferrer, *Beyond Edge Computing*, https://doi.org/10.1007/978-3-031-23344-9_1

1

computing platforms in charge of meeting the specific needs of IoT [1]. More specifically, Edge computing is defined as "the enabling technologies allowing computation to be performed at the edge of the network, on downstream data on behalf of cloud services and upstream data on behalf of IoT services" [2]. This definition encompasses the complete set of compute and network devices on their path from IoT data sources to cloud data centres.

Edge computing has undoubtedly taken an initial step towards the decentralisation of Cloud computing by initiating its transformation from the provision of services in dedicated data centres for which resources were perceived as unlimited to a more decentralised approach in where these cloud services are offered in combination with stationary Edge devices [2].

Current Edge computing developments regard the Edge as stationary single device environments which distribute computing and storage services to a set of closely located IoT devices solely viewed as sources of data, while their increasing complexity in terms of computing and storage capacity is disregarded.

However, IoT devices are presently widely proliferating while gaining noteworthy compute resources which lead to a significant expansion of their capacities. Owing to the progression of microprocessor technologies materialised over the last decades by the development of Moore's law, compute units have become "smaller, faster and cheaper" [3] with the passing of the time. This currently allows for compute units to be embedded into a wide diversity of IoT devices. Consequently, the materialisation of IoT is conducive to the presence of computing not only on our smartphones, but also on a wide range of devices (cars, televisions, cameras, etc.).

Current IoT environments encompass simple sensors with 8-bit microprocessors [4] as well as increasingly complex devices which represent assemblies of non-negligible computing and storage resources aggregated together with diverse sensors and actuators.

In this sense, IoT devices are relinquishing their often basic sensing features, and rapidly gaining complexity and sophistication by means of their ability to incorporate considerable computing power. Hence, a significant number of IoT devices are presently becoming de facto, Edge devices.

Moreover, innovative compute devices are being released on the market endowed with application specific processors for AI processing to facilitate embedding compute intelligence into all kinds of IoT devices. IDC [5] predicted that "By 2022, over 40% of organisations' cloud deployments will include edge computing and 25% of endpoint devices and systems will execute AI algorithms." Some examples of extant market developments which pave the way towards supporting this trend are provided as follows: NVIDIA's Jetson systems for processing on-board edge devices [6]; and Intel movidius [7] and Google Edge TPU [8].

Considering the abovementioned context, computing will cease to be confined to certain devices located on large data centres or stationary edge devices, instead it will be embedded and pervasive to virtually everything. This emergence of innovative computing capacity at the edge of the network is expected to have a long-lasting impact with the rise of all kinds of compute enabled connected IoT devices, such as smart fabrics, connected cars and roads, diverse forms of nano-computing, smart cities and robots. These connected devices and scenarios will unquestionably represent an integral part of our daily lives over the short term.

This scenario enables the emergence of an unprecedented computing continuum which ranges from cloud environments to a myriad of devices at the Edge including dedicated Edge and complex IoT devices. The fact that IoT devices are progressively drawing on noteworthy resources points to an unjustifiable underutilization merely employing them as data sources of resource richer computing environments. The growth in the complexity of IoT devices is calling for an evolution in Edge computing approach addressed by Swarm Computing and Ad-hoc Edge Clouds from the perception of IoT devices solely as data sources to the fully exploitation of all compute and storage capacity available in a specific location in all kinds of IoT edge devices.

This development is additionally intensified by the expected rise in compute demand at the Edge in the coming years together with expert assessments regarding the development of micro-processor technologies which might not have the capacity to cope with this demand at the same pace as the one set over the last decades.

OpenAI [9] has recently published a study which states that "the amount of compute used in the largest AI training runs has been increasing exponentially with a 3.4-month doubling time since 2012". Execution of AI computational workloads at the Edge is increasingly regarded as one of the major drivers for Edge computing development in the coming years [10, 11].

Concurrently, confidence in Moore's law to be able to respond to this growing compute demand may slightly be surpassing the physical capacity of providing ever miniaturised cheaper and faster low-power computing units, as it has been the trend for the last 50 years [12]. According to experts, this anticipated slowdown in Moore's low does not directly transmit the message to computing progress to suddenly stall, nevertheless it can indicate that the nature of such progress has to gradually change in two main directions: first, as previously mentioned, by driving the need to exploit hardware heterogeneity with the help of specialised processors to be embedded into all sorts of IoT devices; and secondly, pushing the demand of benefitting from all computing capacity available everywhere [13].

1.2 Swarm Computing and Ah-hoc Edge Clouds

Vast numbers of connected devices have proliferated during the past 10 years. Moreover, currently connected devices are rapidly advancing in sophistication in terms of their ability to carry significant storage and computation capacity, while becoming omnipresent. As a result, computing is now embedded everywhere and is no longer restricted to certain fixed computing devices. This characteristic, when coupled with the ever-increasing demand for rapid data processing at the Edge, highlights the pressing necessity to fully utilise all compute resources at the network's edge.

This represents a significant breakthrough to initial Edge computing developments concentrated on providing low latency compute environments for which IoT devices are solely considered as data sources.

The concept of Swarm computing introduced in this book aims at exploiting existing capacity at the Edge to create an on-demand, autonomic and decentralised self-managed computing infrastructures. Swarm Computing seeks to capitalise on all available highly heterogeneous resources at the Edge of the network, and combine them with fixed capacity in Clouds, to provide a service-based environment which allows for dynamically collecting and managing these massive, diverse, unconnected and highly distributed resources. Swarm computing aims to transform today's pre-configured and static service provisioning orientation into an on-demand, opportunistic and ad-hoc service provision in which service execution rely on dynamic sets of heterogeneous, non-dedicated and distributed compute capacity.

The Swarm computing concept is implemented by the Ad-hoc Edge Cloud architecture detailed in the book. The aim of Ad-hoc Edge Cloud is to define an Edge management system which harnesses the increasingly available computing capacity at the Edge of the network so as to form ephemeral compute infrastructures out of resources available in a certain physical space at a specific point in time.

The distinctive characteristics of the edge devices, which constitute this infrastructure, pose specific challenges to resource management in this context due to heterogeneity, dynamicity, and volatility of resources, resulting in the probability of node churn.

Whilst the proposed decentralised Swarm model represents a major step forward from a Cloud perspective, it is rooted in existing research areas and market developments in the area of Cloud computing, as well as, Mobile Cloud Computing, Mobile Ad hoc Computing and Edge computing. This book performs a state-of-the-art analysis and literature review of works in these fields to determine their role in the definition of Ad-hoc Edge Cloud architectures and future computing development in Swarm computing.

Perhaps more importantly, this work advances a specific approach to Swarm computing by developing its concept and main principles and characteristics. In addition to this, it proposes Ad-hoc Edge Cloud architecture with the purpose of creating dynamic ecosystems of IoT Edge Devices in a distributed and decentralised manner.

The Ad-hoc Edge Cloud architecture consists of two main building blocks: Edge Device and Ad-hoc Edge Cloud Context. Both building blocks are expected to be deployed in any IoT Edge device participating into an Ad-hoc Edge Cloud. Contexts determine the two dimensions we define for the architecture features: the management of a certain node belonging to the infrastructure at a specific point in time, Edge Device Context; and the management of the Edge overall cluster which is fully decentralised and distributed through to the use of distributed coordination systems, Ad-hoc Edge Cloud Context. The main novelties of the presented architecture stem from three main aspects:

– The consideration of IoT Edge devices beyond their ability to gather data, instead developing the approach of considering them as appropriate execution environments of services to be executed at the Edge of the network;
– The fact of considering unreliability of resources a essential characteristic of the proposed architecture by designing it centered on node churn and resource volatility issues as the keystone around which the architecture definition gravitates;
– The view of a fully decentralised architecture which spreads management features over punctual participant devices in infrastructures which can be ephemeral and on-demand created by design. Hence Ad-hoc Edge Cloud avoids a single point of failure, eliminating reliance on external management layers which can hinder operation in anticipation of unreliable connectivity and possesses inherent mechanisms to handle scale.

Additionally, this publication analyses the challenges generated by particularities of IoT Edge devices which form this infrastructure in two main research areas.

At the level of Cognitive Resource management, it elaborates on the mechanisms for enabling dynamic Ad-hoc Edge Cloud cluster formation and management which rely in build-in capabilities of distributed coordination services and consensus algorithm, demonstrating how these can be beneficial in addressing the specific challenges of Resource management in Ad-hoc Edge Clouds.

In terms of Service placement and Management, it presents an Admission Control mechanism together with an associated resource availability prediction model pertaining to the needs evidenced by dynamic behaviour of participant IoT Edge devices and specifically addressing the aspects of resource instability, dynamic availability and probability of node churn.

Finally, this book elaborates on future research challenges in the areas of Edge and Swarm computing highlighting the specific necessities for exploitation of heterogeneity, dynamicity and cognitive management, among others.

1.3   Book Organisation

The books is structured in three main parts, in this manner:

Part I, Current Status of Computing at the Cloud and Network Edges
Part I offers systematic survey of the literature and existing developments in the areas of Cloud computing, Mobile Cloud Computing, Mobile Ad-hoc Computing and Edge computing.

This work aims to assist in identifying their relations and existing developments as potential contributions to the further evolution in the Swarm computing concept realisation. Various chapters in this part analyse Cloud computing market developments and baseline technologies, alongside the heterogeneous models of decentralised cloud encountered in today's literature, including the specific relations among them. Subsequently, it provides the details for these different approaches. For each of the research areas existing challenges and approaches are defined; alongside the analysis of contemporary papers according to the defined taxonomies.

To conclude two crucial elements for the development of the Swarm computing model are examined: the analysis of p2p developments and overlay networks and their role as distributed coordination mechanisms for Ad-hoc Edge Cloud; as well as the difficulties generated by the elicitation of the specific security requirements of Swarm and Ad-hoc Edge Cloud models.

Part II Computing Beyond the Edge: Swarm Computing and Ad-hoc Edge Architectures

Taking as starting point the detailed state-of-the-art analysis, Cloud computing technologies are regarded as indispensable to progress from existing data centre based centralised architectures towards the incorporation of complete decentralised models which prosper from the growing computing capacities at the Edge of the network over all kinds of heterogeneous IoT connected devices.

With market penetration figures of connected devices escalating to unprecedented levels, the ability to exploit growing compute capacity at the Edge of the network available on heterogeneous IoT Edge devices has become paramount. Moreover, acknowledging the fact that these IoT Edge devices have ceased to be considered mere data sources, as they sustain significant compute and storage resources.

With this purpose in mind, we define the concept of Swarm computing as the enabler to dynamically form computing infrastructures out of available IoT devices in a decentralised and distributed manner across the Edge and Cloud computing continuum. Furthermore, we specified the distinctive and novel aspects of Resource management in this context, designing its principles and characteristics and detailing use cases which would benefit from the envisaged computation hyper distribution in Ad-hoc Edge Clouds.

In the interest of bringing the Swarm concept to a concrete concept implementation, the Ad-hoc Edge Cloud architecture has also been defined. The aim of Ad-hoc Edge Cloud architecture is to determine an Edge management system which harnesses the increasingly available computing capacity at the Edge of the network so as to form ephemeral compute infrastructures out of resources available in a particular physical location at a specified moment.

The Ad-hoc Edge Cloud serves the purpose to respond to the rising demands for processing at the Edge driven by the advances of AI via exploiting the existing capacity. Its overall ambition is to enable the on-demand and opportunistic formation of fully decentralised and distributed compute infrastructures by making use of the ever-increasing resources already available on IoT Edge devices.

The Ad-hoc Edge Cloud architecture materialises the idea of Swarm computing to avoid unnecessary latencies and exploit accessible complex compute capacity at the edge of the network.

In this context, we investigate the implications of resource dynamicity to Cognitive Resource management mechanisms in the overall Ad-hoc Edge infrastructure and its performance. Cognitive Resource management mechanisms unravel the implications of resource dynamic addition and removal as well as the analysis of the specific levels of node churn (as sudden resource unavailability to the Ad-hoc Edge infrastructure) which can be supported in order not to hinder the appropriate provision of services from Ad-hoc Edge Cloud infrastructures.

In addition, the Service Placement and Management implications are examined, specifically in Admission Control mechanisms to be employed in Ad-hoc Edge infrastructures and a validation of the use of a resource availability prediction model is provided in this context.

Part III Next Steps for Ad-hoc Edge Cloud and Swarm Computing Realization
The exploitation of the capacity in innovative IoT Edge devices is the basis for Ad-hoc Edge Clouds architectures and the Swarm computing concepts. Beyond the studies presented in previous chapters of this book, many research challenges remain both at levels of Edge and Swarm in order to fully frame the concept. Part III specifically analyses these challenges.

At level of Edge computing, innovative processor architectures, such as neuro-morphic computing, are currently aiming at surpassing von Neumann's architectures by designing compute units which target energy optimal AI workloads execution at the Edge.

This complements an existing source evolution which Cloud providers are already adopting, by means of exploitation of hardware heterogeneity. Developing computing continuum technology compatible with the management of hardware heterogeneity requires finding new ways to optimally embrace heterogeneous special purpose processing units without losing the advantages of abstraction of the utility-based models.

These advances could be materialised by the development of novel virtualisation tools, heterogeneity-aware scheduling at resource and platform levels, in addition to programming models which permit handling heterogeneity in a seamless way. Moreover, taking advantage of hardware heterogeneity (together with specific developments for energy aware metering and scheduling) are key aspects to enabling the advance towards energy aware, optimised and sustainable Edge and Swarm computing services.

Furthermore, the movement towards hyper distribution of the computing continuum envisioned in Swarm computing will have to allow the development of edge and swarm computing scenarios which inherently contemplate intelligent collaboration, self-* (configuration, organisation, management, healing and optimisation) across many and heterogeneous resources present in all kinds of IoT Edge devices, micro edge data centres, private enterprise clouds, federated cloud models and large Cloud set-ups. Orchestration and placement problems in this context will require novel management tools, programming models and approaches potentially p2p and bio-inspired which cope with heterogeneity and hyper distribution of computing while handling security and performance together with extreme scale, parallelisation and fault-tolerance.

References

1. Bonomi, F., Milito, R., Zhu, J., & Addepalli, S. (2012). Fog computing and its role in the internet of things. In *Proceedings of the First Edition of the MCC Workshop on Mobile Cloud Computing* (pp. 13–16). https://doi.org/10.1145/2342509.2342513
2. Shi, W., Cao, J., Zhang, Q., Li, Y., & Xu, L. (2016). Edge computing: Vision and challenges. *IEEE Internet of Things Journal, 3*(5), 637–646. https://doi.org/10.1109/JIOT.2016.2579198
3. Markoff, J. (2016). *The New York Times, Moore's law running out of room, tech looks for a successor*. Retrieved February 23, 2020. https://www.nytimes.com/2016/05/05/technology/moores-law-running-outof-room-tech-looks-for-a-successor.html
4. Chen, D., Cong, J., Gurumani, S., Hwu, W.-m., Rupnow, K., & Zhang, Z. (2016). Platform choices and design demands for IoT platforms: Cost, power, and performance tradeoffs. *IET Cyber-Physical Systems: Theory & Applications, 1*(1), 70–77. https://doi.org/10.1049/iet-cps.2016.0020
5. *IDC FutureScape: Worldwide IT industry 2019 predictions*. (2018). Retrieved October 20, 2019, from https://www.idc.com/getdoc.jsp?containerId=US44403818
6. NVIDIA Jetson. (2019). Retrieved August 15, 2019, from https://www.nvidia.com/en-us/autonomous-machines/embedded-systems/
7. Intel Movidious. (2019). Retrieved August 15, 2019, from https://www.movidius.com/
8. *Google Cloud Edge TPU - Run inference at the edge*. (2019). Retrieved December 1, 2019, from https://cloud.google.com/edge-tpu/
9. Amodei, D., & Hernandez, D. (2018). *AI and compute*. Retrieved December 1, 2019, from https://openai.com/blog/ai-and-compute/
10. Chen, J., & Ran, X. (2019). Deep learning with edge computing: A review. *Proceedings of the IEEE, 107*(8), 1655–1674. https://doi.org/10.1109/jproc.2019.2921977
11. Zhou, Z., Chen, X., Li, E., Zeng, L., Luo, K., & Zhang, J. (2019). Edge intelligence: Paving the last mile of artificial intelligence with edge computing. *Proceedings of the IEEE, 107*(8). https://doi.org/10.1109/JPROC.2019.2918951145
12. Guess, A. (2015). *Ray Kurzweil predicts our phones will be as smart as us by 2020*. Retrieved December 1, 2019, from https://www.dataversity.net/raykurzweil-predicts-our-phones-will-be-as-smart-as-us-by-2020/
13. The Economist. (2016). *After Moore's law, The future of computing*. Retrieved August 1, 2018, from https://www.economist.com/News/Leaders/21694528-Era-Predictable-Improvement-Computer-Hardware-Ending-What-Comes-Next-Future

Part I
Current Status of Computing at the Cloud and Network Edges

Cloud computing initially emerged in the space in which "we transitioned from an era in which underlying computing resources were both scarce and expensive, to an era in which the same resources started to be cheap and abundant" [1]. Current approaches for Cloud computing are based on dedicated Data Centres managed by enterprises where resources are perceived as unlimited and everything is delivered as a service in stationary resources set-ups. Cloud computing has enabled the democratisation of computing. It has created the illusion of infinite computing and allowed for the radical acceleration of commoditization of computing by materialising the concept of utility computing.

Existing Cloud computing developments emerged as part of a centralised paradigm in which large and fully equipped Data Centre concentrate the available computing power. Gartner's Edge Manifesto [2] has demanded "the placement of content, compute and Data Centre resources on the edge of the network, closer to concentrations of users. This augmentation of the traditional centralised Data Centre model ensures a better user experience demanded by digital business".

Initial steps towards decentralisation of Cloud Computing are being taken through the emergence of Fog [3] and Edge computing [4]. These novelties, together with telecommunications conception of Mobile Edge Computing, are recognised to be rooted in the Cloudlet concept in Mobile Computing [5, 6].

Edge and Fog computing are currently being developed under the premise of static computing devices (or sets of them) which serve as computing environments located in the vicinity of data generation areas in order to avoid latencies generated by application of Cloud computing to IoT scenarios. With in this framework, IoT devices are solely considered as mere sources of data presenting minimal actuation capacities.

Nevertheless, the expected benefits relative to the transition from IoT devices to complex IoT Edge devices predict a future in which connected things transcend existing basic data gathering and actuation, and secure enhancements to execute deep learning and AI processing. Therefore, the current evolution will afford novel opportunities to future evolution of Edge computing by grouping ever increasing computing capacities available in complex connected IoT devices at the edge of the network.

Complex IoT devices are assembles of computing and storage resources with diverse actuators and sensors, conceptually similar, to Mobile Devices. Connections among Mobile Cloud Computing and Evolution of Edge Computing do not end here: the fact that these complex IoT devices have a number of constraints regarding size and energy harvesting is also shared with Mobile Cloud computing works.

Additionally, the fact that often complex IoT devices are capable of moving raises novel challenges with regard to resource reliability, unstable connectivity and overall computing environment dynamicity, which for a number of years have been thoroughly analysed in the context of Mobile Cloud Computing. This reinforces the idea that future evolution of Edge computing has an intrinsic relationship with Mobile Cloud Computing.

Beyond existing Mobile Cloud Computing Cloudlet and Edge computing concepts relation, we affirm that Mobile Cloud and Ad-hoc Computing concepts create novel forms of distributed and opportunistic computing which will become a key building block for the evolution of existing Cloud and Edge computing towards the a fully decentralised Cloud model we call Swarm Computing.

This part starts by examining the connections between Cloud and Edge computing, Mobile and Ad-hoc Cloud Computing, and their development towards decentralised cloud models in Chap. 2. The state of these technologies is then thoroughly studied, beginning with a review at the state of the art for cloud computing in Chap. 3.

Based on this, we have identified the diverse models of decentralised cloud we encounter in today's literature including the specific relations among them. The upcoming chapters provide a systematic literature review of works in the areas of Mobile Cloud Computing in Chap. 4, Mobile Ad-hoc Computing in Chap. 5 and Edge computing in Chap. 6. The latter includes both Compute perspectives and Networking works in telco's Mobile Edge computing. Overall the purpose is to facilitate the identification of the relations and existing developments as potential contributions to further evolution decentralised cloud concepts in Swarm computing and Ad-hoc Edge Cloud architectures. These sections elaborate on the details of these different approaches including definition of existing challenges and approaches together with analysis of existing works according to the defined taxonomies. In addition, Chap. 7 explores in two concrete elements which are fundamental for Swarm computing developments: analysis of their specific security requirements; and study of the state-of-the-art technologies in P2P and consensus algorithms.

References

1. Kushida, K., Murray, J., & Zysman, J. (2015). Cloud computing: From scarcity to abundance. *Journal of Industry, Competition and Trade, 15*, 5–19.

2. *Gartner the edge manifesto: Digital business, rich media, latency sensitivity and the use of distributed data centers* (2017). https://www.gartner.com/doc/3104121
3. Bonomi, F., Milito, R., Zhu, J., & Addepalli, S. (2012). Fog computing and its role in the Internet of Things. In *Proceedings of the First Edition of the MCC Workshop on Mobile Cloud Computing* (pp. 13–16). https://doi.org/10.1145/2342509.2342513
4. Garcia Lopez, P., Montresor, A., Epema, D., Datta, A., Higashino, T., Iamnitchi, A., Barcellos, M., Felber, P., & Riviere, E. (2015, 9). Edge-centric computing. *ACM SIGCOMM Computer Communication Review, 45*, 37–42. http://dl.acm.org/citation.cfm?doid=2831347.2831354
5. Satyanarayanan, M., Simoens, P., Xiao, Y., Pillai, P., Chen, Z., Ha, K., Hu, W., & Amos, B. (2015, 4). Edge analytics in the Internet of Things. *IEEE Pervasive Computing, 14*, 24–31. http://ieeexplore.ieee.org/lpdocs/epic03/wrapper.htm?arnumber=7093020
6. Bilal, K., Khalid, O., Erbad, A., & Khan, S. (2018, 1). Potentials, trends, and prospects in edge technologies: Fog, cloudlet, mobile edge, and micro data centers. *Computer Networks, 130*, 94–120.

Chapter 2
Setting the Scene: Cloud, Edge, Mobile and Ad-hoc Computing Context

2.1 Cloud, Edge, Mobile and Ad-hoc Computing Relations

Figure 2.1 illustrates the parallel evolution pathways that Cloud and Edge computing technologies, along with Mobile Cloud Computing, Mobile Ad-hoc Computing, have taken up to this point. We believe that these trajectories will eventually converge in the idea of Swarm computing.

The movement towards Cloud decentralisation represents a novel approach from a Cloud perspective. There is extensive research in the areas of Mobile Cloud Computing, Mobile Ad-hoc Computing and Edge computing, including telco's Mobile Edge Computing, which can be explored so as to gain insight into existing approaches and the challenges they pose. Figure 2.2 provides a high level view identifying connections among these technologies. Table 2.1 details conceptual differences and similarities in their current approaches.

The emergence of Internet of Everything—the networked connection of people, process, data and things—is expected to exponentially increase the number of connected devices worldwide, from billions of units available today, to orders of magnitude of tens of billions of units expected to be deployed in the coming years. At present we are observing evolutionary forms of Cloud Computing, such as Edge and Fog, starting to remove the Data Centre barriers so as to provide novel forms of computing embracing computing power and data resources increasingly obtainable everywhere. These formats are forcing existing Cloud computing environments which emerged as part of a centralisation paradigm to evolve to decentralised environments avoiding drawbacks of large data movements and latency, specifically found in IoT scenarios [1]. These new forms of Cloud are driving the Cloud concept to create a more distributed approach in order to deliver better performance and enabling a wider diversity of application and services, complementary to traditional X-as-a-service cloud models used as resource rich environment.

Major cloud providers such as AWS [2] and Azure [3] are increasingly featuring Edge Computing services, as a way to extend their offerings for IoT scenarios.

© The Author(s), under exclusive license to Springer Nature Switzerland AG 2023
A. Juan Ferrer, *Beyond Edge Computing*, https://doi.org/10.1007/978-3-031-23344-9_2

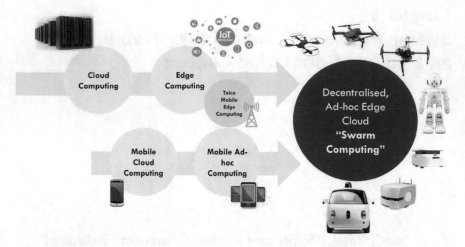

Fig. 2.1 Cloud, Edge, Mobile Cloud and Ad-hoc Cloud Computing evolution paths

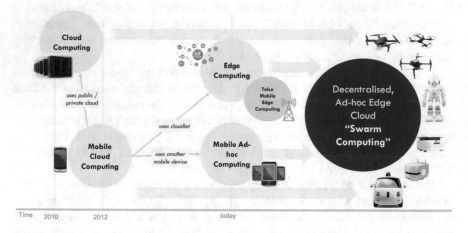

Fig. 2.2 Relations among decentralised Cloud models

In doing so, Edge computing has become an extension of well-established Cloud offerings.

Both for Edge, Fog and Mobile Cloud Computing, traditional Cloud models are perceived as the resource rich environment to be used in order to expand limited capacities of these environments.

In parallel to the hype around Cloud computing, mobile technologies experienced an unprecedented growth both in development and adoption. Mobile Devices and Cloud Computing have increasingly amplified the concept of Mobile Cloud Computing (MCC).

MCC is a research area which "aims at using cloud computing techniques on storage and processing of data mobile devices" [4]. In traditional approaches to

Table 2.1 Cloud, MCC, MAC, Edge computing and MEC concepts comparison

	Cloud computing	Mobile Cloud Computing (MCC)	Mobile Ad-hoc Computing (MAC)	Edge computing	Mobile Edge Computing (MEC)
Motivation	To provide IT services on-demand	To provide additional capacity to resource constrained mobile devices	To provide additional capacity to resource constrained mobile devices	To reduce latency in computation tasks of Data Generated by IoT	To enhance quality of networks data processing
Client	Any application	Mobile applications	Mobile applications	IoT applications	Virtualised Network Functions
Resource nature	Steady servers in Data Centres	Mobile devices complemented with capacity on Cloud computing environments, Steady servers located in the vicinity (cloudlet) or other Mobile devices	Mobile devices complemented with capacity of other Mobile devices	IoT devices complemented with capacity of steady servers located in the vicinity of IoT data generation areas	Steady servers in Data Centres placed at the Edge of the network
Means to acquire additional capacity	Federation with other Clouds	Cloud, Cloudlet and other mobile devices	Other mobile devices	Cloud	Cloud
Optimisation problem	Capacity, QoS	Energy, Capacity	Energy, Capacity	QoS (latency)	QoS (latency)
Commercial offerings	AWS, Azure, Google Cloud	None	None	AWS Greengrass, Azure IoT Edge, FogHorn	AWS Outpost, Wavelength, Azure Edge Zones
Standardisation	NIST, ETSI, SNIA, DMTF, OASIS, etc.	None	None	OpenFog Consortium, ETSI	ETSI

MCC, Cloud computing environments are utilised to overcome Mobile devices limitations. These limitations are often outlined in terms of battery lifetime as well as processing and storage capacity.

In order to overcome mobile devices limitations, three different approaches can be found in literature to augment limited mobile devices capabilities:

- Approaches which boost mobile devices capabilities with resources from Cloud environments by means of public or private environments. These approaches adopt the assumption that employed resources in the Cloud offer rich capacity and ensured availability.
- Approaches which rely on servers located close to the mobile device position, are called Cloudlets.
- Approaches which are dependent on other mobile devices to increment their capacities (therefore relying on resources in principle subject to the same mobile's devices constraints and limitations). These approaches have been coined under the term Mobile Ad-hoc Cloud (MAC) [5].

Mobile Cloud Computing Cloudlet concept [6] serves as a precedent to Edge and Fog computing. It defines the concept of a proximal cloud which brings closer computing capacities so as to avoid latency to the mobile devices its serves. Diverse authors have drawn on this connection. Examples of these are [7, 8] and [9].

The forms of Mobile Cloud Computing (MCC) which consider other Mobile Devices to make use of their available resources have been recently classified as Mobile Ad-hoc Cloud (MAC)[5]. The concept of MAC develops a common umbrella term for a number of works both in MCC and other research environments which consider mobile devices as valid execution resources [5]. Historically, MCC's main motivation has been the need to extend Mobile Devices limited resources to richer execution environments. Fuelled by the increased capabilities of Mobile Devices, this research area aims to go beyond these approaches considering the Mobile Device a valid Cloud resource and therefore capable of taking part in Computing infrastructures. Although the concept had already been addressed in previous MCC works, it presents the characteristic of the opportunistic behaviour of the environments very much of interest for the development of ad-hoc Edge Cloud architectures and Swarm computing concept.

2.2 Decentralisation of Cloud Computing

The call towards the decentralisation of Cloud computing is present in a wide variety of works and under diverse terms. Satyanarayanan [7] contextualises the current trend towards Cloud computing decentralisation in the framework of alternating waves of centralisation and decentralisation which have affected computing since the 1960s. In these alternations, the presence of centralisation of computing has been prevalent in 1960s and 1970s through batch processing and time-sharing and from mid-2000s employing traditional centralised Cloud computing models; whereas alternating with decentralisation in 1980s and 1990s via the emergence of personal computing and in which Edge computing presents the last episode of this on-going trend.

Shi [10], among many authors, has explained the need of decentralisation motivated by the development of richer IoT devices which have changed their role from simple data consumers to rich data providers. Overall rich IoT devices are expected to generate such amounts of data which in the longer term it will become impractical to centralise all their processing.

Garcia-Lopez [11] further expands on the factors which call for placement of computing at the edge with the help of four elements: Proximity, bringing facilities to distribute and communicate information; Intelligence, due to the fact that IoT devices increase computing capacities at a rapid pace; Trust and Control, by permitting data sources to remain in control of generated data and application management; and Humans, making them the centre of all interactions. In addition, Garcia-Lopez recognises further research challenges to be addressed in Cloud computing for realising novel highly distributed Edge architectures and middleware which go beyond Hybrid Cloud developments, coping with specific challenges of decentralisation and "computation trade-offs between mobile terminals and cloud servers". These systems are expected to have to deal with issues affecting stability on the availability of edge devices, such as devices' churn, fault tolerance and elasticity aspects; all of them being core aspects of research in Mobile Cloud Computing in the last years.

A similar approach is taken by Varghese when analysing the future of Cloud computing in the next decades in [12]. It precisely identifies MCC Cloudlet and MAC concepts as foundations for the evolution of Cloud Computing infrastructure towards the decentralised computing infrastructure in which resources are away from the Data Centre boundaries.

At the time of writing, there is still not a term which delimits the above mentioned highly decentralised computing infrastructure. Some authors such as [13] refer to this just as Edge Computing, declaring that existing Edge Computing development solely reflect an embryonic evolution stage of what it can become by utilising the incorporation to the concept of "smartphones, sensor nodes, wearables and on-board units where data analytics and knowledge generation are performed which removes the necessity of a centralised system".

Other authors prefer to define a specific term for this foreseen Edge capacity advancement. This is the case of Villari [14] who defines Osmotic Computing as "a new paradigm to support the efficient execution of IoT services and applications at the network edge". Osmotic Computing considers again application execution distributed across Edge and Cloud elaborating on MCC concepts to define its evolution requirements while acknowledging the need for reverse "mobile (cloud) offloading" mechanisms which move functionalities from Cloud computing to Edge devices. Bojkovic et al. [15] has coined the term Tactile internet for the evolution of Fog (Edge) computing which combined with developments in SDN and NVF is able to address requirements for ultra low latency and high availability required in scenarios such as "autonomous vehicles, haptic healthcare and remote robotics" among others.

Back in 2014, Lee [16] invented the TerraSwarm concept, as a set of technologies able to integrate cyber and physical worlds in a way that "Mobile battery-powered personal devices with advanced capabilities will connect opportunistically to the Cloud and to nearby swarm devices, which will sense and actuate in the physical world". These herald the beginning of a close link which can be detected among MCC and MAC and the future of Cloud and Edge Computing. It is interesting to note that the consideration of Mobile device in TerraSwarm also surpassed existing smartphone technology, considering Autonomous vehicles and Unmanned aerial vehicles (UAVs). While these vehicles may resemble futuristic scenarios, analysis of UAVs as "near user edge devices which are flying" was provided in [17]. The anticipation of the use of mobile cloud computing cloudlet servers in the air on drones as "Data mules", was able to bring data to the best processing location, or by means of the development of "Fly-in, Fly-out infrastructure", able to provide punctual computing services in a specific location.

However, today specific implementations of these uses are starting to emerge, showing their potential to develop in the medium term. Some of the most noteworthy examples are as follows: Jeong et al. [18] who provides a Cloudlet mounted in a UAV which provides offloading capabilities to a series of static mobile devices and [19] which develops an opportunistic computational offloading system among UAVs. All the abovementioned works evidence the nature of UAVs, and generally speaking robots and autonomous vehicles, which share device characteristics with traditional mobile devices in the form that they present constraints in terms of computational and storage capacity, battery and energy supply limitations. Alongside relying on unstable network links due to mobility, which drives specific device reliability and volatility issues not yet explored in stationary resource environments present in Edge and Cloud computing today.

While specific needs of smartphones have driven the development of MCC, we anticipate that the emergence of rich IoT devices in the form of complex IoT Edge devices will push towards the development of Ad-hoc Edge Clouds and Swarm computing concept.

Whereas it is widely recognised that MCC Cloudlet concept is the precursor of Edge computing, further evolution of this concept will be rooted in other forms of Mobile Computing, which has relied on the interconnection of constrained devices to resource richer environments in traditional clouds, and more importantly, in the opportunistic formation of computing infrastructures among mobile devices and MAC.

This will be motivated by the on-going trend towards decentralisation coupled with the increasing pressure to take advantage of all available computing capacity. As the evolution of Moore's law is progressively reaching its limits and computing demands will solely increase with the advent of more complex IoT devices and their expected data deluge generation. Parallel advances in deep learning and artificial intelligence will intensify this need by multiplying the requirement for complex processing at the Edge.

All together it evidences the need for Cloud and Edge computing to drawn inspiration from and explore comprehensive evolutions which have happened in the context of MCC and MAC in order to address novel challenges that Ad-hoc Edge Cloud architectures and Swarm computing are bringing to this context, removing the pre-existing boundaries among these technologies employing resources which are analogous in nature.

2.3 Edge and Fog Computing Terminology

A clarification should be provided about the terms used in the rest of this book. At the time of writing, there is still some controversy regarding the use of Fog and Edge computing terms. OpenFog consortium [20] in its reference architecture [21] alludes to the fact that Fog Computing is often erroneously named Edge Computing, which is pointed out in the differences at levels of Cloud interaction, hierarchy and layers and aspects addressed. In particular indicates that "Fog works with the cloud, whereas edge is defined by the exclusion of cloud. Fog is hierarchical, where edge tends to be limited to a small number of layers. In additional to computation, fog also addresses networking, storage, control and acceleration." [21] Fog Computing is a term coined by CISCO in its enlightening paper "Fog Computing and Its Role in the Internet of Things" [22]. In this publication, Fog computing is defined as a "highly virtualised platform" between end-devices and Data Centre clouds which provides compute, storage, and networking services (see Sect. 5.1 for details on definition). Publications of OpenFog Consortium blog [23] extends this definition, to consider Fog Computing "a continuum or a range of computing that goes from the cloud, to the edge, to the devices".

Many authors are currently considering "Fog Computing" a vendor specific term, and therefore opt for using "Edge Computing" term. ETSI has also coined the term "Mobile-edge Computing" [24], which explicitly focus on the Network aspects of the technology. While the research and standardisation communities are currently debating the appropriate term to use, major cloud and technology providers have released related products, tagged as Edge Computing, to the market. These commercial products do not adjust to the differentiation levels provided by OpenFog Consortium, instead, they consider Edge computing all computing environments outside Data Centre boundaries. The growing popularity of these products, evidenced by Google Trends "Fog Computing" and "Edge Computing" comparison of terms [25], prompts us to opt for using the Edge computing term throughout this book. However, as our work is a literature survey, both terms Fog and Edge Computing will be used as synonyms, making use of the term applied by the referenced author in different analysed studies.

References

1. *Cisco systems fog computing and the Internet of Things: Extend the cloud to where the things are.* (2016). https://www.cisco.com/c/dam/en_us/solutions/trends/iot/docs/computing-overview.pdf
2. *AWS IoT Greengrass*. Retrieved May 26, 2022, from https://aws.amazon.com/greengrass/
3. Azure IoT Edge. Retrieved May 26, 2022, from https://azure.microsoft.com/en-us/services/iot-edge/
4. Guan, L., Ke, X., Song, M., & Song, J. (2011). A survey of research on mobile cloud computing. In *Proceedings - 2011 10th IEEE/ACIS International Conference on Computer and Information Science, ICIS 2011* (pp. 387–392).

5. Yaqoob, I., Ahmed, E., Abdullah, G., Salimah, M., Muhammad, I., & Sghaier, G. (2016). Mobile ad hoc cloud: A survey. *Wireless Communications and Mobile Computing*, *16*, 2572–2589. https://onlinelibrary.wiley.com/doi/abs/10.1002/wcm.2709

6. Satyanarayanan, M., Bahl, P., Caceres, R., & Davies, N. (2009). The case for VM-based cloudlets in mobile computing. *Pervasive Computing, IEEE*, *8*, 14–23.

7. Satyanarayanan, M. (2017). The emergence of edge computing. *Computer*, *50*, 30–39.

8. Satyanarayanan, M., Simoens, P., Xiao, Y., Pillai, P., Chen, Z., Ha, K., Hu, W., & Amos, B. (2015, 4). Edge analytics in the Internet of Things. *IEEE Pervasive Computing*, *14*, 24–31. http://ieeexplore.ieee.org/lpdocs/epic03/wrapper.htm?arnumber=7093020

9. Bilal, K., Khalid, O., Erbad, A., & Khan, S. (2018,1). Potentials, trends, and prospects in edge technologies: Fog, cloudlet, mobile edge, and micro data centers. *Computer Networks*, *130*, 94–120.

10. Shi, W., Cao, J., Zhang, Q., Li, Y., Xu, L. (2016). Edge computing: Vision and challenges. *IEEE Internet of Things Journal*, *3*(5), 637–646. https://doi.org/10.1109/JIOT.2016.2579198

11. Garcia Lopez, P., Montresor, A., Epema, D., Datta, A., Higashino, T., Iamnitchi, A., Barcellos, M., Felber, P., & Riviere, E. (2015,9). Edge-centric computing. *ACM SIGCOMM Computer Communication Review*, *45*, 37–42. http://dl.acm.org/citation.cfm?doid=2831347.2831354

12. Varghese, B., & Buyya, R. (2018). Next generation cloud computing: New trends and research directions. *Future Generation Computer Systems*, *79*, 849–861. http://www.sciencedirect.com/science/article/pii/S0167739X17302224

13. El-Sayed, H., Sankar, S., Prasad, M., Puthal, D., Gupta, A., Mohanty, M., & Lin, C. (2018). Edge of things: The big picture on the integration of edge, IoT and the cloud in a distributed computing environment. *IEEE Access*, *6*, 1706–1717 (2018)

14. Villari, M., Fazio, M., Dustdar, S., Rana, O., & Ranjan, R. (2016). Osmotic computing: A new paradigm for edge/cloud integration. *IEEE Cloud Computing*, *3*, 76–83 (2016). http://ieeexplore.ieee.org/document/7802525/

15. Bojkovic, Z., Bakmaz, B., & Bakmaz, M. (2017, 10). Vision and enabling technologies of tactile internet realization. In *2017 13th International Conference on Advanced Technologies, Systems and Services in Telecommunications (TELSIKS)* (pp. 113–118).

16. Lee, E., Rabaey, J., Hartmann, B., Kubiatowicz, J., Pister, K., Sangiovanni-Vincentelli, A., Seshia, S., Wawrzynek, J., Wessel, D., Rosing, T., Blaauw, D., Dutta, P., Fu, K., Guestrin, C., Taskar, B., Jafari, R., Jones, D., Kumar, V., Mangharam, R., Pappas, G., Murray, R., & Rowe, A. (2014, 6). The swarm at the edge of the cloud. *IEEE Design & Test*, *31*, 8–20. http://ieeexplore.ieee.org/lpdocs/epic03/wrapper.htm?arnumber=6781658

17. Loke, S., Napier, K., Alali, A., Fernando, N., & Rahayu, W. (2015, 2). Mobile computations with surrounding devices. *ACM Transactions on Embedded Computing Systems*, *14*, 1–25. http://dl.acm.org/citation.cfm?id=2737797.2656214

18. Jeong, S., Simeone, O., & Kang, J. (2018). Mobile edge computing via a UAV-mounted cloudlet: Optimization of bit allocation and path planning. *IEEE Transactions on Vehicular Technology*, *67*, 2049–2063.

19. Valentino, R., Jung, W., & Ko, Y. (2018, 2). Opportunistic computational offloading system for clusters of drones. In *2018 20th International Conference on Advanced Communication Technology (ICACT)* (pp. 303–306).

20. OpenFog Consortium. (2016). https://www.openfogconsortium.org

21. Group, O., et al. (2017). OpenFog reference architecture for fog computing. *OPFRA001*, *20817*, 162.

22. Bonomi, F., Milito, R., Zhu, J., & Addepalli, S. (2012). Fog computing and its role in the internet of things. In *Proceedings of the First Edition of the MCC Workshop on Mobile Cloud Computing* (pp. 13–16). https://doi.org/10.1145/2342509.2342513

23. Kubik, S. (2017). *A plain language post about fog computing (that anyone can understand)*. Retrieved May 13, 2018, from https://www.openfogconsortium.org/a-plain-language-post-about-fog-computing-that-anyone-can-understand/

24. Hu, Y., Patel, M., Sabella, D., Sprecher, N., & Young, V. (2015). Mobile edge computing—A key technology towards 5G. *ETSI White Paper*, *11*, 1–16.

25. *Google Trends, fog computing vs Edge Computing*. (2022). Retrieved May 26, 2022, from https://trends.google.com/trends/explore?q=fog%20computing,edge%20computing

Chapter 3
Cloud Computing

3.1 Introduction to Cloud Computing

Cloud computing [1] initial developments revolved around the Infrastructure as a Service, having Amazon Web Services Elastic Compute [2] as its main representative. In this day and age, Cloud computing is considered both a business and a delivery model which permits the acquisition of a wide range of IT capabilities encompassing from infrastructure, development environments and security features to final user applications. Thus, nurturing the ambition of providing an infinite all-purpose elastic IT utility in which everything is accessible by any individual, regardless of the location "as-a-Service".

The emergence of Cloud computing was facilitated by the convergence of certain already existing technologies and concepts:

1. Virtualisation, acting as the main enabler to achieve economic benefits and economies of scale for cloud providers.
2. Grid computing, which created advances in distributed systems essential to develop cloud management systems.
3. Utility computing, which derived from Grid Computing and anticipated the concepts of 'pay per use' and 'as a service' provisioning model.

Cloud computing triggered a considerable disruption in the way IT services are consumed which evolved from the purchase of products in the classic on-premises and license based models, towards the possibility to get an IT feature by means of the on-line sign-up of contracts with third party providers in order to obtain elastically the same functionality in on-demand and pay-per-use models.

Figure 3.1 depicts a taxonomy of Cloud computing, illustrating its core elements and services, outlined in the upcoming subsections.

A. Juan Ferrer, *Beyond Edge Computing*, https://doi.org/10.1007/978-3-031-23344-9_3

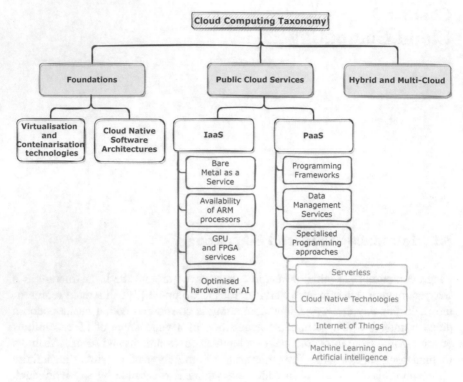

Fig. 3.1   Cloud Computing taxonomy

3.2   Basic Definitions, Benefits and Drawbacks

The US National Institute of Standards and Technology [1] back in 2012 offered the following basic definitions for Cloud computing:

On-demand self-service   "A consumer can unilaterally provision computing capabilities, such as server time and network storage, as needed automatically without requiring human interaction with each service provider."

Broad network access   "Capabilities are available over the network and accessed through standard mechanisms that promote use by heterogeneous thin or thick client platforms (e.g., mobile phones, tablets, laptops, and workstations)."

Resource pooling   "The provider's computing resources are pooled to serve multiple consumers using a multi-tenant model, with different physical and virtual resources dynamically assigned and reassigned according to consumer demand. There is a sense of location independence in that the customer generally has no control or knowledge over the exact location of the provided resources but may be able to specify location at a higher level of abstraction (e.g., country, state, or datacenter). Examples of resources include storage, processing, memory, and network bandwidth."

Rapid elasticity   "Capabilities can be elastically provisioned and released, in some cases automatically, to scale rapidly outward and inward commensurate with demand. To the consumer, the capabilities available for provisioning often appear to be unlimited and can be appropriated in any quantity at any time."

Measured service   "Cloud systems automatically control and optimise resource use by leveraging a metering capability at some level of abstraction appropriate to the type of service (e.g., storage, processing, bandwidth, and active user accounts). Resource usage can be monitored, controlled, and reported, providing transparency for both the provider and consumer of the utilised service."

In addition, NIST also defined the cloud stack elements as follows:

Software as a Service (SaaS)   "The capability provided to the consumer is to use the provider's applications running on a cloud infrastructure. The applications are accessible from various client devices through a thin client interface such as a web browser (e.g., web-based email). The consumer does not manage or control the underlying cloud infrastructure including network, servers, operating systems, storage, or even individual application capabilities, with the possible exception of limited user-specific application configuration settings."

Platform as a Service (PaaS)   "The capability provided to the consumer is to deploy onto the cloud infrastructure consumer-created or acquired applications created using programming languages and tools supported by the provider. The consumer does not manage or control the underlying cloud infrastructure including network, servers, operating systems, or storage, but has control over the deployed applications and possibly application hosting environment configurations."

Infrastructure as a Service (IaaS)   "The capability provided to the consumer is to provision processing, storage, networks, and other fundamental computing resources where the consumer is able to deploy and run arbitrary software, which can include operating systems and applications. The consumer does not manage or control the underlying cloud infrastructure but has control over operating systems, storage, deployed applications, and possibly limited control of select networking components (e.g., host firewalls)."

Depending on the model of choice for the installation and consumption of Cloud services, there can be the following differentiation:

Private cloud   Refers to cloud installations solely dedicated to the use of one organisation.

Community clouds   In which several organisations with pre-existing agreements share the capacity in their private cloud installations. This model is frequently used by academic and scientific organisations, such as the European Science Cloud.

Public clouds   Are the clouds offered to the general public for consumption of their services on-demand and pay per use. They typically encompass all layers of the cloud stack (Iaas, PaaS, SaaS) or only certain parts of these (sets of these services). Public Cloud is the model employed by the most popular cloud offerings, Amazon Web Services, Google Cloud and Azure.

Hybrid cloud   Denominates the combined use of private and public cloud.

Cloud computing main benefits include:

Reduction of capital investment   By converting the acquisition of IT products into the consumption of services, Cloud computing transforms the IT capital investments of organisations, to variable operational expenditures, dependant on the actual consumption necessities of the organisation.

On demand scalability   Cloud Computing has the potential to reduce the risk of over and under provisioning, offering the possibility to dynamically adapt the consumption of services to the actual organization needs. In addition, the elastic capability provided by Cloud Computing bypasses the need to predict future capacity of services or the necessary demand, as capacity can be dynamically adapted to business requirements.

Reduction of Operating costs   Cloud services are multi-tenant which means that multiple customers share infrastructure and services at cloud provider installations. Multi-tenancy enables Cloud providers to achieve economies of scale increasing business benefit. This is further enhanced by Cloud providers via high levels of standardisation in their architectures and physical infrastructures, resulting in cost effective optimised services operation. These two factors co-jointly are considered to provide significantly reduced prices in front of traditional in-house IT service operation.

Metered usage and billing   While outsourcing of IT services and hosting of IT infrastructures were already popular prior to the popularisation of Cloud computing, the on-demand Cloud nature and its pay per use model, allowed for the to change from recurring fees or a flat rate in how outsourcing services were billed, to new models based on the actual service consumption of the services, ensuring for a more fine-grained IT costs assessment.

In spite of the fact that Cloud computing is a current reality in the market, certain risks and drawbacks are still identified:

Vendor lock-in   The most popular public Cloud providers have built very attractive ecosystems of services for final users, however they do not facilitate the switching among providers and overall seek to firmly retain customers adhered to their ecosystems of services.

Uncertainty on final cost   Inappropriate user environment configurations together with the fact that usage of a cloud provider service may imply the need to contract a series of additional services in the same provider to render the final solution operational, causing some cases of initial cost-effective offers, not to be economically sustainable over time.

Security   Cloud computing environments in public clouds are inherently shared among multiple users. Cloud security presents the specific characteristic of being a joint responsibility among the cloud user and the provider in order to provide end-to-end security. The intrinsic loss of control from the user in the security measures in place at cloud providers is still often perceived as a risk for cloud adoption.

SLAs   SLAs offered in existing public cloud providers solely contemplate percentages of service available as the factor affecting their service levels. In this context, many other factors which can affect the quality of the service obtained from the service use are only offered in a best effort approach.

3.3   Cloud Foundations

In this section we perform an analysis of the current status of technologies considered foundational for Cloud computing developments such as virtualisation and the works of the Cloud Native Computing Foundation.

3.3.1   *Virtualisation and Containerisation Technologies*

Server virtualisation is a software-enabled capability which allows the perception of a single physical server as multiple isolated virtual divisions of the server, virtual machines (VMs). From this perspective, a VM represents a software partition of the physical server in which operating systems and application are executed similarly to being executed in the physical server. The software technology which enables this physical server abstraction is the Hypervisor.

Server virtualisation is pre-existent to Cloud computing. Server virtualisation was widely used during the decades of the 1960s and 1970s with the purpose of segmenting the use of mainframe computers among diverse user groups, granting the sharing of this highly costly and single resource. The popularisation of the x86 server Virtualisation technique during the 1990s by VMware, attracted once again the attention of the industry, identifying its potential for server consolidation, enhanced fault tolerance and resource optimisation. The advances made over that period facilitated by the development of x86 server virtualisation completely disrupted the common practices in data centre management systems, allowing the dissolution of the pre-existing one to one association between a physical server and an application and becoming a pre-cursor of Cloud.

Virtualisation represents a secure technology foundation for Cloud service provisioning. Virtualisation empowers Cloud providers to achieve economies of scale and multi-tenancy over their computing infrastructures. Traditionally the following different classes of server virtualisation techniques, or types of hypervisors, have been considered:

Full virtualization   Software platform offering to the virtual machine an interface identical to the one provided by the underlying hardware.

Para-virtualization   Software whose objective is to extend to the virtual machine an interface that is comparable to the one of the underlying hardware, hence, adaptations in the guest operating system are necessary to improve obtained performance.

Hardware-assisted virtualization   Delivers new instructions to support direct calls by a Para virtualized guest SO into the hypervisor.

Native or Bare-metal virtualization   Does not presuppose the existence of a underlying operating system, due to the fact that it directly controls CPU.

In the context of standarisation activities in relation to Virtualisation it is worth mentioning Open Virtualization Format (OVF) [3]. OVF was defined by DMTF and is part of the ISO/IEC 17203:2017 [3]. OVF defines a "standard packaging format for software solutions based on virtual systems". It allows the portability of VMs across hypervisors that support it.

Libvirt [4] is described as a "a toolkit to manage virtualization platforms". It displays a common management API on top of diverse hypervisors. Libvirt utilises APIs to monitor and handle the resources available on the physical server in terms of CPUs, memory, storage and networking, as well as guest OS. At current state of developments it supports virtualisation tools such as KVM, QEMU, Xen, VMWare ESX and LXC.

Table 3.1 contains a comparison among existing virtualisation technologies, highlighting their approaches in terms of Host and Supported OS, VM formats and support for Libvirt.

At the level of hypervisor-based virtual machine provisioning in public Cloud providers, they make use of a mixture of tailored open source hypervisors (Xen, KVM) as well as, proprietary solutions developed independently. User reports existing from the open source private cloud management system Open Stack recognize KVM as the most used hypervisor [8].

Until a few years ago, server virtualization was the most common alternative to share a server's capacity among multiple applications. The emergence of container technologies, such as Docker [9] or LXC [10], presently constitutes a widely employed technique to further achieve this objective.

Containers are currently employed as an alternative to OS-level virtualization to run multiple isolated systems on a single server, or used in combination with VMs in order to keep the appropriate levels of isolation. Container technologies build on top of the idea of process isolation explored by Solaris Zones [11]. Container technologies exploit novel technologies developed in the Linux kernel which enable process isolations based on cgroups for resources (CPU, memory, block I/O, network, etc.) and namespaces (to detach application's view from the operating environment in terms of process, network, user and file systems).

Table 3.1 Comparison among existing virtualisation technologies

Hypervisor		Host OS	Supported OS	VM format	Libvirt support
Xen [5]	Hypervisor based on para-virtualization. Originated as a research project in University of Cambridge in 2003, and acquired afterwards by Citrix systems. GNU General Public License (GPL2)	Linux, Solaris among others	Xen is based in para-virtualization which means the guest OS has to be modified in order to "collaborate" with the hypervisor. It is supported by specific systems on windows and other os such as NetBSD, FreeBSD, and OpenSolaris	Own. OVF Supported	Yes
KVM [6]	Based on Full virtualisation. Very popular in conjunction with Open Source Cloud management systems. GPL license	Linux, Windows, FreeBSD, Solaris among others	Same as host	Own. OVF not supported	Yes
VMware [7]	Forerunner in x86 server virtualization. Based on full virtualization. Covering a range of products from virtualization to cloud management. Very popular Virtualisation commercial solution	Depending on products: Linux, Windows	DOS, Linux, Mac OS X Server, FreeBSD, Haiku, OS/2, Solaris, Syllable, Windows	Own. Support for OVF	Yes

Containerization is considered to be more lightweight than VMs due to the fact that they do not require inclusion of the complete software packages of a Linux distribution of the guest OS. Instead, containers solely require of the Linux runtime libraries demanded by the application. When the container is instantiated at the physical or virtual server it has to be executed in, the container format indicates the host Linux kernel it necessitates to be executed under, and the host provisions the essential operating system libraries.

Container technologies are part of the mainstream, as they constitute the origin of the technological baseline Cloud Native technologies. The Flexera 2021 State of Cloud report [12], stated that in the present climate the most widely employed containerisation technologies in cloud are centred around Open-source tools, having Docker and LXC as its figureheads. These developments are increasingly complemented by popular tools which act at higher abstraction levels addressing container orchestration toolsets, such as Kubernetes [13].

In this context, LXC is considered as a de-facto standard for the containerisation of Linux and Unix environments [14]. Nevertheless, the noteworthy uptake of Docker is explained by the fact that it had an early release as an open source, as a result of building on top of LXC technologies [15] together with its prevalent availability in a variety of executions environments (notably in predominant container orchestration tools (Kubernetes) and all major public Clouds). Recently, technologies which address the possibility of having more lightweight implementations of virtualisation and containerization technologies are starting to emerge on the market. Some examples are the following: Firecraker [16], Unikernels [17], Kata Containers [18] or gVisor [19]. These developments are expected to be particularly of interest for constrained Edge computing execution environments.

3.3.2 Cloud Native Software Architectures

The Cloud Native Computing Foundation [20] defines Cloud native technologies as the technologies which "empower organizations to build and run scalable applications in modern, dynamic environments such as public, private, and hybrid clouds. Containers, service meshes, microservices, immutable infrastructure, and declarative APIs exemplify this approach." [21]

Cloud Native Technologies are presently considered the most up-to-date approach for the design and implementation of cloud applications, irrespectively of the cloud model chosen private, public clouds, and progressively embracing Edge computing execution models as well. Business analysts such as Gartner [22] predict that "cloud-native platforms will serve as the foundation for more than 95% of new digital initiatives by 2025—up from less than 40% in 2021" [22].

The CNCF defines the three main properties of cloud native systems:

Container packaged   Running applications and processes in software containers as an isolated unit of application deployment, and as a mechanism to achieve high levels of resource isolation.
Dynamically managed   Actively scheduled and actively managed by a central orchestrating process.
Micro-services oriented   Loosely coupled with dependencies explicitly described (e.g., through service endpoints).

In addition, the following characteristics have been identified for applications and services to be deployed to a cloud infrastructure according to CNCF Cloud Native Definition [23]

Location independence   The ability to move across hosts in the event of a server
        failure, with no loss of state.

Fast startup   Cloud nodes are expected to fail and restart, therefore the startup time
        of services must be ultra fast, ideally measured in single-digit seconds.

Fault-tolerance   In-memory state will be lost when a node crashes, therefore
        stateful applications and services running on cloud infrastructure must
        have a robust recovery mechanism.

Reliable communications   Other processes will continue to communicate with a
        service or application which has crashed, therefore they must have a
        mechanism for reliable communications in the event of a downed node.

Distributed state   Cloud-native services must support in-memory state and have a
        mechanism for recovery in case of service failure and restart.

Cloud Native Architectures have been fully adopted by public Cloud providers.
All major Cloud providers currently render the necessary tools and services for
development and deployment of Cloud Native architectures (see Sect. 3.3.2 for
details in these services). Aside from that, the Cloud Native Computing Foundation
being part of the Linux Foundation, supports open source and vendor neutral solutions for cloud applications and services. At time of writing it hosts 16 Graduated
projects (counting on widely used tools such as Kubernetes and Prometheus), 26
Incubating projects and 67 Sandbox projects (for cutting-edge innovation projects)
[24]. The overall CNCF landscape [25] comprises a comprehensive ecosystem of
Cloud solutions, most which are hosted as part of the community.

3.4 Services in Public Clouds

Services in public cloud providers extend a wide variety of services with a highly
mature status of development. In this section, we provide a glimpse into the set
of offerings which are considered closely related to the developments of Swarm
Computing. More specifically we observe cloud services support for heterogeneous
processing, and container technologies for IaaS and PaaS. For the latter, we can
establish their relation to aspects of interest for Edge computing, for instance for
dedicated Hybrid Cloud, IoT, Machine learning and Artificial intelligence

3.4.1 Infrastructure-as-a-Service (IaaS)

IaaS was the precursor of the usage of Cloud services, kick-started by the launch
of AWS EC2 services in 2006. Infrastructure as a Service is the Cloud computing
model which has the highest market share [26] and on which major public Cloud
providers (AWS, Google, Azure) have relied as starting point to build their Cloud
services ecosystems.

From a user viewpoint, making use of IaaS models is the closest experience to running their applications and services on-premises. As highlighted by the NIST definition of IaaS previously provided, in IaaS, the provider is responsible for the provision of basic infrastructure services (servers, storage and networking) on top of which they typically offer added value services for the user's management of the infrastructure (i.e. security, monitoring, logging and backups).

From a provider's perspective, the IaaS model is the cloud provision model found at a higher risk of becoming a commodity. In the Iaas model, public cloud vendors encounter more difficulties to differentiate their services from the ones available in other providers. For this reason, public Cloud providers continuously innovate and enhance the typologies of infrastructures they make available to their customers. Initial offerings in public Cloud providers focused on providing diverse flavours of x86 servers by means of virtual machines. Nowadays, all major public cloud providers dispense container-based services—as an interplay among PaaS and IaaS—but also services with extra value, such as the possibility to execute Kubernetes Clusters as a Service.

Moreover, public Cloud providers constantly innovate in integrating a diversity of hardware options into their services with the purpose of guaranteeing access to a wide range of solutions covering the needs of all kinds of applications. Examples of these innovations are as follows:

Bare Metal as a Service   Bare metal as a service refers to services which provide dedicated services instead of virtual infrastructure. These are intended to address the needs of applications with stringent performance requirements which make them not suitable to run on top of virtualisation platforms. These offerings are today available in all major public cloud providers AWS [27], Azure [28] and Google Cloud [29].

Availability of ARM processors   ARM processors are recognised as more cost-effective and energy efficient processors. Likewise, they are natural platform for execution of mobile applications and various uses cases from mobile application development to gaming. In order to satisfy the needs of these scenarios public cloud providers increasingly offer a diversity of VM flavours into their compute services [30–32].

GPU and FPGA services   Back in 2010, AWS was a forerunner to provider GPU capabilities by means of dedicated instances [33]. From the initial GPU offerings, AWS currently has an array of offerings [34], based on accelerated computing instances which comprises access to NVIDIA GPUs of diverse sizes and flavours. The instance type P2 is intended for general-purpose GPU compute applications. The utilisation of these instances is supported by programming models such as CUDA and OpenCL. AWS recommends P2 instances for the execution of deep learning applications. Additional accelerated instances part of AWS offerings include: G2, a set of instances including optimisations for graphics-intensive applications and F1 instances providing dedicated FPGAs. These offerings have been

promptly followed by equivalent services in other cloud providers such as
IBM [35], Azure [36], and GoogleCloud [37].

Optimised hardware for Artificial intelligence process execution   In   order   to
achieve the performance levels public Cloud providers aim to incorporate
into their services, Cloud providers are increasingly supporting the design
of specialised hardware to address the needs of their services. This line
of innovation is currently focused on a fierce competition to provide the
best AI execution environments. Examples on this innovation consider
the GPU services previously mentioned but also specific developments as
Google TPU [38].

3.4.2   Platform-as-a-Service (PaaS)

Parallel to the emergence of Infrastructure-as-a-Service, boosted by the significance
acquired by Amazon Web Services, Salesforce.com started to offer Software-as-a-
Service. Salesforce's SaaS offering included a tool for its SaaS offering customiza-
tion, force.com. In the short term, driven by the market presence of force.com and
significantly complemented by the Google's development of Google's App Engine,
the necessity to be contemplated as part of the Cloud stack became widely accepted,
as a new middleware layer in between IaaS and SaaS: Platform-as-a-Service (PaaS).
Subsequently, PaaS has been considered the intermediate layer of the Cloud stack
which enables simplified consumption of Cloud infrastructure and sustains the
development of Cloud applications [39].

PaaS layer commonly encompasses programming toolsets and data management
services which can be packaged as a service, or alternatively, as a software
stack to be deployed in-house offering deployment and application management
features on top of private and public cloud offerings. At the level of application
development tools, public Cloud provider strategy has been to cover countless
software development necessities in order to extend a wide range of tools addressing
an increasing diversity of application developer communities and requirements.

Since its initial development, PaaS layer has undergone a significant transformation. Initial PaaS developments concentrated into offerings of two large players as
Microsoft (Azure) [40] and Google (App Engine) [41]. Today, it currently covers a
wide variety of solutions, capabilities and programming languages and approaches.

Present PaaS offerings range from all types of programming frameworks and
tools, to a wide diversity of data managing services, in addition to specialised programming approaches such as Artificial Intelligence and IoT solutions, Serverless
and even, Cloud robotics services. Moreover, the increased popularisation of Cloud
Native technologies has facilitated the incorporation by Cloud providers in their
offerings' of container and Kubernetes as a service services. Hand in hand with these
developments, a number of software platforms which act as PaaS, enable to support
of multi-cloud strategies for certain types of applications. The upcoming subsections

will present a high level overview on the variety of PaaS services currently available on the market.

In consonance with the diversity of PaaS offerings in the market, PaaS providers are also diversified. These providers comprise:

Vendors whose main service is SaaS   offer platform tools to permit the customisation of their services with the purpose of increasing customer loyalty and establishing a wider marketplace around their offering;

IaaS public Cloud providers   who wish to overcome the intrinsic risk of IaaS commoditisation by offering added value services on top of infrastructures. All together the combination of IaaS and PaaS services in these market actors, define a very well-integrated vendor ecosystems which lock-in the customer to a specific ecosystem selection and prevents the customer from switching to another vendor without incurring into substantial cost;

Technology providers of multi-cloud solutions   who aim to offer risk-free solutions of vendor lock-in previously described by offering software platforms which support multi-cloud customer strategies. Although this kind of products previously existed on the market, the emergence of Cloud Native Architectures constitutes a key market driver for their adoption.

Table 3.2 provides an overview of this classification and market examples which have implemented these approaches.

3.4.2.1   Programming Frameworks and Tools

Most known platforms supplying programming frameworks and tools have been historically Azure .Net environment [40] and Google App Engine [41].

Google App Engine empowers developers to build applications in-house and to deploy them to the Google Cloud. Google App Engine aims to facilitate application

Table 3.2 Classification of Platform-as-a-service offerings

Type of PaaS provider	Description	Examples
SaaS providers, services customisation	Tailor and extend the capabilities of a SaaS application	Salesforce Platform [42]
IaaS public Cloud providers, added value services and ecosystem	May provide general capabilities but can be used only in the context of a determined public cloud provider products and services, offering a tightly integrated vendor ecosystem	Amazon Web Services [2], Microsoft Azure [43], Google Cloud [44]
Technology providers of multi-cloud solutions	Enabling the customer to utilise services across diverse public cloud providers. Offer specific security measures and enhances service management mechanisms	Red Hat OpenShift [45], VMware Tanzu [46]

development tasks by offering rapid deployment and easier application management. It introduces ondemand automated scalability for Node.js, Java, Ruby, C#, Go, Python, and PHP based applications. Similarly to many other PaaS offerings, Google App Engine have been scrutinised in relation to the lack of transparency and user control over the execution infrastructure, due to the fact that developers do not exert direct control over resource allocation and detailed monitoring.

Azure Platform places specific focus on the .NET framework. It is a part of Microsoft's Cloud computing strategy, complementing their IaaS and SaaS Cloud developments. The main services and products offered are consequent to previous in-house Microsoft .Net offer: a Cloud-based, scale-out version of SQL Server, Azure App Service, facilitating to build and deploy web applications and webservices developed in ASP.NET but also on Node.js, PHP, Java, Python and Ruby on Rails. It enables high availability and automated scalability and supports both Windows and Linux execution environments.

3.4.2.2   Data Management Services

Complementary to their application development services all public Cloud providers have an extensive catalogue of databases services as well as data storage services as part of their PaaS offerings.

Managed Databases services mainly offer the same functionalities to the corresponding alternatives to be deployed in house, combined with the fact that databases underlining infrastructure is fully managed for the users. As a drawback, in certain cases data security concerns may appear in these models.

Managed Databases services in public Cloud providers PaaS offer NoSQL databases (such as Cassandra, MongoDB and Apache CouchDB) and relational databases (including for instance MySQL, SQLServer, Oracle Database). In addition, these services comprise license-based databases, which in certain cases can also be managed as IaaS offerings and open source databases, depending on the necessity of specific configurations required by users. In terms of Databases management options available in public Cloud providers, it is interesting to remark the scalability options presented which include: horizontal scaling via clustered instances, vertical scaling, by means of the addition of memory, compute and storage capacity and read-replicas, altogether to enhance the read and write performance of the database.

Almost any existing database is currently accessible as a cloud-based service. Overall, major public Cloud services exhibit rather equivalent offerings [47] with specific services characteristics to be explored case by case depending on the specific offerings.

3.4.2.3 Specialised Programming Approaches

Under this category we will explore the services supplied by Cloud service providers for the development of specific types of applications and services. Similarly to the analysis of databases services evidenced in the previous section, the current extension of the public Cloud catalogue that it only allows for a high level overview as part of this work.

Serverless

During the past decade, cloud computing and virtualization have enabled applications deployment models to change from monolithic n-tier approaches to more flexible and scalable methodologies. In spite of all benefits gained, IaaS, and to some extend PaaS deployment models, do not eliminate the burden of infrastructure management for cloud users [48].

Driven by the motto "No server is easier to manage than no server" [49], serverless computing has recently emerged with the ambition of eliminating this burden by providing tools and mechanisms which removed the need to handle infrastructure for deploying, running and managing event-driven and stateless applications. Cloud Native Computing Foundation (CNCF) Serverless Whitepaper through its CNCF Serverless Working Group provides a detailed overview of the technology [50].

Although there is not a formal definition of the serverless concept, a highly comprehensive one was provided by Barga in [49] as "a cloud-native platform for short-running, stateless computation and event-driven applications which scales up and down instantly and automatically and charges for actual usage at a millisecond granularity".

Following the popularity gained by concept's initiator, AWS Lambda [51], a myriad of commercial cloud providers offerings and open-source frameworks have emerged to provide its own technological alternatives. In terms of public Cloud offerings Google's Cloud Functions [52] and Microsoft's Azure Functions [53] follow the path initiated by AWS, currently offering comparable solutions to Lambda, including cost wise [54]. At open source level solutions such as Apache OpenWhisk [55], and Kubernetes' Knative [56] intend to deliver similar functionalities independently of offerings of cloud providers.

Cloud Native Technologies Services: Container-as-a-Service,
Kubernetes-as-a-Service and Container Serverless

The popularity gained by Containerization technologies and Cloud Native Architectures has led to the availability of related services on all public Cloud providers. These resources commonly comprise Container as a Service standalone service offerings, Kubernetes as a Service, as the de-facto standard for container orchestration solution; and the most recent Container serverless offerings, which allow for the deployment of containers making use of orchestration facilities provisioned by the public cloud provider. In further in detail:

Container as a Service   As previously introduced in Sect. 3.3.1, modern applications rely on Cloud Native Architectures built by means of containers.
Containers ease resource providing for application developers, supply
more rapid deployment and facilitate portability. At this stage, all main
cloud providers offer Container as a service based on the most widespread
containerisation solution [9]. These offerings are usually complemented
with "Container Registry as a Service" services, which take on board container lifecycle management including functionalities, such as container
versioning and secure container management. Container as a Service
offerings are considered to be midway between PaaS and IaaS, given that
the user handles all process for building the container on its own albeit
not directly managing the infrastructure. These services operate at the
level of standalone containers which can be limiting for many types of
applications reliant on the orchestration of several containers. Kubernetes
is currently considered a de-facto standard for Container orchestration
solutions.

Kubernetes as a Service   In order to cope with the necessities of modern complex
applications which require container orchestration solutions, main public
cloud providers have released to the market Kubernetes as a service
offerings. Initially developed by Google, it has grown into a key open-
source initiative part of Cloud Native Computing Foundation, Kubernetes
[13] is "an open-source system for managing containerized applications
across multiple hosts. It provides basic mechanisms for deployment,
maintenance, and scaling of applications." [57]. User surveys in the
CNFN community acknowledge today's Kubernetes role as a mainstream
technology alongside its participation in multi-cloud industrial strategies
[58]. Being the Kubernetes technology author, Google already provide
the most mature and automated solution for Kubernetes as a Service vs
the existing offerings of principal public Cloud providers [59].

Serverless containers   Serverless containers term refers to an approach followed
by principal Cloud providers which allow the execution of container
orchestrations without having to handle the underlying infrastructure (as
opposite to Kubernetes as a Services offerings). By doing so, execution
of containers mimic the serverless approach in as much as the user solely
needs to provide the container files and expected quality of service parameters and configurations; the service will be fully provisioned by the cloud
provider to meet these requirements handling the necessary elasticity and
fault tolerance. Azure by means of Azure Container Instances [60] was
the first Cloud provider to implement this approach [60]. Other examples
of these services in public cloud providers are: Google Cloud Run [61]
and AWS Fargate [62].

Internet of Things (IoT) Services

Early IoT platforms were entirely provided by specific solutions vendors who focused on presenting an end-to-end IoT solutions to a vertical. While these kind of IoT platforms are still present in the market, public Cloud providers have developed a new approach in relation to these services, the provision of Cloud IoT Platforms. These solutions, instead of centering on use case particular solutions, follow a Platform approach by delivering a set of services to be combined as building blocks to develop a IoT solutions a part from the services of the selected public Cloud provider.

All Cloud market leaders, AWS, Azure and Google have released Cloud IoT platforms namely AWS IoT Core [63], Azure IoT Core [64] and Google Cloud IoT Core [65]. In all cases, they link these solutions to Edge computing developments. The analysis of offerings in this section will omit this part, which will be covered in the upcoming Edge computing section.

The IoT services from public Cloud providers display three main types of features:

IoT Device Management   Support remotely handling IoT devices configurations, IoT device security, firmware updates as well as device monitoring.

IoT Data Management   Detail the set of protocols to communicate with the IoT devices and obtain the generated data in addition to facilitating storing and processing it.

IoT Application Management   Specify all services which allow the development of applications managing IoT devices data, containing features such as message brokers, rules engines and digital twins.

Following the usual dynamics, AWS was the first public Cloud provider to launch IoT services on the market back in 2015. AWS IoT was shortly followed by Azure equivalent services. Google Cloud still maintains a limited offering in this field concentrating only on IoT device management features in addition to their application management services [66].

It is essential to highlight that both AWS and Azure are currently supporting the development of real time operating systems (RTOS), also as part of their IoT services strategy. AWS has taken over the support of FreeRTOS [67] and Azure commercial use of ThreadX as Azure RTOS [68].

Machine Learning (ML) and Artificial Intelligence (AI) Services

In the past few years, public Cloud providers have been allocating gigantic amounts of resources to address the most trending IT area, artificial intelligence.

These investments result in more and more sophisticated services customers of these cloud providers can integrate into their applications and services or use to develop their own machine learning models. Public Cloud providers follow the same approach previously introduced for Internet of Things services, they provide a set of services which act as building blocks users can integrate in order to build customer solutions in these two main categories:

Artificial Intelligence Services   make it possible to apply AI features into user applications avoiding to develop user machine learning models with the aid of pre-trained models developed by the Cloud providers. Common services available in this area are: Computer vision services; services for automated data extraction and analysis, such as natural language processing; particular services in relation to language, including charbots and virtual agent services, automated speech recognition and text-to-speech solutions; software code analysis services; in addition to data anomaly and on-line fraud detection. Notably, certain cloud providers start to offer sector specific AI services which address the specific needs of a vertical sectors. Examples of these are AWS Industrial AI solutions [69] to detect abnormal machine conditions or to perform predictive maintenance and Healthcare AI Services, for storage, analysis and extraction of health data.

Machine learning services   render existing tools and services available at Cloud providers to encourage users to develop their own machine learning models. In this field public Cloud providers offer machine learning IDEs or integrated studios which assist the user in managing the lifecycle of their models building and deployment as well as tools for data exploration and validation of results. These tools lend support to use Juniper notebooks and MLOps approaches in addition to enabling the use of multiple frameworks such as TensorFlow and PyTorch among others. Examples of these are AWS Sage Maker [70], Azure Machine Learning studio [71] and Google Cloud AutoML [72]. Typically accessible by means of these tools, public Cloud providers provide a wide set of built-in algorithms for common features such as classification, regression, clustering, anomaly detection, recommendation and ranking [73].

3.5   Hybrid and Multi-Cloud Management

The Cloud market has witnessed a gradual trend to employ hybrid and multi-cloud models, as a mechanism to avoid vendor lock-in as well as perceived data security and privacy risks, and to obtain legal compliance. Figures provided by user survey in the State of Cloud report 2022, seize this trend in a 89% of respondent users having a multi-cloud strategy while "80% recognised to have a hybrid approach by uniting use of public and private clouds" [74]. In the absence of a widely accepted definition of multi-cloud and hybrid cloud terms, several market and academic research works have advanced certain specifications:

Multi-Cloud   Multi-Cloud is demarcated as the "serial or simultaneous use of services from diverse providers to execute an application" in [75]. Diverse authors such as [76] have used the term Inter-Cloud to refer to these inter-connection models across diverse clouds.

Hybrid Cloud   Gartner as part of its glossary, defines Hybrid cloud computing as a "policy-based and coordinated service provisioning, use and management across a mixture of internal and external cloud services" [77].

Juan Ferrer et al. [78] has examined a diversity of scenarios which explore coordinated and simultaneous utilisation of diverse Cloud offerings in the context of private and public cloud interplay:

Cloud bursting   Cloud bursting is presented as the simplest and most popular hybrid/multi-cloud model. In this scenario, an application in execution in a private cloud is moved, "busts", into a public cloud when the demand for capacity exceeds its available capacity.

Federated Cloud   In a federated Cloud environment a cloud provider obtains additional capacity from other providers while offering spare capacity to group of cloud providers, a federation, when available.

Multi-cloud   In a multi-provider scenario, a user or a broker acting on behalf of the user, handles the provision of cloud services choosing the best fitting offerings from multiple providers.

The interconnection among cloud environments envisaged by the multi-cloud and hybrid cloud scenarios previously presented poses a number of requirements in terms of Cloud Interoperability and Portability. The interoperable Europe initiative of the European Commission employs the following definitions for both terms [79]:

Interoperability   within the cloud computing context refers to "the capability of public and private clouds to use an agreed language to use each others' access interfaces and to transmit data in machine to machine communications. Achieving high levels of interoperability is critical for the ability of a cloud service customer to exchange data within and between cloud services. Nevertheless, this capability is still not universally available."

Portability   is referred as the "capability of a program to be executed on various types of data processing systems without converting the program to a different language and with little or no modification". For Cloud computing it capitalises on the capacity to transmit both applications and data which have been initially developed and generated by a provider to another Cloud Service Provider without significant porting or transformation costs.

As the demand for Multi-Cloud hybrid cloud grows, two types of market approaches aim to address this user requirement:

Offerings by technology vendors of PaaS multi-cloud solutions   which as introduced previously in Sect. 3.4.2 enables the customer to utilise services across diverse public cloud provider. While Interoperability based on standards is not yet a market reality, these solutions provide plug-ins to public cloud offerings which enable this feature. Portability is achieved by adopting de-facto market standards such as Kubernetes. Examples of these offerings are Vmware Tanzu

[46] and Redhat OpenShift [45]. These offerings enable Kubernetes provision in public Cloud offerings and include added value services such as self-service provisioning, application catalogues and life-cycle management, high availability and fault tolerance.

Offerings by public cloud providers   which aim at responding to Hybrid and Multi-Cloud user demand by offering platforms which permit in-house deployment complementing their public cloud offerings. The need for portability and interoperability is typically suppressed by putting forward one single vendor fully compatible ecosystem of services. This approach particularly consents to the private and public cloud interplay while continuing to bounce the cloud users to an ecosystem of choice. While public Cloud providers enable private cloud developments and hybrid cloud provision by means of their targeted products Microsoft Azure Stack [80], AWS Outpost [81] and Google Anthos [82], these products are frequently engaged in their Edge computing strategies addressing Telco providers. At the time of writing one of the main public cloud providers, Google Cloud, assuredly admits the multi-cloud user requirement by concrete developments in its Anthos offering to support Azure and AWS via its Anthos Multi-Cloud API [83] to handle Kubernetes clusters on top of AWS and Azure services.

References

1. Mell, P., & Grance, T. SP 800-145. *The NIST definition of cloud computing*. (National Institute of Standards & Technology, 2011, 9)
2. *Amazon Web Services, Cloud Computing Services - Amazon Web Services (AWS)*. https://aws.amazon.com/
3. *ISO/IEC 17203:2017 Information technology — open virtualization format (OVF) specification*. https://www.iso.org/standard/72081.html
4. *libvirt Virtualisation API*. https://libvirt.org/
5. Xen. http://www.xen.org/
6. *Kernelbased Virtual Machine*. http://www.linuxkvm.org/page/Main_Page
7. VMware. http://www.vmware.com/
8. OpenStack, *Choosing a hypervisor*. https://docs.openstack.org/arch-design/design-compute/design-compute-hypervisor.html
9. *Docker: Enterprise container platform for high-velocity innovation*. Retrieved May 26, 2022, from https://www.docker.com/
10. Linux Containers. Retrieved May 26, 2022, from https://linuxcontainers.org/
11. Drewanz, D., & Grimme, L. (2012). *The role of Oracle Solaris Zones and Linux containers in a virtualization strategy*. https://www.oracle.com/technical-resources/articles/it-infrastructure/admin-zones-containers-virtualization.html
12. *Flexera 2021 State of Cloud report*. https://info.flexera.com/CM-REPORT-State-of-the-Cloud
13. Kubernetes, *Production-Grade container orchestration*. https://kubernetes.io
14. Pahl, C., Brogi, A., Soldani, J., & Jamshidi, P. Cloud container technologies: A state-of-the-art review. *IEEE Transactions On Cloud Computing*, *7*, 677–692 (2019)
15. Bernstein, D. Containers and cloud: From LXC to Docker to Kubernetes. *IEEE Cloud Computing*, *1*, 81–84 (2014)
16. Firecraker. https://firecracker-microvm.github.io/

17. Unikernels. http://unikernel.org/
18. Kata Containers. https://katacontainers.io/
19. Gvisor. https://github.com/google/gvisor
20. Cloud Native Computing Foundation. https://www.cncf.io/
21. CNCF Cloud Native Definition v1.0. https://github.com/cncf/toc/blob/main/DEFINITION.md
22. *Gartner Identifies the Top Strategic Technology Trends for 2022.* https://www.gartner.com/en/newsroom/press-releases/2021-10-18-gartner-identifies-the-top-strategic-technology-trends-for-2022
23. Webber, K., Goodwin, J. & Safari, A. *Migrating Java to the Cloud.* (O'Reilly Media, Incorporated, 2017). https://books.google.lu/books?id=wnU6zQEACAAJ
24. CNCF Graduated and Incubating projects. https://www.cncf.io/projects/
25. CNCF Landscape. https://landscape.cncf.io/
26. Statista, *Worldwide infrastructure as a service (IaaS) and platform as a service (PaaS) hyperscaler market share from 2020 to 2022, by vendor.* https://www.statista.com/statistics/1202770/hyperscaler-iaas-paas-market-share/
27. *Introducing two new Amazon EC2 bare metal instances.* https://aws.amazon.com/about-aws/whats-new/2021/11/amazon-ec2-bare-metal-instances/
28. Azure Dedicated Host. https://azure.microsoft.com/enus/services/virtualmachines/dedicated-host/#overview
29. *Bare Metal Solution: Enabling specialized workloads in Google Cloud.* https://cloud.google.com/blog/products/compute/bare-metal-solution-enabling-specialized-workloads-in-google-cloud
30. *AWS and NVIDIA to bring Arm-based Graviton2 instances with GPUs to the cloud.* https://aws.amazon.com/blogs/machinelearning/awsandnvidiatobringarmbasedinstanceswithgpustothecloud/
31. *AWS New – EC2 Instances (A1) Powered by Arm-Based AWS Graviton Processors.* https://aws.amazon.com/blogs/aws/newec2instancesa1poweredbyarmbasedawsgravitonprocessors/
32. *Now in preview: Azure Virtual Machines with Ampere Altra Arm-based processors.* https://azure.microsoft.com/enus/blog/nowinpreviewazurevirtualmachineswithamperealtraarmbasedprocessors/
33. *Jeff Barr, AWS News Blog, in the works – Amazon EC2 elastic GPUs.* https://aws.amazon.com/blogs/aws/intheworkamazonec2elasticgpus/
34. *AWS, Linux accelerated computing instances.* http://docs.aws.amazon.com/AWSEC2/latest/UserGuide/acceleratedcomputinginstances.html
35. *IBM GPU Cloud Server Overview.* https://www.ibm.com/cloud/gpu
36. Azure, *GPU optimized virtual machine sizes.* https://docs.microsoft.com/en-us/azure/virtual-machines/sizesgpu
37. GoogleCloud, Cloud GPUs. https://cloud.google.com/gpu
38. Sebastian Moss, *Google launches TPU v4 chips, builds 9 exaflops AI cluster.* https://www.datacenterdynamics.com/en/news/googlelaunchestpuv4chipsbuilds9exaflopsaicluster/
39. Ferrer, A., Pérez, D., & González, R. Multi-cloud platform-as-a-service model, functionalities and approaches. *Procedia Computer Science, 97,* 63–72 (2016). https://www.sciencedirect.com/science/article/pii/S187705091632097X, 2nd International Conference on Cloud Forward: From Distributed to Complete Computing
40. .Net applications on Azure. https://azure.microsoft.com/en-us/develop/net/
41. Google Cloud, App Engine https://cloud.google.com/appengine
42. Salesforce platform. https://www.salesforce.com/products/platform/products/force/?sfdc-redirect=300
43. Microsoft Azure, Cloud Computing Services. https://azure.microsoft.com/en-us/
44. Google Cloud, Cloud Computing Services. https://cloud.google.com/
45. Red Hat OpenShift. https://www.redhat.com/en/technologies/cloud-computing/openshift
46. VMware Tanzu. https://tanzu.vmware.com/
47. Rob Moore, *AWS vs Azure vs GCP cloud comparison: Databases.* https://acloudguru.com/blog/engineering/aws-vs-azure-vs-gcp-cloud-comparison-databases

48. Shafiei, H., Khonsari, A., & Mousavi, P. (2022). Serverless computing: a survey of opportunities, challenges, and applications. ACM Computing Surveys, 54(11s), 1–32. https://doi.org/10.1145/3510611
49. Serverless Computing: Patterns and Road Ahead Roger Barga, Amazon Web Services. https://www.serverlesscomputing.org/wosc17/presentations/barga-keynote-serverless.pdf
50. *CNCF Serverless Whitepaper v1.0.* https://github.com/cncf/wg-serverless/tree/master/whitepaper
51. AWS Lambda. https://aws.amazon.com/lambda
52. GoogleCloud. *Cloud Functions.* https://cloud.google.com/functions/
53. Azure Functions. https://azure.microsoft.com/en-us/services/functions/
54. Moneer Rifai, *Serverless showdown: AWS Lambda vs Azure Functions vs Google Cloud Functions.* https://acloudguru.com/blog/engineering/serverless-showdown-aws-lambda-vs-azure-functions-vs-google-cloud-functions
55. Apache OpenWhisk. https://openwhisk.apache.org/
56. Knative. https://github.com/knative/
57. Kubernetes (K8s). https://github.com/kubernetes/kubernetes
58. State of Kubernetes 2022. https://tanzu.s3.useast2.amazonaws.com/campaigns/pdfs/StateOfKubernetes2022_eBook.pdf
59. Alexander Potasnick, *AKS vs EKS vs GKE: Managed Kubernetes services compared.* https://acloudguru.com/blog/engineering/aksvseksvsgkemanagedkubernetesservices-compared
60. Azure, *Azure Container Instances documentation.* https://docs.microsoft.com/en-us/azure/containerinstances/
61. GoogleCloud, Cloud Run. https://cloud.google.com/run
62. AWS Fargate. https://aws.amazon.com/fargate/
63. AWS IoT Core. https://aws.amazon.com/iot-core/
64. Azure IoT. https://azure.microsoft.com/en-us/overview/iot/
65. Google Cloud IoT Core. https://cloud.google.com/iot-core
66. Mohammad Hasan, *The IoT cloud: Microsoft Azure vs. AWS vs. Google Cloud*, February 2022. https://iot-analytics.com/iot-cloud/
67. FreeRTOS FAQ – Amazon. https://www.freertos.org/FAQ_Amazon.html
68. Azure RTOS. https://azure.microsoft.com/en-au/services/rtos/
69. AWS Explore AWS AI services. https://aws.amazon.com/machine-learning/aiservices/
70. Amazon SageMaker. https://aws.amazon.com/sagemaker/?nc2=h_a1
71. Azure Machine Learning studio. https://docs.microsoft.com/enus/azure/machine-learning/overviewwhatismachinelearningstudio
72. GoogleCloud, AutoML. https://cloud.google.com/automl/
73. AltexSoft, *Comparing Machine Learning as a Service: Amazon, Microsoft Azure, Google Cloud AI, IBM Watson* (2021). https://www.altexsoft.com/blog/datascicncc/comparing-machine-learning-as-a-service-amazon-microsoft-azure-google-cloud-ai-ibm-watson/
74. Flexera 2022 State of Cloud report, https://info.flexera.com/CM-REPORT-State-of-the-Cloud?lead_source=Website%20Visitor&id=Blog
75. Petcu, D. Multi-Cloud: expectations and current approaches. In *MultiCloud 2013 - Proceedings of the International Workshop on Multi-Cloud Applications and Federated Clouds* (pp. 1–6) (2013,4)
76. Toosi, A., Calheiros, R., & Buyya, R. Interconnected cloud computing environments: Challenges, taxonomy, and survey. *ACM Computing Survey, 47* (2014, 5). https://doi.org/10.1145/2593512
77. Gartner Glossary, Hybrid Cloud Computing. https://www.gartner.com/en/information-technology/glossary/hybrid-cloud-computing
78. Juan Ferrer, A., Hernández, F., Tordsson, J., Elmroth, E., Ali-Eldin, A., Zsigri, C., Sirvent, R., Guitart, J., Badia, R., Djemame, K., Ziegler, W., Dimitrakos, T., Nair, S., Kousiouris, G., Konstanteli, K., Varvarigou, T., Hudzia, B., Kipp, A., Wesner, S., Corrales, M., Forgó, N., Sharif, T., & Sheridan, C. OPTIMIS: A holistic approach to cloud service provisioning. *Future Generation Computer Systems, 28*, 66–77 (2012). https://www.sciencedirect.com/science/article/pii/S0167739X1100104X

79. European Commission. *ICT Standards for procurement, Interoperability and porta-bility*. https://joinup.ec.europa.eu/collection/ict-standards-procurement/interoperability-and-portability
80. Azure, Azure Stack. https://azure.microsoft.com/en-us/overview/azure-stack/
81. AWS, *AWS infrastructure and services on premises – AWS Outposts*. https://aws.amazon.com/outposts/
82. Google Cloud, *Hybrid Cloud Management with Anthos | Google Cloud*. https://cloud.google.com/anthos
83. Google Cloud, *Anthos Multi-Cloud API*. https://cloud.google.com/anthos/clusters/docs/multi-cloud/reference/rest

Chapter 4
Mobile Cloud Computing

4.1 Introduction to Mobile Cloud Computing

MCC is an area of research meant to connect Mobile Computing [1–3], Cloud computing [4] and even, certain aspects of networks management [5]. There are manifold approaches and definitions, yet in general they all have the same principle at their core which is to apply to mobile's devices compute and storage processes techniques from cloud computing [6].

Some examples of these definitions are provided below:

- Sanaei et al. [7] defines MCC as "a rich mobile computing technology that leverages unified elastic resources of varied clouds and network technologies toward unrestricted functionality, storage, and mobility to serve a multitude of mobile devices anywhere, anytime through the channel of Ethernet or Internet regardless of heterogeneous environments and platforms based on the pay-as-you-use principle".
- For [8] MCC represents "an emergent mobile cloud paradigm which leverage mobile computing, networking, and cloud computing to study mobile service models, develop mobile cloud infrastructures, platforms, and service applications for mobile clients. Its primary objective is to delivery location-aware mobile services with mobility to users based on scalable mobile cloud resources in networks, computers, storages, and mobile devices. Its goal is to deliver them with secure mobile cloud resources, service applications, and data using energy-efficient mobile cloud resources in a pay-as-you-use model".
- Kovachev et al. [9] describes MCC as "a model for transparent elastic augmentation of mobile device capabilities via ubiquitous wireless access to cloud storage and computing resources, with context-aware dynamic adjusting of offloading in respect to change in operating conditions, while preserving available sensing and interactivity capabilities of mobile devices".

MCC has been recognised as a beneficial technology for diverse fields of mobile applications in [10]. By means of concrete application examples, it details mobile

© The Author(s), under exclusive license to Springer Nature Switzerland AG 2023   43
A. Juan Ferrer, *Beyond Edge Computing*, https://doi.org/10.1007/978-3-031-23344-9_4

applications that take advantage of MCC in areas which comprise: Mobile commerce, using MCC as the mechanism that allows handling mobility in operations such as "mobile transactions and payments and mobile messaging and mobile ticketing" [10]; Mobile learning, applying MCC in order to overcome shortcomings in terms of devices costs, available network, computing and storage resources, as well as, access to limited educational resources; Mobile healthcare, in which MCC is employed as a tool that permits efficient access to information making specific emphasis in the necessary security and data protection aspects; Mobile gaming, enabling these kind of applications to access resource richer environments. In addition to these, MCC is considered admittedly useful for content sharing, searching services and collaborative applications [10].

4.2 MCC Challenges

Challenges in the scope of Mobile Cloud fall into four groups: Firstly, we can mention the ones inherent to the use of mobile devices. These are related on the one hand to the limitations of mobile devices in resources and battery and, on the other hand, those associated to the ability to perceive context and location. In addition to these, three groups of challenges related to the different approaches favoured to deal with these constraints such as Network Connectivity, Security and Off-loading and Application Partitioning are detailed. These are represented in Fig. 4.1.

4.2.1 Inherent Mobile Devices Challenges

Scarcity in Resource and Energy   While initial works in the area of Mobile Computing considered overcoming devices' limitations as the major issue for performance associated to resources hardware characteristics [2, 11]. Authors today acknowledge the substantial augmentation of devices capacities in terms of CPU, memory, storage and others, such as the size of screen or associated sensors [12]. Nevertheless, battery lifetime is still often perceived as a main roadblock due to the effect it has on mobile resource availability. With this regard, [7] acknowledges existing efforts to optimise, by means of applying offloading techniques, energy utilisation on the mobile device and the fact that this cannot always reduce energy. Other authors do not regard energy management and battery restriction as an issue for present-day Mobile Cloud Computing [10, 13]. Specifically [10] presents MCC as a promising solution that can help to reduce power consumption in mobile devices without having to perform changes into the devices structure or hardware and taking advantage of software off-loading techniques.

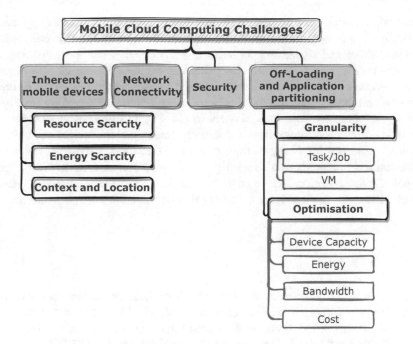

Fig. 4.1 Mobile Cloud Computing taxonomy

Context and Location   Guan in [6] underlines the fact that mobile devices allow
        the assessment of certain information from the device itself without the
        user's interaction. In the information that can be extracted without user
        interaction two types of contexts are identified: spatial context, related to
        location, position and proximity; as well as, social context, extracted from
        the user's or groups social interactions. Sanaei et al. [7] describes obstacles
        which radiate from the management of the social context owing to the
        exponential growth of this context due to multiple social interactions in
        diverse networks and social dynamism. The identified obstacles are related
        to storage, management and processing of these context data on resource
        constrained mobile devices.

4.2.2 Network Connectivity

The nomadic nature of Mobile devices and the fact that they rely on wireless
networks is a challenge for Mobile Cloud in [12]. Wireless networks are "characterised by low-bandwidth, intermittent and lower reliable network protocols is
considered as a factor that affects latency and therefore, unfavourably affects energy
consumption and response time" [7]. Hoang et al. [10] adds to this list availability

issues and heterogeneity among different wireless networks interfaces applied. It explicitly cites as sources for availability issues, the aspects of traffic congestion, network failure and signal loss. In terms of heterogeneity, considers diversity on the radio access technologies, precisely determining the MCC needs with regards to continuous connectivity, on-demand scalability and energy efficiency. In order to address all these issues, approaches based in local clouds or cloudlets have been developed. These are examined in detail in [14–17]. In this context, [18] tackles the aspect of wireless intermittent connectivity among mobile devices and cloudlet environments, as a MCC key distinctive aspect. It develops a dynamic offloading algorithm which regards user's mobility patterns and connectivity to diverse geographically disperse cloudlets. In addition, it examines cloudlet's admission control policies based on user's distance to the cloudlet and cloudlet's coverage areas.

4.2.3 Security

Fernando et al. [19] concedes the fact that although many authors cite the need to provide the appropriate security context for Mobile Cloud Computing Services execution, the issue has been barely touched upon thus far. Specific analysis of Authentication and Privacy and Security issues are exhibited in [20, 21].

Shiraz et al. [22] underlines that fact that "privacy measures are required to ensure execution of mobile applications in isolated and trustworthy environments while security procedures are necessary to protect against threads, mainly at network level". The analysis of privacy and security issues featured in [23] does not specifically concentrate on Mobile Cloud Computing issues, but rather reports well-known issues in the context of Cloud computing which involve the providers access to to user's virtual infrastructure or mobile physical threads associated with lending, lost or thieve of mobile devices or connection to public open network infrastructures.

Conversely, [24] provides a careful analysis and draws a detailed comparison of existing Mobile Cloud Computing security frameworks. Conclusions point to the fact that the majority of security frameworks overlook the trade-off between energy consumption and security requirements. It identifies hurdles which can be surmounted at the level of "data security, network security, data locality, data integrity, web application security, data segregation, data access, authentication, authorisation, data confidentiality, data breach issues, and various other factors"[24].

4.2.4 Off-Loading and Application Partitioning

Many of Mobile Cloud Computing perspectives today revolve around application offloading and partitioning techniques in order to augment mobile device capacities [19]. Off-loading consist of moving part of the mobile computational workload to more resource-rich servers in heterogeneous Cloud models [25]. Research in Offloading techniques [26] often contemplates a set of well-delimited phases which include:

Decision to offload   Offloading has been viewed as a means to save energy and/or improve performance of mobile devices; however both feasibility and acquired benefits depend on factors such as available network link and amount of data to be transmitted. Considering the trade-off between offloading costs (commonly in terms of time, data transmission, economic costs, overall performance and energy) versus local processing costs, plays a key role in reaching offloading decisions.

Decision of application parts to off-load   The offloading granularity can be taken statically; this is pre-determined in the mobile application execution flow at application development time; or dynamically, determined at runtime based on the execution context at a given time[25, 26]. The granularity of parts of the application candidates to be offloaded ranges from offloading the complete application, so called coarse-grained methods; to fine-grained methods which consider specific application parts both at level of object, method, class, function and even tasks [27].

Selection/Definition of infrastructures to off-load   Both specific framework analysis and literature surveys in the offloading topic consider this step, not as the selection of a computing infrastructure, but a specific server or surrogate selection in a pre-defined infrastructure [25–27]. Very frequently, application partitioning mechanisms include mechanisms to optimize mobile device at the level of processor augmentation, energy savings, execution cost and bandwidth utilisation [12, 19, 22, 23].

4.3   MCC Models

Multiple papers tackle the issue of workload offloading from mobile devices to resource richer environments. These can be classified according to four main perspectives, depicted in Fig. 4.2:

Off-loading to Server   Under this classification we consider works that perform offloading to specific servers, which can be located or not in a Cloud environment. The pre-configured server has the mission to provide resources to alleviate mobile resource constraints and are by design limited to the initially defined server configuration. Analysis of articles that fit in this category is provided in Sect. 4.4.1.

Off-loading to Cloud   Through use of private or public Cloud computing infrastructures, this classification considers the execution of off-loaded application parts often to virtual machine executing in a IaaS provider [28]. Works in this class are detailed in Sect. 4.4.2.

Off-loading to Cloudlet   By means of using of Local computing infrastructures or Cloudlets [17], works classified under this category (see Sect. 4.4.3) aim

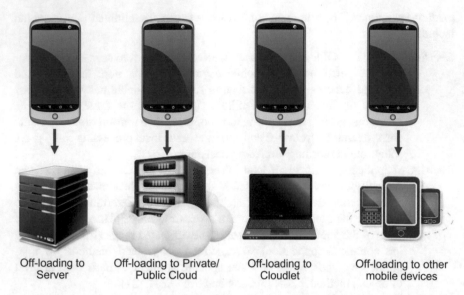

| Off-loading to | Off-loading to Private/ | Off-loading to | Off-loading to other |
| Server | Public Cloud | Cloudlet | mobile devices |

Fig. 4.2 Classification of Mobile Cloud Computing models

to reduce the overhead network latency derived from the use of distant traditional cloud infrastructures by using local infrastructures, cloudlets, closer to the mobile device location. Satyanarayanan et al. [29] further develops this concept by regarding the cloudlet as an intermediary step between the mobile device and the cloud, in a three-tier hierarchy in which the cloudlet is deemed to be a "Data Centre in a box" set-up so as to "bring the cloud closer" to the device [30], therefore reducing latency. Conceptually, the idea of Cloudlet is the building block which sustains both Edge and Fog Computing. This is further developed in Chap. 6.

Off-loading to device   Works in this category rely on using additional mobile devices capacity, commonly labelled as surrogates. These works are detailed in Sect. 4.4.4. Recently, under this standpoint a novel concept has been formulated through the development of Mobile Ad-hoc cloud (MAC) concept.

This classification serves us to structure the analysis of existing works in MCC in Sect. 4.4 presented hereby.

4.4   Analysis of Existing Works in MCC

Drawing on the previously identified Mobile Cloud Computing Challenges and Models we define the taxonomy that is depicted in Fig. 4.1. In the sections that follow we employ the Mobile Cloud Computing models for categorisation of existing works.

4.4.1 Approaches Based on Off-Loading to a Server

The model considers off-loading from Mobile device to a fixed external server, which can be or not hosted in a cloud environment.

4.4.1.1 MAUI, Making Smartphones Last Longer with Code Offload

MAUI [31] targets reducing energy consumed by mobile devices while executing resource intensive applications. It offers fine-grained application off-loading at level of method. MAUI was defined by Microsoft research in 2010, being one of Mobile Cloud Computing precursor works, role in which is commonly referenced [10, 19].

MAUI's design goal is to overcome battery limitations of mobile devices. This work identifies the three most energy voracious categories of applications: video games and streaming, as well as, applications which focus on analysing data streams coming from mobile device's sensors. By means of .Net code portability features, MAUI maintains two versions of the application to offload; one executing at the mobile device (equipped with Windows mobile in an ARM architecture) and one running at the server (x86 CPU). MAUI architecture presents components which execute both on the mobile device and the server. MAUI programming model, based C# and Microsoft .NET Common Language Runtime (CLR), allows developers to annotate methods as remotable. These annotated methods are instrumented at compilation time with the aim of allowing application state transfer when offloading. In order to minimize the amount of transfer of serialized application state, it uses an incremental approach, solely engaged in transmitting differences between mobile and remote states in different method invocations. At runtime the MAUI determines for all instrumented methods whether to execute it on the mobile device or remotely in the server before each execution.

Experimentation over MAUI's performance has been performed using four distinct applications, three of them are pre-build and currently running on Windows mobile phones (face-recognition, interactive video game and chess game applications), whereas a forth application was developed from scratch, a voice-based Spanish to English translator. For the first three, analysis of energy consumption and performance has been performed by comparing standalone execution of the application of the mobile application versus remote server execution based on a set of application metrics defined per each one of the mobile applications and considering several network conditions.

4.4.1.2 Cuckoo, a Computation Offloading Framework for Smartphones

Cuckoo framework [32] targets application offloading for Android platform. Cuckoo design goals focus on providing a framework for mobile phones computation offload which allows energy consumption reduction, along with increased speed on execution of compute intensive applications for the Android mobile platform. The framework includes a programming model based on Java, conjoined with a Runtime environment. It allows mobile to server fine-grained method offloading which presents two optimization models: minimizing computation time and mobile device energy consumption. Server side execution requires any environment running a complete Java Virtual Machine, whether it is a dedicated server, a local cluster, a VM in a Cloud environment or any other capable environment.

To a certain extent, Cuckoo can be considered an analogous work in Java and Android platforms to previous .Net and Windows Mobile developments in MAUI. Having its main difference in the fact that Cuckoo permits to distinguish among code versions to be executed in the mobile device and the server [32] bringing new capabilities for user system configurability. This mechanism, while being powerful in some cases, has been identified as a drawback in previous mobile cloud computing surveys due to the need of providing two versions of the same application code [19]. By the use of Ibis High performance computing system Cuckoo acquires new capabilities for remote server configurability compared to other Server Off-loading existing works. Cuckoo permits dynamic deployment and interoperability with remote servers in diverse execution environments. This way, Cuckoo is able to consider Off-loading to Server model, in remote servers in diverse execution environments (dedicated server, a local cluster, a VM in a Cloud environment, etc.) in a transparent manner enabled by the interoperability layer that Ibis facilitates.

Cuckoo has been validated using two example applications: First, eyeDentify, an application which performs image pattern recognition, and simultaneously computing and memory intensive. eyeDentify was re-factored to use the Cuckoo programming environment. The second application was Photoshoot which is a distributed augmented reality mobile application.

4.4.2   Approaches Based on Off-Loading to Public/Private Cloud Computing

These approaches focus primarily on augmenting mobile device capabilities enabled by the use of more powerful resources in traditional date centre Clouds, both considering in private or public cloud environments and different levels of the Cloud stack (IaaS, PaaS and SaaS).

4.4.2.1   CloneCloud, Elastic Execution Between Mobile Device and Cloud

CloneCloud presents a system which aspires to "augment mobile devices" [33] capabilities by means of offloading methods to device clones executed in a computational cloud. Vision was presented in [33] while its implementation is reported in [34]. CloneCloud design goal is enable automatic transformation of mobile applications to profit from Cloud.

Significantly different from previous works Cuckoo and MAUI, CloneCloud is not dependent on the programmer in order to create application partitions. Instead, its purpose is to make application partitioning seamless and automatic for the programmer. In order to do so, it applies an offline method in which both static program analysis and dynamic program profiling are performed to define application partitions. Application partitions, in this case, are a choice of execution points where the application migrates a part of its execution and state from the device to the clone. Analyses can be executed considering several execution characteristics (considering CPU, network and energy consumption) leading to the creation of diverse partitions for the same application.

Static program analysis aims to identify "legal" choices whereby migration and re-integration execution between the device and the cloud are made possible. The system defines these migration points as method entry and exit points. "Legal" partitions are pre-computed and stored in a database. These are used in combination with dynamic application profiler to manage the distributed execution of the application across the mobile device and the device clone in the cloud.

CloneCloud is reliant on the concept of Application layer VMs, specifically in the Java VM available on Android devices, DalvikVM. This supports the migration of application pieces between the mobile device and the clone despite the differences in the CPU instruction set architectures, ARM and x86. Migration in CloneCloud is at level of thread and relies in a private Cloud environment based on VMware ESX.

4.4.2.2 ThinkAir

ThinkAir [35, 36] ambition is to simply developers tasks in migrating their applications to Cloud. In order to so, it presents a framework that facilitates method level computation offloading to Cloud environments.

Main novelties provided by ThinkAir adopt a more sophisticated use of Cloud computing environment directed at exploiting Cloud potential with regard to elasticity and scalability for Mobile Cloud benefit. ThinkAir provides on-demand cloud resource allocation in order to comply with specific requirements of mobile applications to offload at level of CPU and memory resources. Unlike CloneCloud, ThinkAir makes use of public commercial Cloud offerings and does not store pre-defined off loadable code partitions. ThinkAir relies instead on annotations provided by the developer to identify parts of code candidate to be off-loaded.

Furthermore, it enables parallelization by dynamically managing virtual infrastructure in the Cloud environment, therefore reducing both cloud server's side and overall application's execution time and energy consumption. The primary server in the ThinkAir architecture is a VM which clones of the mobile device replicating both data and applications (additional information about how these clones are synchronised and kept up-to-date is not present in the analysed works). This primary server is always set-up ready to be contacted by the mobile device. Other

VMs distinct from the primary server, called secondary servers, are instantiated on-demand by the user. The primary server manages communications from the mobile, the life-cycle of these secondary servers, as well as task, allocation in case of parallelization; however no concrete details about this mechanism are readily available.

4.4.3 Approaches Based on Off-Loading to Cloudlets

Satyanarayanan et al. [17] formulated the concept of cloudlet as "a trusted, resource rich computer or cluster of computers that is well-connected to the internet and it is available for nearby mobile devices". In this concept, the mobile device acts as thin-client to services deployed in the cloudlet by means of VMs and that are accessible by wireless LAN.

As opposed to previously described approaches subject to distant servers or clouds, the overall aim of these models is to decrease the overhead network latency derived from the use of distant traditional cloud infrastructures. This is achieved by using local clouds or infrastructures, cloudlets, closer to the mobile device location. Proximity intends to ensure the predictability of the cloudlet's response time in order of magnitude of milliseconds. From this definition it derives the intrinsic linkage among cloudlet concept defined by Satyanarayanan in 2009 and posterior Edge and Fog computing definitions [37, 38]. Generally speaking, the cloudlet vision defined by Satyanarayanan et al. [17] constructs scenarios where cloudlets shape "decentralised and widely disperse" computing infrastructures spread over the Internet. It is similar to enriching WIFI access points today with an easily deployable, long-lasting and self-managing "datacenter-in-a-box" resource. It is relevant to note, that [17] circumscribe cloudlet to WLAN connectivity.

4.4.3.1   The Case for VM-Based Cloudlets in Mobile Computing

While [17] defined the concept of cloudlet it also provided an architecture in order to turn the concept into reality. Several authors, including those of the recently developed Edge Computing area, do not dramatically differ in the concept articulation, but in its realisation: in MCC context developing the concept of workload offloading from mobile devices while in Edge and Fog contexts, responding to processing needs of IoT scenarios.. Some of these works are described in the sections that follow.

Overall design ambition of this work is to unveil potential of mobile computing as a mechanism which "seamlessly augments cognitive abilities of users using compute-intensive capabilities such as speech recognition, natural language processing, computer vision and graphics, machine learning, augmented reality, planning and decision-making". This ambition, articulated more than a decade ago, is today demonstrated ahead of its time and visionary by dint of existing Edge computing and Swarm computing foreseen evolution. The architecture proposed in this paper [17] is contingent upon "transient customisation of cloudlet infrastructure" in which, VMs are temporarily created, used and, afterwards, discarded from the cloudlet infrastructure in a dynamic manner and in order to provide a specific service to a mobile device located nearby. VM technology creates the necessary isolation and compatibility for cloudlet sustainability.

4.4.3.2 Gabriel

Following the example described in previous work [17], Gabriel [39] applies the Cloudlet concept to wearable devices in order to exploit its potential in Cognitive assistance processes. Gabriel relies on Cloudlets, with a view to reduce end-to-end latency while addressing battery and processing constraints of these wearable devices.

The concept is developed for the cognitive assistance scenarios include applications such as Face, Object, and Optical character recognition and Motion classifier. These require the interaction with wearable device (Google Glasses in this case) while placing high demands on both computation level capacity and latency requirements. The system design considers offloading from wearable devices to cloudlets and considering transiency among diverse cloudlets.

Also it takes the account that cloudlets could have interactions to public/private clouds. Another notable aspect is that Cloudlets could be implemented with resource richer (not smartphones) movable devices such as laptops and netbooks. These bring different options for deployment of Gabriel framework itself, however are not developed in its architecture so to enable interoperability and seamless integration with a variety of execution environments. In Gabriel offloading normally occurs between the wearable device and the cloudlet located nearby. The wearable device discovers and associates to it.

In the absence of a cloudlet set-up, a proposed solution is to offload to cloud. This alternative workaround does not offer the cloudlet advantages incurring into the WAN latency and bandwidth issues in accessing distant Clouds initially avoided with cloudlets.

In addition, this framework considers the situation of not having internet connection accessible, the alternative solution proposed is the use of a mobile device or a laptop carried by the user as a direct device to offload. The vision proposed is that as smartphones increasingly come with more processing power, they can morph into viable offloading devices in the near future. Gabriel deploys each cognitive application in a separated VM in the cloudlet cluster. This cluster is also utilised in order to perform computational task parallelization required by the various applications.

4.4.4   Approaches Based on Off-Loading to Other Mobile Devices

Hitherto, approaches regarding the mobile device part of the cloud are the least explored ones. The works under this classification significantly differ from previous MCC presented works. Both for Server, Public/Private Cloud and Cloudlet based MCC approaches, the mobile resource acts as a thin client and main motivation is to extend its limited capacities by acquiring additional capacity in resource richer environments. These resource richer environments are witnessed as infinite, in terms of the resources they can bring to the mobile application execution, neither presenting limitations in terms of battery and network instability under these approaches consideration. Here, the perspective changes. First, due to the consideration of mobile devices, which changes perception from just been seen as a thin client, to be considered a valid execution environment to complement capacity of other resources in its network. But also, from the view that the resource in which workload is offloaded presents the same volatility and instability characteristics than the resource which has originated the workload. The notable evolution which commenced a decade ago thanks to Moore's Law, has led to the increase of power and functionality of mobile phones [40].

Specialists expect this trend to continue up to a certain limit, as previously presented. Mobile battery is also an extended area of research both at industry and academia driven by requirements generated by the developments of wearable technologies.

Initial works driving to off-loading to additional mobile devices were presented in 2009–2010 and coined under the MCC term. Starting in 2016 with [41] some authors have used the term Mobile Ad-hoc Cloud computing to refer to similar approaches. These are presented in the upcoming Sect. 5.1.

4.4.4.1   Hyrax, Cloud Computing on Mobile Devices Using Map Reduce

Hyrax [42] is "a platform derived from Hadoop that supports cloud computing on Android devices". Hyrax is constructed on the basis of a vision in which mobile computing is "an extension of cloud computing for which foundational hardware is at least partially made up of mobile devices" [42].

Hyrax's overall goal is to evaluate feasibility of mobile devices' hardware and network infrastructure to become a sort of cloud provider which uses local data and computational resources, analogous to traditional clouds. The envisaged type of clouds would be made of the opportunistic creation of networked connections of smartphones in which smartphones perform individual local computations in support of a larger system-wide objective which aggregates smartphone's local computations to meet goals of an overall application. The following principles guide the proposed mobile cloud computing infrastructure: "(a) each node is owned by different user; (b) each node is likely to be mobile; (c) each node is battery powered and (d) network topology is more dynamic" [42].

The following are understood as advantages of the approach: Avoidance of large data transfers to centralized remote services to perform computational jobs, instead of using local or vicinity capacity processing mobile multimedia and sensor data immediately; Enablement of more efficient access and sharing of data stored on smartphone devices through local area or peer-to-peer networks; As well as, distributed hardware ownership and maintenance.

Hyrax has based its work on porting Apache Hadoop 1.0 (Map Reduce) to be executed in the proposed Mobile Cloud infrastructure, rather than traditional commodity hardware as it is by definition intended. It is important to note that although mobile nodes are intended to be distributed, implementation of Hyrax utilizes an approach based on centralised management. Additionally, Hyrax to some extend oversimplifies the problem by relying solely on existing Hadoop fault tolerance mechanisms to overcome issues derived from use of mobile resources of the infrastructure. In addition, Hyrax does not take into account any of the application offloading and partitioning techniques for mobile application in previous works, instead it focuses on providing a already existing data analytics infrastructure in which worker nodes are mobile devices which offered functionality is equivalent to traditional clouds. Thereby, Hyrax is significantly divergent to previous MCC works however, completely in line with on-going and expected developments of Edge and Swarm computing approaches, which almost a decade after still ambition similar goals.

4.4.4.2 A Virtual Cloud Computing Provider for Mobile Devices

Huerta-Canepa work on "virtual cloud computing provider for mobile devices" is described in [43]. Its overall ambition is to overcome mobile resource limitations by simulating a cloud environment with other mobile resources available in the vicinity for situations in which connection to cloud is inaccessible or too costly. This work is unique in MCC field by defining an infrastructure which is solely created out of mobile devices as an ad-hoc p2p cloud. The work provides remarkable inputs in relation to context management adapted to particularities of mobile devices. Specifically in this work partitioning of an application takes into account local resource availability and application resource needs. The selection of subrogates to which to offload and assign application partitions uses the amount and type of resources requested by the application execution and the amount of these resources available at candidate surrogates. This takes into account the mobile devices context defined as: social context, including relationships among users; location; and number devices in the vicinity. In addition, the works put forward a model for application partitioning that considers energy and time constraints; a failure prevention mechanism based on context; plus an adaptable trust mechanism that enables to open the platform to unknown nodes. Huerta Cánepa [44] depicts the set of policies and processes involved in the proposed Context-aware offloading policy schema. The schema details the following steps: Monitoring, Partitioning, Selection of surrogate candidate and Offloading. Implementation of this architecture is reported to be based on Hadoop running on top of PhoneME. PhoneME is Sun Microsystems project to provide a JVM and Java ME reference implementation.

4.4.5   Features Comparison

Table 4.1 provides a feature comparison using the concepts defined in Mobile Cloud Computing Taxonomy, adding additional information about implementation status, maturity and use cases. In previous subsections we have analysed existing MCC works according to the MCC defined models for offloading: to server, cloud, cloudlet and mobile device.

Independently of its system architectural approach, all analysed studies except of Hyrax, build on top of two main concepts: overall aim to optimise mobile device constrained resources and subsequent need for workload off-loading. From the analysed works only Gabriel (by use of wearable devices) is exploiting the MCC optimisation models and techniques for other available constrained devices than mobile devices, while these have huge potential for development in IoT and Swarm computing context.

Reinfurt et al. [45] provides a systematic classification of IoT devices in form of patterns. In this, it is recognised that many IoT devices are mobile and are located off the power grid and recognises the need for these to optimise energy use, similarly to mobile devices addressed by MCC works. We claim that similarly to how MCC Cloudlet concept has recently been conceptually used in the development of Edge Computing concept. Tools and techniques for task off-loading and energy optimisation developed in the context of MCC will soon have to be employed in IoT and decentralised cloud context, together with the need of optimising IoT devices resources and taking advantage of all existing computing capabilities at the Edge.

According to this analysis we observe that the criteria most often used for optimisation of offloading decision are Energy and Execution time. The consideration of the Energy criteria is devoted to MCC traditional overall approach to preserve mobile devices resources. We foresee this need will remain with the application of MCC techniques to IoT context. It is noteworthy that so far consideration of security in MCC has been only marginally addressed. This is particularly critical while considering more advanced scenarios for MCC in Swarm Computing context, as mobile devices and, generally speaking IoT devices, act sources of data which will soon become critical to protect.

Table 4.1 MCC frameworks feature comparison

Works	MAUI	Cuckoo	Clone cloud	ThinkAir	VM-based cloudlets	Gabriel	Hyrax	Virtual cloud
Resource scarcity	X	X	X	X			X	X
Energy scarcity	X	X	X	X				
Context and location			X	X		X		X
Network	X		X	X	X	X	X	
Security								
Off-loading granularity	Method	JVM	JVM	Method	VM	VM	JVM	
Off-loading optimisation	Energy	Energy	Energy	Cost		Latency		Energy, Time
MCC model	Off. to Server	Off. to Server	Off. to Cloud	Off. to Cloud	Off. to Cloudlet	Off. to Cloudlet	Off. to Mobile Device	Off. to Mobile Device
Prog. Model/ Language	Windows Mobile/.Net	Android/ Java	Android/ Java	Javascript/ Java, C#		Android/ Java	Java/ Hadoop	PhoneMe, Java/Hadoop
Maturity	Prototype	Prototype	Prototype	Prototype	Architecture	Prototype	Prototype	Prototype
Use cases	Image Recog, Gamme	Image conv., Aug. Reality	Virus scan, image search, adver.	Image proc., aug. reality and video		Object recog., OCR	Video search and sharing	

References

1. Satyanarayanan, M. (1993, 9). Mobile computing. *Computer, 26*, 81–82. http://ieeexplore.ieee. org/lpdocs/epic03/wrapper.htm?arnumber=231283
2. Satyanarayanan, M. (1996). Fundamental challenges in mobile computing. In *Proceedings of the Fifteenth Annual ACM Symposium on Principles of Distributed Computing* (pp. 1–7). https://doi.org/10.1145/248052.248053
3. Stojmenovic, I. (2012, 1). Keynote 1: Mobile cloud and green computing. *Procedia Computer Science, 10*, 18–19. http://linkinghub.elsevier.com/retrieve/pii/S1877050912003614
4. Mell, P., & Grance, T. (2011, 9). SP 800-145. *The NIST definition of cloud computing*. National Institute of Standards & Technology.
5. Sanaei, Z., Abolfazli, S., Gani, A., & Hafeez, R. (2012). Tripod of requirements in horizontal heterogeneous mobile cloud computing. In *Proceedings - First International Conference on Computing, Information Systems, and Communications*.
6. Guan, L., Ke, X., Song, M., & Song, J. (2011). A survey of research on mobile cloud computing. In *Proceedings - 2011 10th IEEE/ACIS International Conference on Computer and Information Science, ICIS 2011* (pp. 387–392).
7. Sanaei, Z., Abolfazli, S., Gani, A., & Buyya, R. (2014). Heterogeneity in mobile cloud computing: Taxonomy and open challenges. *IEEE Communications Surveys and Tutorials, 16*, 369–392. http://ieeexplore.ieee.org/lpdocs/epic03/wrapper.htm?arnumber=6517049
8. Chang, R., Gao, J., Gruhn, V., He, J., Roussos, G., & Tsai, W. (2013). Mobile cloud computing research - Issues, challenges, and needs. In *Proceedings - 2013 IEEE 7th International Symposium on Service-Oriented System Engineering, SOSE 2013* (pp. 442–453).
9. Kovachev, D., Cao, Y., & Klamma, R. (2011). Mobile cloud computing: A comparison of application models. *CoRR, abs/1107.4*. http://arxiv.org/abs/1107.4940
10. Hoang, D., Lee, C., Niyato, D., & Wang, P. (2013). A survey of mobile cloud computing: Architecture, applications, and approaches. *Wireless Communications and Mobile Computing, 13*, 1587–1611. https://onlinelibrary.wiley.com/doi/abs/10.1002/wcm.1203
11. Chang, J., Balan, R., & Satyanarayanan, S. (2005). *Exploiting rich mobile environments*. http://reports-archive.adm.cs.cmu.edu/anon/anon/usr0/ftp/home/ftp/2005/CMU-CS-05-199.pdf
12. Qi, H., & Gani, A. (2012, 5). Research on mobile cloud computing: Review, trend and perspectives. In *2012 Second International Conference on Digital Information and Communication Technology and It's Applications (DICTAP)* (pp. 195–202).
13. Zhong, L., Wang, B., & Wei, H. (2012, 7). Cloud computing applied in the mobile Internet. In *2012 7th International Conference on Computer Science & Education (ICCSE)* (pp. 218–221). http://ieeexplore.ieee.org/lpdocs/epic03/wrapper.htm?arnumber=6295061
14. Fernando, N., Loke, S., & Rahayu, W. (2011). Dynamic mobile cloud computing: Ad hoc and opportunistic job sharing. In *Utility and Cloud Computing (UCC), 2011 Fourth IEEE International Conference on* (pp. 281–286).
15. Gkatzikis, L., & Koutsopoulos, I. (2013). Migrate or not? Exploiting dynamic task migration in mobile cloud computing systems. *Wireless Communications, IEEE, 20*, 24–32.
16. Sanaei, Z., Abolfazli, S., Gani, A., & Shiraz, M. (2012, 8). SAMI: Service-based arbitrated multi-tier infrastructure for Mobile Cloud Computing. In *2012 1st IEEE International Conference on Communications in China Workshops (ICCC)* (pp. 14–19).
17. Satyanarayanan, M., Bahl, P., Caceres, R., & Davies, N. (2009). The case for VM-based cloudlets in mobile computing. *Pervasive Computing, IEEE, 8*, 14–23.
18. Zhang, Y., Niyato, D., & Wang, P. (2015, 12). Offloading in mobile cloudlet systems with intermittent connectivity. *IEEE Transactions on Mobile Computing, 14*, 2516–2529.
19. Fernando, N., Loke, S., & Rahayu, W. (2013). Mobile cloud computing: A survey. *Future Generation Computer Systems, 29*, 84–106. http://www.sciencedirect.com/science/article/pii/S0167739X12001318

20. Alizadeh, M., Abolfazli, S., Zamani, M., Baaaharun, S., & Sakurai, K. (2016, 2). Authentication in mobile cloud computing: A survey. *Journal of Network and Computer Applications*, *61*, 59–80.
21. Mollah, M., Azad, M., & Vasilakos, A. (2017). Security and privacy challenges in mobile cloud computing: Survey and way ahead. *Journal of Network and Computer Applications*, *84*, 38–54 . http://www.sciencedirect.com/science/article/pii/S1084804517300632
22. Shiraz, M., Gani, A., Khokhar, R., & Buyya, R. (2013, 3). A review on distributed application processing frameworks in smart mobile devices for mobile cloud computing. *IEEE Communications Surveys Tutorials*, *15*, 1294–1313.
23. Gao, J., Gruhn, V., He, J., Roussos, G., & Tsai, W. (2013, 3). Mobile cloud computing research - Issues, challenges and needs. In *2013 IEEE Seventh International Symposium on Service-Oriented System Engineering* (pp. 442–453). http://ieeexplore.ieee.org/lpdocs/epic03/wrapper.htm?arnumber=6525561
24. Khan, A., Kiah, M., Khan, S., & Madani, S. Towards secure mobile cloud computing: A survey. *Future Generation Computer Systems*, *29*, 1278–1299 (2013). http://www.sciencedirect.com/science/article/pii/S0167739X12001598
25. Kumar, K., Liu, J., Lu, Y., & Bhargava, B. (2012, 4). A survey of computation offloading for mobile systems. *Mobile Networks and Applications*, *18*, 129–140. http://link.springer.com/10.1007/s11036-012-0368-0
26. La, H., & Kim, S. (2014, 11). A taxonomy of offloading in mobile cloud computing. In *2014 IEEE 7th International Conference on Service-Oriented Computing and Applications* (pp. 147–153). http://ieeexplore.ieee.org/lpdocs/epic03/wrapper.htm?arnumber=6978603
27. Enzai, N., & Tang, M. (2014, 4). A taxonomy of computation offloading in mobile cloud computing. In *2014 2nd IEEE International Conference on Mobile Cloud Computing, Services, and Engineering* (pp. 19–28). http://ieeexplore.ieee.org/lpdocs/epic03/wrapper.htm?arnumber=6834942
28. Abolfazli, S., Sanaei, Z., Ahmed, E., Gani, A., & Buyya, R. (2014, 3). Cloud-based augmentation for mobile devices: Motivation, taxonomies, and open challenges. *IEEE Communications Surveys and Tutorials*, *16*, 337–368.
29. Satyanarayanan, M., Schuster, R., Ebling, M., Fettweis, G., Flinck, H., Joshi, K., & Sabnani, K. (2015, 3). An open ecosystem for mobile-cloud convergence. *IEEE Communications Magazine*, *53*, 63–70. http://ieeexplore.ieee.org/lpdocs/epic03/wrapper.htm?arnumber=7060484
30. Satyanarayanan, M., Chen, Z., Ha, K., Hu, W., Richter, W., & Pillai, P. (2014). Cloudlets: At the leading edge of mobile-cloud convergence. In *Proceedings of the 6th International Conference on Mobile Computing, Applications and Services* (pp. 1–9). http://eudl.eu/doi/10.4108/icst.mobicase.2014.257757
31. Cuervo, E., Balasubramanian, A., Cho, D., Wolman, A., Saroiu, S., Chandra, R., & Bahl, P. (2010). MAUI: Making smartphones last longer with code offload. In *Proceedings of the 8th International Conference on Mobile Systems, Applications, and Services* (pp. 49–62). http://doi.acm.org/10.1145/1814433.1814441
32. Kemp, R., Palmer, N., Kielmann, T., & Bal, H. (2012). Cuckoo: A computation offloading framework for smartphones. In *Mobile Computing, Applications, and Services* (pp. 59–79).
33. Chun, B., & Maniatis, P. (2009). Augmented smartphone applications through clone cloud execution. In *Proceedings of the 12th Conference on Hot Topics in Operating Systems* (pp. 8). http://dl.acm.org/citation.cfm?id=1855568.1855576
34. Chun, B., Ihm, S., Maniatis, P., Naik, M., & Patti, A. (2011). CloneCloud: Elastic execution between mobile device and cloud. In *Proceedings of the Sixth Conference on Computer Systems* (pp. 301–314). http://doi.acm.org/10.1145/1966445.1966473
35. Kosta, S., Aucinas, A., Hui, P., Mortier, R., & Zhang, X. (2011). Unleashing the power of mobile cloud computing using ThinkAir. *CoRR*, *abs/1105.3*.
36. Kosta, S., Aucinas, A., & Mortier, R. (2012, 3). ThinkAir: Dynamic resource allocation and parallel execution in the cloud for mobile code offloading. In *2012 Proceedings IEEE INFOCOM* (pp. 945–953). http://ieeexplore.ieee.org/lpdocs/epic03/wrapper.htm?arnumber=6195845

37. Bonomi, F., Milito, R., Zhu, J., & Addepalli, S. (2012). Fog computing and its role in the internet of things. In *Proceedings of the First Edition of the MCC Workshop on Mobile Cloud Computing* (pp. 13–16). https://doi.org/10.1145/2342509.2342513

38. Shi, W., Cao, J., Zhang, Q., Li, Y., & Xu, L. (2016). Edge computing: Vision and challenges. *IEEE Internet of Things Journal, 3*(5), 637–646. https://doi.org/10.1109/JIOT.2016.2579198

39. Ha, K., Chen, Z., Hu, W., Richter, W., Pillai, P., & Satyanarayanan, M. (2014). Towards wearable cognitive assistance. In *Proceedings of the 12th Annual International Conference on Mobile Systems, Applications, and Services* (pp. 68–81). https://doi.org/10.1145/2594368.2594383

40. Triggs Robert. (2022). Does Moore's Law still apply to smartphones in 2020? Retrieved May 26, 2022, from https://www.androidauthority.com/moores-law-smartphones-1088760/

41. Yaqoob, I., Ahmed, E., Abdullah, G., Salimah, M., Muhammad, I., & Sghaier, G. (2016). Mobile ad hoc cloud: A survey. *Wireless Communications and Mobile Computing, 16*, 2572–2589. https://onlinelibrary.wiley.com/doi/abs/10.1002/wcm.2709

42. Marinelli, E. (2009, 9). Hyrax: Cloud computing on mobile devices using MapReduce. *Science, 389*, 1–123. http://www.contrib.andrew.cmu.edu/

43. Huerta-Canepa, G., & Lee, D. (2010). A virtual cloud computing provider for mobile devices. In *Proceedings of the 1st ACM Workshop on Mobile Cloud Computing & Services: Social Networks and Beyond*. https://doi.org/10.1145/1810931.1810937

44. Huerta Cánepa, G. (2012). *A Context-aware Application Offloading Scheme for a Mobile Peer-to-peer Environment*. Ph. D. dissertation, KAIST, South Korea.

45. Reinfurt, L., Breitenbücher, U., Falkenthal, M., Leymann, F., & Riegg, A. (2016). Internet of Things patterns. In *Proceedings of the 21st European Conference on Pattern Languages of Programs*. https://doi.org/10.1145/3011784.3011789

Chapter 5
Mobile Ad-hoc Cloud Computing

5.1 Introduction to Mobile Ad-hoc Cloud Computing (MAC)

The concept of MAC has been only recently coined in [1] in which is recognised as a novel area of research which is still in its infancy. In this work, MAC is understood as a new research domain that aims to "augment various mobile devices in terms of computing intensive tasks execution by leveraging heterogeneous resources of available devices in the local vicinity".

More concise definition is provided in [2], "MAC enables the use of a multitude of proximate resource-rich mobile devices to provide computational services in the vicinity". Balasubramanian [3] further extends MAC definition by adding cooperation factors among participant mobile devices "A MAC is a pool of devices with high computational capabilities and is closer to the user. This low-cost computational environment is deployed over a network where all nodes cooperatively maintain the network". To the best of our knowledge, there is not yet a formal definition of MAC.

MAC motivation is to address situations in MCC for which connectivity to cloud environment is not feasible, such as absence or intermittent network connection [1]. This motivation was already the driver for MCC "offloading to mobile device" works, specifically central to [4, 5]. It has to be noted that neither motivation nor MAC definitions denote substantial differences with previous MCC works instead; MAC appears as a novel term to denominate more recent works.

MAC is recognised to have its roots into MCC but also in opportunistic computing [1]. The definition of opportunistic computing [6] provides additional considerations relevant for a system solely constituted by mobile devices. These are the concepts related to resource volatility and churn which can support further formal definition of MAC: "Opportunistic computing can be described as distributed computing with the caveats of intermittent connectivity and delay tolerance. Indeed, mobile and pervasive computing paradigms are also considered natural evolutions of traditional distributed computing. However, in mobile and pervasive computing systems, the disconnection or sleep device situations are treated as aberrations, while in opportunistic computing, opportunistic connectivity leads to accessing essential resources and information" [6].

Kirby [7] develops the desired features for ad-hoc clouds as: "An ad hoc cloud should be self-managing in terms of resilience, performance and balancing potentially conflicting policy goals. For resilience it should maintain service avail-ability in the presence of membership churn and failure. For performance it should be self-optimizing, taking account of quality of service requirements. It should be acceptable to machine owners, by minimizing intrusiveness and supporting appropriate security and trust mechanisms" [7].

Shila in [8] provides a distinction among mobile and static ad-hoc clouds. The latter, are including Edge computing and cloudlet environments and elaborating links among these novel cloud models and volunteer computing, as a way to opti-mise use of spare devices in mobile and other edge devices. Similar consideration is made by Varghese and Buyya [9] considering this a as major trend for changing cloud infrastructures.

5.2   MAC Challenges

Challenges in MAC are inherit from MCC. However the consideration of Mobile devices as the single source of resources brings specific challenges to be considered in the context of MAC. These are depicted in Fig. 5.1.

QoS and Fault tolerance   As described in [10] mobile devices present specific characteristics with regards to resource availability (connectivity instabil-ity, battery limitation, communication bandwidth, or location variations). This makes it specifically relevant in the context of MAC the consideration of service management issues related to fault tolerance, availability and

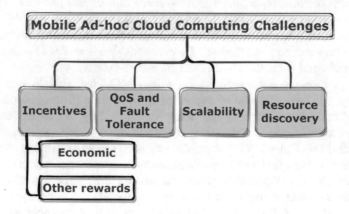

Fig. 5.1 Mobile Ad-hoc Cloud computing taxonomy

performance aspects. This work [10] highlights the importance of Fault tolerance mechanism considering the nature of mobile devices and its volatility. In addition, it remarks the need of incorporating additional aspects for QoS management in Mobile Cloud Computing which entail frequent loss of connectivity and low bandwidth and computational resources. Management of volatility of mobile resources and the availability issues derived from this fact is as a result the main identified challenge. Related work in the area for Mobile Cloud Computing based on Cloudlets recognizes as main problems the limited and highly demand resources and mobility of users. Yaqoob et al. [1] reinforces the need of additional research of stability issues related to ad-hoc and distributed clouds. Similarly to some aspects of Service Management, few authors so far have analysed the problem of Admission control (the mechanisms to decide whether to accept or not a service to be executed on a cloud infrastructure). It is likely due to the fact that it is solely applicable in the context of MAC. In addition to this, expected autonomic nature of MAC, calls for management procedures which are self-managed. This autonomic management has to consider self-healing mechanisms so as to optimize provided QoS taking into account levels of fault tolerance and device's churn.

Scalability   Mobile Ad-hoc Clouds could potentially sustain the provision of services over a massive number of resources with limited availability. Specifically on this aspect, authors such as [11] only contemplate network QoS factors relevant for Mobile Cloud Computing, relying on local clouds and cloudlets as the simple solution for these issues. Particularly, [11] identifies challenges in this area such as the distribution of processing, networking and storage capacity, in addition to the management trade-offs among cost and quality of experience. Both aspects, when extrapolated from MCC to MAC context, become critical in order to further develop this technology at scale.

Incentives   Incentives for participation represent a key aspect for MAC and generally speaking to any volunteer computing system [12]. Previous research in the area of volunteer Computing has demonstrated that temporal and voluntary resource donation is linked to different types of social, cultural and economic incentives with respect to service and data exchange, financial and collaboration aspirations. User's willingness to contribute is a key aspect for any contributory system. Although this area has been barely analysed in the MAC context, [12] presents motivations to contribute in the eScience area where most of the Volunteer computing work has been developed. Findings relate motivations mainly to "do good" and social contribution.

Resource Heterogeneity   Generally speaking, Mobile Ad-hoc Clouds are particularly susceptible to the heterogeneity of devices. As resources set-in up the Ad-hoc Cloud environment are not confined to the data centre boundaries,

but instead are extracted from sets of available resources, management
frameworks have to consider device heterogeneity as key enabler.

Resource Discovery   The dynamic behaviour of devices in terms or intermittent
availability and its consequent possibility of resource churn in MAC,
makes it necessary to take into account processes that permit the discovery of resources potentially available to join the MAC system. These
processes for resource discovery in MAC have specific requirements with
regard to the need to manage the environment dynamicity as well as
to act in close relation with incentives mechanisms. Resource discovery
methods for MAC could act in diverse logical network models including
decentralised and centralised models. These methods could also consider
diverse degrees of clustering and hierarchy depending on specific requirements in terms of scalability or fault-tolerance.

5.3   MAC Models

The analysis of existing literature in MAC, as well as general ad-hoc Cloud and
opportunistic computing enables the definition of the following potential models for
MAC (depicted in Fig. 5.2).

Distributed   Similarly to existing works in Contributory or Voluntary Computing,
MAC could be based on the temporary resource donation, which is

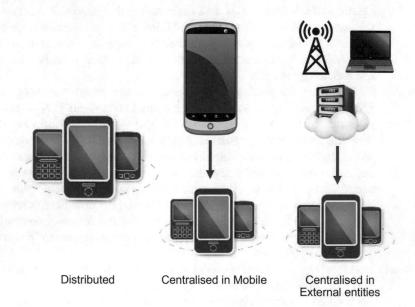

      Distributed   Centralised in Mobile   Centralised in
                                                     External entities

Fig. 5.2 Classification of Mobile Ad-hoc Cloud Computing models

voluntarily contributed to set-up the ad-hoc mobile cloud. In this case, mobile resources would act at the same time as resource contributors and as resource users, by executing tasks or jobs in the MAC environment. Rooted in the contributory approach, mobile devices capacity is expected to be bestowed for an undetermined time period and can be disconnected at any time; as well as, it is decentralised and purely distributed, we can note the absence of any dedicated resource to its management.

Centralised in Mobile   These represent models in which one of the mobile devices taking part in the MAC does act as a Master for the Ad-hoc cluster, having the rest of devices as "surrogates". This model is inherited directly from previous work in MCC in which the concept of surrogate was described.

Centralised in External   This model considers external entities providing management features to the environment. This model categorises these cases in which the mobile device is deemed not to have sufficient resources to perform the ad-hoc cloud management, and other resource richer entities are selected as master. This model therefore only views mobile devices as "workers" or "surrogates". In the observed cases, the master election is a static decision, and not considering operational environments.

The taxonomy in Fig. 5.1 for MAC challenges defines previously described characteristics for MAC. This taxonomy is used in Table 5.1 to classify existing works presented in next section.

5.4   Analysis of Existing Works in MAC

This section presents a detailed analysis of previous works in MAC.

5.4.1   Dynamic Mobile Cloud Computing: Ad Hoc and Opportunistic Job Sharing

Fernando et al. [13, 14] elaborate on various aspects of dynamic mobile cloud computing framework. This framework aims to exploit the cloud when it is defined as "a cloud if local resources utilised to achieve a common goal in a distributed manner". The aim of this work is to explore the feasibility of such local cloud in order to support mobility in mobile computing and associated concerns such as: sparseness and hazardousness of the resources in addition to limited energy source and connectivity. This framework aspires to respond to the following characteristics, being: "(a) Dynamic, in the way it can handle different resources and connectivity changes; (b) Proactive, so that costs can be pre-estimated; (c) Opportunistic, it makes use of resources as they are encountered; (d) Cost-effective, in a manner that allows task distribution based on a cost model benefiting all participant resources;

(e) Not limited to mobile devices, but able to manage low end devices such as sensors" [14]. As opposed to previous works analysed it considers parallel task execution using simultaneously diverse surrogate devices, however details on the approach to do so, are not provided.

The system architecture is organised in a cluster, in which one of the end-user devices acts as master, with a set of associated surrogate mobile devices performing slave tasks. Although authors intention in this set of works is to handle diverse end-user devices in the IoT spectrum, experimentation performed focus on PCs and mobile devices.

5.4.2   MoCCA, A Mobile Cellular Cloud Architecture

MoCCA [15] is described as a "cellular Cloud architecture for building mobile clouds using small-footprint microservers running on cell phones". MoCCA's objective is to avoid costs incurred in the set-up of traditional cloud data centres by taking advantage of already existing infrastructure elements. MoCCA advances the idea of benefiting from already existing telecommunications and networking elements in GSM cellular systems in order to build its architecture. Thus, the resources included in the architecture are smartphones, base stations, base stations controllers and mobile switching centres. Five aspects are identified as main concerns for Mobile Cloud design in this work: (1) Connectivity, bandwidth limitation, lack of direct connectivity among mobile devices, and the need to consider frequent network disconnections; (2) Computational limitation, due to mobile device resource limitations; (3) Churn, due to users mobility and devices' volatility; (4) Energy, with the approach of conserving energy in the mobile device; (5) and Incentives to users to participate with their mobile device in the Mobile Cloud infrastructure. The architecture proposed consists of two main parts: MoCCA Client and MoCCA manager. The latter, provides centralised control from the base station controller resource and executes from this location. The MoCCA client is powered with an execution sandbox with stores function codes to be executed, in addition to Client controller and Audit and logging functions.

MoCCA has been evaluated with computer bound applications. The only notable issue regarding Mobile Cloud Design which has been evaluated is Energy consumption from data reception and transmission. The remaining concerns (connectivity, churn, computational limitations and incentives) have yet to be considered in their architectural design and evaluation.

MoCCA's differentiation aspect from previous MCC and MAC works is that MoCCA adopts GSM cellular network infrastructure as part of the MAC. This fixed infrastructure acts as the MAC coordinator. The idea of using network equipment as part of the computing infrastructure at the Edge is now intensively examined as part of Edge computing research.

5.4.3 Ad-hoc Cloud as a Service

Zaghdoudi et al. [16, 17] present a "protocol and a preliminary architecture for the deployment of Ad-hoc MCC on top of MANET Ad-hoc networks". It addresses the need of solving dependence of mobile devices with remote cloud by exploiting capacities of surrounding devices. In these, two main entities are considered: Providers, offering nodes acting as resource providers; and Customers, that request resources. The resultant protocol, C-Protocol "governs the interaction and the communication among Ad-hoc nodes and provides the dynamic management of providers and customers" [16, 17].

The proposed architecture presents two layers: The C-protocol layer, a meta-layer intended to provide required network services; The CloudSim layer: a simulation layer using CloudSim simulation aiming to model and simulate a data centre environment and virtualised infrastructure based on mobile devices. The protocol considers members adding and departure processes, as well as Customer inclusion. No specific details about potential implementation of these, such as mechanisms for customer or provider registry or fault tolerance, monitoring mechanisms, workload considerations are constituent of this work.

The originality of this work lies in the joint consideration of network and compute aspects (although the latter are not developed with full details) and specifically the joint consideration of MAC and spontaneous networks such as MANETs. Initial experimentation has used 9 laptops equipped with Windows and Linux operating systems simulating mobile nodes connected over WIFI Adapters. The objective of the experimentation was to analyse the feasibility of three metrics: Time to set-up, Time for customer to join and Time to add a provider in the MAC system.

5.4.4 MobiCloud

MobiCloud [18] is presented as a "reliable collaborative mobilecloud management system". which enables the efficient and collaborative use of available mobile phone resources. This work coins the novel term mobilecloud in order to refer to the overall objective of exploitation of computing capacities of mobile and field devices even when no internet connectivity is available. The detailed architecture comprises two types of nodes: a field control node, named Cloud Agent and participant nodes (mobile or field nodes). The Cloud Agent is the agent requesting to form a Cloud and provides centralized Cloud controller functionalities. When an application is submitted to the CloudAgent it localizes from the set of available registered resources those which match the defined application requirements.

The reliability of the resources is assessed by means of a Trust management system which takes into account QoS offered by the participant nodes.

Available nodes are priorised resting on: first, number of available CPUs, and then on, time employed in data transmission. The differentiation aspect of this work is declared to rely on the node reliability mechanism and its reputation system based on user's feedback. Other works in the past [4, 5] have provided fully automated processes built upon collection of historical node behaviour. Evaluation of MobiCloud has been performed using an extension of CloudSim simulation and has included the homogeneous computing capacities of nodes, complete availability of all nodes and uniform distribution of connectivity speed. The metric evaluated in simulation has been application execution time.

5.4.5   mClouds

mClouds [19] build on the vision future mobile devices will become core components of mobile cloud computing architectures and not just thin clients to cloud environments. It particularly elaborates in the assumption that "computation and memory will likely increase considerably while battery and network capacity will not grow at the same pace" with the overall aim of reducing saturation of cellular data networks [19]. The initial analysis of mClouds architecture is divided into two main aspects: distributed mCloud processing and specific resource discovery procedures; and Incentives management.

Distributed mCloud processing architecture comprises mDevs, mobile devices able to execute mTasks. An mTask is a part of a larger computing task that can be parallelised. Distributed mCloud processing advocates on a simple initial principle, execute locally whenever possible. For cases for which this is not feasible due to lack of resources in the task originator device (master), look for mobile resources to form a mCloud.

This work presents the interesting novelty of elaborating in incentives strategies for mCloud participation. Incentives mechanisms consider the mobile carrier as clearing house, in order to reduce network congestions at certain locations. mClouds is conceived as a commentary approach to previous MAC and MCC works developing tools and mechanisms for application partitioning and offloading.

5.4.6   Aura

Aura [20] aims at providing IoT based Cloud computing models in which mobile devices, acting as clients, are able to offload computation tasks to nearby IoT devices. Therefore, creating ad-hoc cloud out of low power IoT devices in a specific location to which proximal mobile devices can outsource computation tasks.

Motivation for this approach is twofold: firstly, in order to provide a local computation environment that reduces latency and keeps data privacy; and secondly, with the intention of avoiding the costs of deploying data centre clouds located near to the client. The use of Aura is exemplified in a Smart building scenario. Compared to previous works, Aura brings the innovation of already considering IoT devices in the Smart Building scenario as part of the MAC system considering them not only as data sources but as valid MAC resources, depending on their specific characteristics.

A proof of concept of the approach has been developed for Aura with an Android mobile application for Mobile Agent implementation; Controller as a Desktop Java application; and IoT devices capabilities represented by MapReduce ported to Contiki IoT platform. A number of IoT devices were simulated with Cooja framework. The experimentation was conducted by offloading wordcount implemented in MapReduce for optimisation of execution time.

5.5 Features Comparison

Table 5.1 provides a feature comparison using the concepts outlined in the Mobile Ad-hoc Cloud Computing Taxonomy (Fig. 5.1), introducing additional information about implementation status, maturity and use cases. At model level, we observe that so far the preferred model in existing works is to provide ad-hoc mobile cloud functionality from an external entity. This external entity in the analyses works is offered from Cloud environments, IoT devices and even, Network equipment. Centralised management in a mobile that manages ad-hoc clouds in other mobiles acting as "surrogates" is also a model which is gaining popularity emerging together with the increment of computing capacities of mobile devices. In both cases, there is a single point of failure for these architectures due to centralised design. Complete decentralisation and distribution has been an area of study in Volunteer and P2P systems in the past. This model of management is feasible and performant, as demonstrated in previous volunteer and p2p computing works, and provides interesting features at levels of mechanism for handling complexity of volatile resources, high scalability and self-management, foreseen as specifically of interest for the evolution of mobile and steady ad-hoc clouds.

Until now only some specific MAC works have gone beyond the smartphone as main source of resources. Tools such as Aura describe initial steps towards the inclusion of IoT in mobile ad-hoc architectures. In our view, future evolution of MAC in Swarm computing will not only reinforce existing initial works addressing IoT devices but to focus its evolution on them, as available processing capacities in heterogeneous devices growth. The exceptional forecasted development on the number and complexity of IoT connected devices will force this evolution as a mandatory requirement. The overall computing available at the Edge of the network is growing in number of devices but also in their capacity, coming from diverse and heterogeneous sources in form of robots, drones and autonomous vehicles. At level of challenges addressed we observe consideration of location is yet to be addressed, as well as, QoS and massive scalability necessary in this context.

As observable in Table 5.1, yet the attention to hardware heterogeneity in the management of MAC is not a reality in any of the analysed MAC works. This is in

Table 5.1 MAC frameworks feature comparison

Works	Job sharing	MoCCA	Ad-hoc cloud	MobiCloud	mClouds	Aura
QoS and fault tolerance						
Scalability						
Incentives	Economic				Economic	
Resource heterogeneity						
Resource discovery			X		X	X
MAC model	Centralised in mobile	Centralised in external entity	Centralised in mobile	Centralised in external entity	Centralised in mobile	Centralised in external entity
Prog. Env.	Java	Java				Android/Java
Maturity	Prototype	Prototype	Simulation	Simulation	Model	Prototype
Use cases	Distributed Mandelbrot set generation	Cholesky decomposition fast Fourier transform				MapReduce word count

our view, another clear source of evolution in the coming years for MAC and Swarm Computing in general.

Over the last decades, Moore's law has enabled the substantial computing capacity growth in microprocessors. Recently, we are witnessing the emergence of built-in artificial intelligence processing units into mobile devices which are expected to soon power many other IoT devices.

The foreseen slow down progress expected for Moore's Law in the future will call for taking better advantage of all available compute resources, therefore forcing MAC systems and Ad-hoc Edge Clouds to manage heterogeneity so to exploit all available compute sources.

References

1. Yaqoob, I., Ahmed, E., Abdullah, G., Salimah, M., Muhammad, I., & Sghaier, G. (2016). Mobile ad hoc cloud: A survey. *Wireless Communications and Mobile Computing, 16*, 2572–2589. https://onlinelibrary.wiley.com/doi/abs/10.1002/wcm.2709
2. Yaqoob, I., Ahmed, E., Gani, A., Mokhtar, S., & Imran, M. (2017). Heterogeneity-aware task allocation in mobile ad hoc cloud. *IEEE Access, 5*, 1779–1795.
3. Balasubramanian, V., & Karmouch, A. (2017, 3). An infrastructure as a service for mobile ad-hoc cloud. In *2017 IEEE 7th Annual Computing and Communication Workshop and Conference, CCWC 2017* (pp. 1–7).
4. Huerta-Canepa, G., & Lee, D. (2010). A virtual cloud computing provider for mobile devices. In *Proceedings of the 1st ACM Workshop on Mobile Cloud Computing & Services: Social Networks and Beyond*. https://doi.org/10.1145/1810931.1810937

5. Huerta Cánepa, G. (2012). *A Context-aware Application Offloading Scheme for a Mobile Peer-to-peer Environment*. Ph. D. dissertation, KAIST, South Korea.
6. Conti, M., & Kumar, M. (2010). Opportunities in opportunistic computing. *Computer*, *43*, 42–50.
7. Kirby, G., Dearle, A., Macdonald, A., & Fernandes, A. (2010). An approach to ad hoc cloud computing. *Arxiv Preprint ArXiv*, 2–5. http://arxiv.org/abs/1002.4738
8. Shila, D., Shen, W., Cheng, Y., Tian, X., & Shen, X. (2017). AMCloud: Toward a secure autonomic mobile ad hoc cloud computing system. *IEEE Wireless Communications*, *24*, 74–81.
9. Varghese, B., & Buyya, R. (2018). Next generation cloud computing: New trends and research directions. *Future Generation Computer Systems*, *79*, 849–861. http://www.sciencedirect.com/science/article/pii/S0167739X17302224
10. Shiraz, M., Gani, A., Khokhar, R., & Buyya, R. (2013, 3). A review on distributed application processing frameworks in smart mobile devices for mobile cloud computing. *IEEE Communications Surveys Tutorials*, *15*, 1294–1313.
11. Hoang, D., Lee, C., Niyato, D., & Wang, P. (2013). A survey of mobile cloud computing: Architecture, applications, and approaches. *Wireless Communications and Mobile Computing*, *13*, 1587–1611. https://onlinelibrary.wiley.com/doi/abs/10.1002/wcm.1203
12. Nov, O., Anderson, D., & Arazy, O. (2010). Volunteer computing: A model of the factors determining contribution to community-based scientific research. In *Proceedings of the 19th International Conference on World Wide Web* (pp. 741–750). https://doi.org/10.1145/1772690.1772766
13. Fernando, N., Loke, S., & Rahayu, W. (2011). Dynamic mobile cloud computing: Ad hoc and opportunistic job sharing. In *Utility and Cloud Computing (UCC), 2011 Fourth IEEE International Conference on* (pp. 281–286).
14. Fernando, N., Loke, S., & Rahayu, W. (2012). Mobile crowd computing with work stealing. In *2012 15th International Conference on Network-Based Information Systems* (pp. 660–665).
15. Mishra, A., & Masson, G. (2013). MoCCA: A mobile cellular cloud architecture. *Journal of Cyber Security and Mobility*, *2*, 105–125. http://www.riverpublishers.com/journal%7B%5C_%7Darticle.php?j=JCSM/2/2/1
16. Zaghdoudi, B., Ayed, H., & Gnichi, I. (2017). A protocol for setting up ad hoc mobile clouds over spontaneous MANETs: A proof of concept. In *2016 Cloudification of the Internet of Things, CIoT 2016* (pp. 1–6).
17. Zaghdoudi, B., Ayed, H., & Riabi, I. (2015). Ad hoc cloud as a service: A protocol for setting up an ad hoc cloud over MANETs. *Procedia Computer Science*, *56*, 573–579. http://www.sciencedirect.com/science/article/pii/S1877050915017378
18. Hammam, A., & Senbel, S. A reputation trust management system for ad-hoc mobile clouds. *Intelligent Systems Reference Library*, *70*, 519–539 (2014)
19. Miluzzo, E., Cáceres, R., & Chen, Y. (2012). Vision: MClouds - Computing on clouds of mobile devices. In *Proceedings of the Third ACM Workshop on Mobile Cloud Computing and Services* (pp. 9–14). https://doi.org/10.1145/2307849.2307854
20. Hasan, R., Hossain, M., & Khan, R. (2015, 3). Aura: An IoT based cloud infrastructure for localized mobile computation outsourcing. In *2015 3rd IEEE International Conference on Mobile Cloud Computing, Services, and Engineering* (pp. 183–188). http://ieeexplore.ieee.org/lpdocs/epic03/wrapper.htm?arnumber=7130885

Chapter 6
Edge and Fog Computing

6.1 Computing Perspective, Edge and Cloud

Cloud computing today has transformed into a massive centralised infrastructure acting as a central keystone for compute power, storage, process, integration, and decision making in numerous environments. Following the pattern we have thus far in the existing IoT set-ups, generated sensor data would have to be transmitted over the network in order to be centralised, processed and analysed in the Cloud.

With a view to cope with IoT proliferation this scenario has to change, providing an infrastructure which takes into account billions of devices connected at the edge and offering more rapid processing and decision making. Therefore, the idea under Edge Computing is to enable the decentralisation of the cloud, approximating computation and storage to the sources, at the edge of the network: avoiding unessential network transmission and getting data and computation at the right place and right time.

Edge computing paradigm [1] "extends Cloud Computing to the Edge of the network". Both Edge and Cloud manage computation, network and storage resources applying similar techniques such as virtualisation and multi-tenancy [2]. However, Edge computing's main aim is to address the latency issues detected in the application of Cloud Computing to large IoT scenarios [3].

Edge computing is defined by Shi [4] as: "Edge computing refers to the enabling technologies allowing computation to be performed at the edge of the network, on downstream data on behalf of cloud services and upstream data on behalf of IoT services.". This work frames Edge "as any computing and network resources along the path between data sources and cloud data centres" [4].

The term Fog Computing has been instead proposed by Cisco [5]: "Fog Computing is a paradigm that extends Cloud computing and services to the edge of the network. Similar to Cloud, Fog provides data, compute, storage, and application

A. Juan Ferrer, *Beyond Edge Computing*, https://doi.org/10.1007/978-3-031-23344-9_6

services to end-users. The distinguishing Fog characteristics are its proximity to end-users, its dense geographical distribution, and its support for mobility". Also from CISCO, Bonomi in its introductory work "Fog Computing and its role on the internet of Things" [1] proposes the following definition for Fog computing: "Fog Computing is a highly virtualised platform that provides compute, storage, and networking services between end devices and traditional Cloud Computing Data Centres, typically, but not exclusively located at the edge of network".

The definition provided by Vaquero and Rodero-Merino [6] does not confine technology choices to virtualisation and adds a cooperation factor: "Fog computing is a scenario where a huge number of heterogeneous (wireless and sometimes autonomous) ubiquitous and decentralised devices communicate and potentially cooperate among them and with the network to perform storage and processing tasks without the intervention of third-parties. These tasks can be for supporting basic network functions or new services and applications that run in a sandboxed environment. Users leasing part of their devices to host these services get incentives for doing so".

Overall Bonomi's approach refers to the fact that IoT platforms will, in the short term generate large volumes of data, which will stand in need of analytics platforms to be geo-distributed; in a way of "moving the processing to the data". Therefore, creating the need for "distributed intelligent platform at the Edge Computing that manages distributed compute, networking and storage resources".

Edge and Fog Computing are not devised as competitors to Cloud; quite the contrary, it is conceived as the perfect ally for use cases and applications for which traditional Cloud Computing is not sufficient. Further extended in [2] the Edge vision was created to "address applications and services that do not fit well the paradigm of the Cloud". Edge approach is very much aligned with Mobile Cloud Computing works, as recognised in [3, 7, 8].

When observing evolution of the market, again, the major Cloud provider, Amazon Web Services (AWS) appears as a pioneer in the area of Edge computing by its AWS Greengrass product [9]. This has recently being followed by MS Azure Edge platform [10], as will be presented in Sect. 6.1.4.

These advances have been soon followed by developments in open-source communities in existing projects of the Cloud Native Computing Foundation, Eclipse Foundation, Openstack and Open Nebula communities. The status of developments of these communities is presented in Sect. 6.1.5.

6.1.1 Edge Computing Challenges

Below we elaborate on a series of Edge computing challenges and characteristics necessary to be developed in order to make the described concepts a reality. These are also represented in Fig. 6.1.

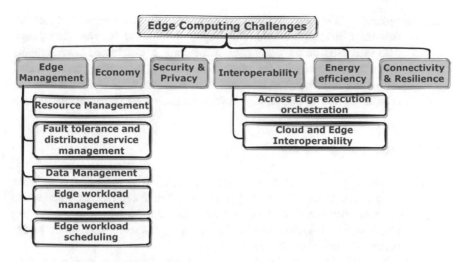

Fig. 6.1 Edge Computing taxonomy

6.1.1.1 Edge Management

Resource Management   Management of massive number of small diverse devices and sensors in Edge computing set-ups will necessitate new management styles, potentially decentralised and able to scale to degrees that nowadays are unprecedented in existing architectures [6].

Fault tolerance and distributed service management   Fault tolerance, availability and performance have yet to be addressed in Edge computing. Edge management systems need of including supplementary aspects for QoS management, scalability and heterogeneity in resources, as well as integration of special devices including hardware accelerators, FPGAs and GPUs.

Workload management   Edge systems able to deal with different application encapsulation approaches will be necessary to prepare the workloads depending on the final execution environment, considering the diversity of processor types. These mechanisms adapted to switch between high-performance processor and low power processor should shortly be taken into consideration.

Workload Scheduling   Workload or task scheduling in Edge and Fog computing has to take into account specificities of the Edge devices, such as energy constraints and QoS (usually in terms of latency optimisation). Diverse works have recently analysed the problem from diverse perspectives. Some works handle it as a joint optimisation problem among the Edge and Cloud resources: with the aim of addressing different application classes [11]; focusing on performance and cost optimisation [12]; and aiming to optimise delay and power consumption [13]. Others, such as Bitam [14] devises it with the innovative approach of bio-inspired optimization.

Data management   The need for Edge computing has been primarily driven by
            data-intensive applications. Edge systems have to be able to manage
            data dispersed on an Edge heterogeneous and distributed environments
            and must contend with the complexities of the underlying sophisticated
            infrastructure comprised by smart devices, sensors, as well as traditional
            computing nodes. Conversely, developers must focus on data quality [15].

6.1.1.2   Edge Interoperability

Orchestration across Edge   Edge set-ups are envisaged to be spread covering wide
            geographic areas. For serving applications and services that make use
            of these distributed set-ups, mechanisms for deployment, provisioning,
            placement and scaling service instances across execution zones in the
            distributed Edge set-ups are necessary.
Interoperability with Edge and Cloud   Current status of Edge computing develop-
            ments very much relies on specific vendor solutions. In order for these
            to interoperate among them and with traditional clouds, new standards
            would have to appear to manage the expected scale of edge set-ups and
            the interoperability of devices and sensors.

6.1.1.3   Cognitive Techniques: AI and ML Applied to Edge Management

Zhou et al. [16] recognises Edge computing, as an essential element for AI
democratisation—this is embedding AI into a wide diversity of objects and application scenarios—providing the advantages of affordability and proximity to the user.
This work denominates Edge intelligence to the ability of exploiting all computing
continuum from the Edge to the Cloud for benefit of AI workloads, and envisions
an scenario in which compute capacity of end Edge devices is fully exploited.

At the same time, the utilisation of cognitive and machine learning techniques
for resource and Edge infrastructure management has recently gained significant
attention in the research community. Le Luc in [17] explores application of these
techniques for reliable resource provisioning for edge-cloud application in the
areas of workload analysis and prediction, placement and consolidation, elasticity
and remediation and network function placement. It performs a deep literature
review of works in the area of application placement at the level of existing
resources in data centre installations in Cloud environments and mobile Cloud
computing computation offloading. The latter, as identified in [18], typically refer
to determining the parts of an application that is in execution on a mobile device to
be transferred to resource richer environments in Clouds.

More in detail, Ilager in [19] proposes a conceptual model for AI-centric resource
management systems in modern distributed systems that encompass Edge and
Cloud. It explores two scenarios in which to apply AI techniques in Cloud computing scope: a resource management on large scale data centre for energy optimisation

in interception stage for Microsoft Azure Cloud; and a AI based mechanism for configuration of GPU Cloud configuration for workload scheduling. These scenarios show the potential of the employment of AI for resource management at Cloud, however it misses the complexity that the consideration of Edge computing resources and its inherent dynamicity add to the scene. Rodrigues in [20] explores specifically works related to the application of AI to Edge computing advocating for the use of machine learning in front of heuristic and convex optimisation problem solving, at the same time it recognises the need for additional research in order to enable Edge device collaboration, as we foresee in our work.

Differently [21] develops the concept of Social Edge Intelligence, that proposes the integration of artificial intelligence with human intelligence to address critical research challenges of Edge computing. In this context, it proposes the challenge of efficient resource management that exploit the heterogeneity present in the Edge devices and diagnoses the need of additional research to enable seamless device collaboration for timely task execution.

6.1.1.4 Economy

Cloud computing has been recognised as a bridge between distributed systems and economics. Cloud computing providers offer a number of services to users using pricing schemes relying on incurred resource consumption. Existing commercial Edge computing environments, although based on simple devices, are being deployed in complex economic models which combine pay per use and licensed based (see Sect. 6.1.4). Further investigation is vital for designing models ready to cope with challenges and diversities of existing Edge Cloud models.

6.1.1.5 Eco-Efficiency

A significant challenge associated with Edge deployments is potent power provisioning for locally deployed infrastructure. While substantial advances have been made for data centre and Cloud Energy Efficiency, particular challenges remain in order to optimise energy consumption and availability of energy sources in edge environments. It is important to note that the diversity of resources and potential energy sources potentially involved in Edge computing provisioning add additional challenges to this matter. Another environmental concern linked with Edge computing is the lifecycle of all devices which are disseminated. Approaches for device management of objects that incorporate a battery and matter potentially harmful to the environment would have to be considered in the future.

6.1.1.6 Security and Privacy

Edge computing, similarly to traditional cloud, is viewed as multi-tenant, and therefore actual set-ups will require of concrete isolation mechanisms so as to avoid security and privacy concerns.

6.1.1.7 Connectivity and Resilience

Resiliency is another essential element required for Edge computing architectures, specifically for mission critical IoT systems. These services need to continue to function from the Edge even when links to Cloud are lost or not operational. Diverse techniques are being studied to provide connectivity resilience, including fault tolerance systems connecting diverse Edge installations in the vicinity and for unconnected Edge limited operation. In addition to this, it is important to remark that a wide area of research exist (which is considered out of scope in this book) addressing specific research challenges in future networks in relation to 5G and SDN/NFV, and Edge computing from Telco perspective.

6.1.2   Edge Computing Models

Existing approaches to Edge Computing can be classified according to the following criteria. These different Edge models are depicted in Fig. 6.2 based on their topology, and in Fig. 6.3 based on the offered service model.

Edge Server   approaches are those which consider the Edge environment a device, which we name server, that provides computing and storage capacities to a series of Edge sensors and other resource poorer devices that are connected to it in a locally close environment. These so-called "servers" can be represented by devices which range from Raspberry Pis to servers, but so can devices such as connected cars, network equipment, or other rich smart IoT devices, as long as they provide a minimum computing and storage capacity. With this regards project HEADS has provided the following classification [22] among devices which comprises: Tiny, Small and Large. These can be described as: Tiny: Very limited devices such as Arduino UNO; Small: Devices with a specific OS and restricted hardware characteristics (less than 128 kB program memory and less than 64 kB data memory); Large: Devices supporting general purpose OS. Edge Server approaches are the ones we encounter today in commercial products such as Amazon Greengrass, and Azure IoT Edge using the so called "Large" devices. Also from equipment vendors such as Dell we found pure and traditional servers to be deployed (Dell PowerEdge Series).

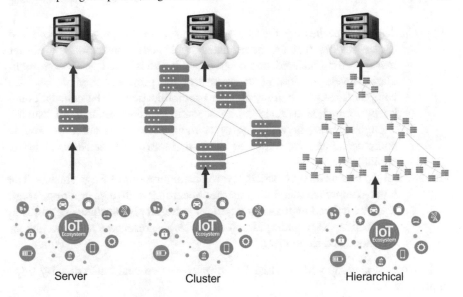

Fig. 6.2 Classification of Edge Computing models according to their topology

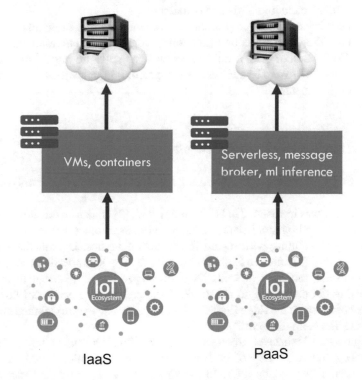

Fig. 6.3 Classification of Edge Computing models by delivered service

Edge Cluster   approaches are those considering sets of the previously so-called
server devices that are coordinated by a node considered the cluster
master. This clustered approach could be considered at diverse granularity levels in view of the nature of the proposed scenario and the
compute/storage requirements. An exemplification of the concept could
be performed in a smart home scenario considering that all "smart"
enough devices, servers, aggregate their capacity in order to provide
compute/storage capacities to other more resource constrained home
appliances.

Hierarchical   classification considers layered configurations of Edge clusters. The
layered approach could be construed according to diverse criterion. These
include: layered approaches based on increasingly resources capabilities
or location (aggregating at diverse levels i.e. resources at home, neighbourhood and smart city).

Making an analogy with existing Cloud offerings we could also classify Edge
approaches as:

IaaS   Those offering compute and storage capacities in diverse virtualisation
formats including VMs and containers.

PaaS   Offering access to programming environments (the more advanced ones
providing Serverless and functional programming environments such as
AWS Lambda), ML tool-sets as well as software capabilities such as
message brokers to facilitate development of applications on top of these
environments.

6.1.3   Existing Works in Research

6.1.3.1   Fog Computing, a Platform for Internet of Things and Analytics

Fog computing was introduced in [1]. Bonomi et al. [2] enhances this initial work in
order to propose a Fog architecture including new requirements that IoT scenarios
pose on Fog Computing with regard to big data analytics. Overall the approach
is based on the fact that IoT platforms will, in the short term generate large
volumes of data, requiring of analytics platforms to be geo-distributed; in a way
that "moving the processing to the data". Thus, creating the need for "distributed
intelligent platform at the Edge (Fog Computing) that manages distributed compute,
networking and storage resources".

The proposed high level architecture has the following three key objectives:
transparency, heterogeneity (of both resources and applications) and distributed
orchestration. Transparency refers to the ability to manage in an abstract manner
resource elements at edge, cloud and network. Heterogeneity is related to the
diversity of previously mentioned resources but also to need of supporting multiple
applications from diverse sectors. Finally, orchestration has to be driven by defined

policies that consider scalability at local and global levels. Bonomi's work coined the term Fog computing. Although cloudlet concept is not specifically referenced in this work diverse authors have recognised its direct links in spite of different motivation for decentralisation: IoT infrastructure scalability, for fog computing; versus mobile applications performance for cloudlet [23].

6.1.3.2 ANGELS for Distributed Analytics in IoT

ANGELS stands for "Available Network Gateways in Edge Locations for Sensors" and it is presented in [24]. ANGELS presents on-going work and explores the idea of using smart edge devices (sensor gateways, personal laptops, play-stations, and smartphones) as envisaged in the Fog paradigm in order to perform parallel execution of data processing jobs in IoT, using idle capability of these devices. Overall ambition of this work is to take advantage of unused computing capacity at the edge of the network at homes and around these, in order to cope with demands for data analytics computation expected from the development of IoT systems. This architecture targets the class of applications which presents a data parallelization approach: namely, applications capable of processing data divisible into several subsets, partitions, which can be processed in parallel, similar to the MapReduce approach.

So far this architecture is working under the assumption that edge devices are available. Next steps detail the consideration of dynamic availability patterns of edge devices. A new element of ANGELS is the contributory/volunteer computing element it brings, by means of taking advantage of idle of smart edge devices. However, it recognises that due to Edge devices resources constraints and their mobility, edge devices will have to be complemented with fully powered resource richer servers.

6.1.3.3 Mobile Fog

Mobile Fog [25] presents a "high level programming model", or a PaaS, "for applications that are geographically distributed, large scale and sensitive to latency"[25]. Authors position this work as an alternative for Cloud PaaS which focus on web applications, by developing a solution that specifically addresses needs of data analytics for IoT.

The objectives of Mobile Fog Programming model are: to ease application development on highly distributed heterogeneous devices; and to support scalability both at Edge and Cloud. In this work Edge devices resources considered go beyond typical mobile phones, but also considering connected vehicles. In Mobile Fog an application is a group of distributed processes which have to be assigned into a set of disperse computing instances in edge devices, and fog or cloud environments. It is considered a physical hierarchy of devices in which a process in an edge device is a leaf, and processes in the edge cloud are intermediate nodes and processes in cloud are considered the root. In this set-up each Mobile Fog Node manages workload from a specific geo-spatial location. Scalability management is performed through scaling policies that determine behaviour reliant on monitoring metrics such as CPU or bandwidth. Scalability mechanisms address instances at the same network level. Further work is expected in runtime systems implementation and process placement algorithms. This work recognises to be complementary to fog architecture presented by Bonomi et al. [1, 2] by addressing on programmability aspects in Fog context.

6.1.3.4 Nebula

Nebula [26–28] is presented as a "dispersed edge cloud infrastructure that explores the use of voluntary resources for both computation and data storage". Nebula motivations are: to reduce data upload to traditional clouds by offering disperse computing environments and to eliminate overhead of virtual infrastructure instantiation in Clouds. Nebula relies on volunteer computing mechanisms as tools that allow widely distributed environment. While supporting distributed data intensive applications, Nebula deems data movement and origination problems, considering geographical distributed execution. In order to do so, scheduling of computing has to take into account execution time, but also data movement costs. Nebula system architecture includes the use of dedicated servers for central platform level operations, together with a set of donated nodes both providing computation or data storage resources.

   Data Nodes donate storage space in order to store application files. They provide operations to get and store data. Compute nodes, offer computation resources to the environment. With a view to maintaining isolation among the donated resources and applications executed by means of Nebulas, it employs NaCI sandbox provided by Google Chrome browser. By means of this sandbox, Nebulas orchestrates the execution of NaCI executables into the contributed resources. Evaluation has been provided for Nebulas MapReduce Scheduler comparing it to current Volunteer computing models BOINC and MapReduce-tuned BOINC. This evaluation has employed an experimental set-up using 52 Nodes in PlanetLab using a Word Count MapReduce Like application. Similarly to ANGELS [24], NEBULAS develops the idea of volunteer contribution of Edge resources, however, elaborating by-design management of fault-tolerance to edge devices churn and volatility.

6.1.3.5 Resource Provisioning for IoT Services in the Fog

Skarlat et al. [29] main objective is to provide both theoretical and practical foundations for resource provisioning in Fog environments. It provides a systematic classification of Edge resources. This classification comprises the following classes for resources: fog cells, single IoT devices that control a series of other IoT resources while providing virtualised resources; and fog colonies, described as micro-data centres built-up from a series of fog cells. In the proposed architecture:

The Cloud-Fog control middleware is the central unit that supports the management of underlying Fog colonies. The management of fog colonies incorporates execution of fault tolerance processes over fog cells as well as novel device discovery, and re-organisation of colonies if needed; Fog Orchestration Control Node supports a fog Colony constituted by diverse Fog Cells; and Fog Cells are software components running on Fog devices. Both the Fog orchestration control node and Cloud-Fog control middleware need to implement placement optimisation for tasks execution. The selected optimisation criterion in this work is twofold, first to optimise resource utilisation at fog cells and secondly to minimise delays in propagating data to cloud. This hierarchical architecture is more complex than MobileFog's one, developing various Fog levels. Evaluation of the proposed model has been performed using an extension of CloudSim simulation framework for Fog Computing, resulting in 39% delays reduction.

6.1.4 Existing Products in the Market

6.1.4.1 Azure IoT Edge

Azure IoT Suite Reference architecture [30] considers three central aspects for a typical IoT solution: device connectivity, data processing, analytics and manage-ment; and presentation and business connectivity. Recently Azure has announced the availability of Azure IoT Edge [10] as Open Source [31]. The provided open source software can run on Windows and Linux/Mac powered devices. IoT Edge modules are executed as Docker compatible containers. The IoT Edge Runtime provides monitoring and workload execution functionalities at the Edge.

It allows data pre-processing on-premises before sending it to Azure Cloud environments. The Microsoft services which can run on these devices include Azure Machine Learning, Stream Analytics Azure Functions, Microsoft's AI services and the Azure IoT Hub. Azure IoT Hub component contains device registry and identity store, as well as, device-to-edge and edge-to-device messaging features, acting as the entry point to access the rest of IoT suite services at Edge side. Azure IoT Hub presents an SDK that allows interoperability with custom gateways and simplified programming. Stream Analytics component offers real-time event processing so to support stream data analysis by processing telemetry, data aggregation, and event detection. On the Cloud side, Azure Storage offers long term data and object storage. This can be used in conjunction with Azure Web Apps and Microsoft Power BI, so as to have data visualisation means. At time of writing Azure IoT Edge can be used free of charge while associated use of Cloud services is billed based on usage.

6.1.4.2 AWS Greengrass

AWS Greengrass [9, 32] offers an Edge computing platform which propounds local computing using AWS Serverless technology (AWS Lambda), messaging, data catching sync and ML inference while providing interoperability with AWS IoT Cloud services. It is a software stack available for any ARM and x86 device with minimum required capacity (1GHz of compute, 128 Mb of RAM plus additional resources for workload and message throughput). At time of writing, AWS Greengrass documentation details that compatibility tests have been validated with more than 40 devices. In addition it offers direct communication and operation with Amazon FreeRTOS micro-controllers. The software stack is divided into three main pieces: AWS Greengrass Core, AWS GreenGrass SDK and AWS IoT Device SDK. The Greengrass core allows for: local deployment of applications using lambda functions developed in Python 2.7, Node.JS 6.10 and Java 8; enables secured local messaging based on OPC-UA protocol; provides device management and device clones; and authentication and authorisation in device to cloud communication. AWS Greengrass SDK permits Lambda functions to interact with Core services. The extended IoT Device SDK endowed with Greengrass offers an extension to existing AWS IoT Device SDK so as to support constrained devices (supporting TLS) to communicate with Greengrass core. In addition, devices can use Greengrass discovery API to locate and manage secure communication to Greengrass core. A very interesting feature added recently is Greengrass ML. This feature allows ML models that have been developed and trained in the cloud, to be deployed and executed locally in the Greengrass core equipped device. This is reported to support GPU utilisation for devices which have it present.

It is important to remark that AWS Greengrass supports the possibility to work offline (without Internet connection to the Cloud) performing synchronisation process when connectivity is ensured to the device. Logically, this has to be limited to the resources available on the device powering the AWS Greengrass Core, albeit no concrete information is presently found in the product information. Pricing for AWS Greengrass considers a combination of devices installed plus the usage of Cloud services these make. The price for devices can be charged monthly or with a fixed yearly amount.

6.1.5 Existing Open-Source Initiatives

6.1.5.1 K3s

K3S [33, 34], provides a lightweight and certified Kubernetes distribution which purpose is to provide an execution environment for workloads making use of resource-constrained ARM64 and ARMv7 Edge servers or IoT devices. At time of writing, it is a sandbox project of Cloud Native Computing Foundation.

K3S [35] optimizes the baseline Kubernetes by: reducing the memory footprint necessary for operation, enabled by executing Kubernetes main components in a single process; and because of its packaging as a smaller single binary, thanks to the removal of third-party storage drivers and cloud providers.

K3S architecture is exactly the same than baseline Kubernetes. It is designed to function together with SUSE Rancher [33] which can handle the lifecycle of Edge k3s clusters identically to any other Kubernetes cluster.

6.1.5.2 Microk8s

Microk8s [36] presents itself as the minimal, CNCF-certified distribution of Kubernetes. More in detail, Microk8s offers an "open-source system for automating deployment, scaling, and management of containerised applications" [37] by offering a lightweight distribution of Kubernetes enabling it to execute in more resource constrained environments.

From a functional perspective, it offers at time of writing similar functionalities to k3s, although differentiation exist at the level of processor architectures supported. Micro-k8s supports the configuration of GPUs on NVIDIA DGX family of servers and workstations, which are specifically designed for AI process execution.

6.1.5.3 KubeEdge

KubeEdge [38] is an open-source Edge management tool included in the Linux Edge chapter of the Cloud Native Computing Foundation. KubeEdge offers a "native containerized application orchestration capabilities to hosts at Edge". Overall, KubeEdge architecture considers a centralized control from the Cloud to the Edge. It takes into consideration services for network configuration, application lifecycle and data and meta-data synchronization across Edge and Cloud environments.

Its architecture covers both an Edge and Cloud parts. At Edge Level, the EdgeD component manages the lifecycle of applications (pods) at a single node level. It allows the configuration of monitoring probes, secrets, container runtimes and volumes. The EventBus allows to send and receive messages based on MQTT topics. The DeviceTwin stores a registry of available Edge devices to this Edge node. The Meta-Manager processes messages among EdgeD and EdgeHub. It also permits to manage metadata from/to lightweight Edge nodes. Lastly, the EdgeHub centralises the interaction among the different Edge components and the Cloud. At the Cloud level, the EdgeController acts as an extended Kubernetes controller for Edge nodes. The DeviceController is responsible of IoT device management. It makes use of Kubernetes Custom Resource Definitions for device description. Device instances belong to a model and allow to get static device data (specification) and dynamic data about its status. Finally, the CloudHub enables the interaction among the Cloud and Edge layer.

6.1.5.4 Starlingx

Starlingx [39] is the Edge management project offered by the OpenStack community. It is defined as "a complete cloud infrastructure software stack for the edge used by the most demanding applications in industrial IOT, telecom, video delivery and other ultra-low latency use cases". Starlingx developments build on top of a series of existing open-source tools which include baseline OpenStack, Kubernetes and Hardened Linux [40].

At deployment level, Starlingx considers geographically distributed Edge sites of diverse sizes governed under a central data center which offers orchestration and synchronization services. Starlingx Edge Virtualisation platform includes deployment options for bare metal, VM and container based workloads. Its technological approach is structured in the main areas: Infrastructure management includes components for: configuration management, providing node discovery and nodes configuration management; Host Management, incorporating host interfaces and monitoring; Service management: considering high availability, messaging and service monitoring; Fault Management, allowing user definition of alarms and events; Software management (in progress) aiming to support node software update and patches handling; offering a container platform based on Kubernetes Cluster software components and including application management based in Helm; in addition it supports integration with openstack services and installation.

6.1.5.5   ONEDge

ONEedge [41] is defined as "a platform for extending private cloud orchestration capabilities to resources at the edge". ONEdge builds on top of the open source OpenNebula VM Manager and aims at applying "a distributed cloud model to dynamically, and on-demand, build and manage private edge clouds to run edge applications".

ONEedge [42] considers two models for building Edge Cloud architectures: Distributed Control Plane model and Centralized Control Plane model. The kind of execution environments considered at the Edge are Edge Data Centres in both models. The Distributed Control Plane model employs as baseline the Datacentre Federation functionality in OpenNebula for federation among Edge "zones" and On-premises data centres. In this model, the diverse data centers share user accounts, groups and permission configuration, however, configuration of the instances remain independent and resilient to network failures to the on-premises data centre. Differently, the Centralized Control Plane model takes the approach of a distributed data centre across diverse locations and therefore establishing a dependency between the on-premises data centre configurations and the rest of Edge federated instances.

ONEedge Solution Framework [43] is articulated on five main components: EdgeScape (Edge Instance Manager) handles the installation, management and monitoring of the Edge Management Platform; EdgeNebula (Edge Workload Orchestration and Management) orchestrates the edge cloud infrastructure resources and manages the life-cycle of the applications instantiated in the Edge environment; EdgeCatalog (Edge Provider Selection) keeps an inventory of edge resource providers federated to a ONEedge instance; EdgeProvision (Edge Infrastructure Allocation and Deployment) permits to handle the provision and life-cycle management of independent edge locations. Finally, the EdgeMarket (Edge Applications Marketplace) acts a yellow-pages for all instances and applications available to deploy.

6.1.5.6 IoFog

IoFog [44] is described as a platform for "deploying, running, and networking distributed microservices at the edge". IoFog develops the concept of an Edge Compute Network as mechanism to implement cluster features among Edge devices. IoFog is part of Eclipse Open Source Community.

At architectural level the IoFog architecture of a Edge Compute Network requires of a centralized ioFog Controller which is in charge of orchestrating the rest of ioFog building blocks: Agents, Microservices, Routers and users. An ioFog Controller can reside in one of the Network hosts or externally in a Cloud provider. Edge hosts are equipped with the software ioFog Agents that act as workers for the controller and are responsible of one or more micro-services deployed in an Edge node. Microservices represent uscr applications and can be deployed using LCX. A Router enables the diverse microservices to communicate among them.

6.1.5.7 EdgeX Foundry

EdgeX Foundry [45, 46] is defined as "a highly flexible and scalable open source software framework that facilitates interoperability among devices and applications at the IoT Edge". EdgeX Foundry supplies a micro-services software platform which allows building an IoT gateway functionality on top of an Edge device. EdgeX Foundry software components offer the functionalities to obtain data from the so-called South Side (IoT objects within the physical realm) with Cloud Services (North Side) in which data can be stored, aggregated, analysed and converted into actionable information. It is important to remark that the framework also contemplates actuation processes from north side to south side.

The following building blocks are identified as part of the EdgeX Foundry architecture. This architecture is structured in the following service layers. Core Services offer the set of services with communicates and orchestrates north and south sides. These services include: Core data, a persistent data repository and associated services for data obtained from south side objects; Command that enables the actuation requests from Cloud (north side) to IoT objects (south side); Metadata which offers a repository and management service which stores metadata the IoT objects connected to EdgeX Foundry instance; Registry and Config which allow the EdgeX Foundry instance configuration. The Supporting Services offer monitoring, alert and notification services; analytics understood as simple rules engine (Drools) over collected data and mechanisms for scheduling data clean-up once transmitted to north side. System Management components enable EdgeX Foundry services lifecycle management (installation, upgrade, start, stop) as well as mechanisms to obtain monitoring information about the framework services. Export Services Layer permits the integration to North side services implemented by means of three different mechanisms: Direct integration with Google IoT Core; integration with Client defined service with receives notifications of data being available; and by means of a Distribution mechanism implemented on top of Spring integration with enables data distribution thought REST, MQTT, or 0MQ to client defined endpoints. Device Services Layer provides a set of services which allows the interaction with IoT devices. It offers an extensible mechanism to build EdgeX Foundry Device Service microservice for new devices.

6.1.6 Features Comparison

In Table 6.1 we present a comparison of features among all analysed architectures in research works, while Tables 6.2 and 6.3 correspond to commercial and open source efforts. The analysis compares features considered by research works and commercial offerings. In this analysis, the observed maturity of market developments possesses a remarkable nature. These today are considering advanced capabilities with regard to Data management, Edge workload execution models adapted to the last trends on the market and even consideration of machine learning frameworks. At the same time analysed works in research elaborate on conceptual approaches and future requirements while existing implemented architectures are yet scarce. It is interesting to note that OpenFog architecture limits Edge computing to intermediary nodes among IoT devices and Cloud, while considering Fog, as the computing continuum that embraces end to end management from IoT devices to Cloud. However, from the provided descriptions, it is clear that commercial Edge computing offerings, and specifically Amazon Greengrass, go far beyond providing an intermediate computing layer. Instead, these develop end to end solution for both IoT devices, computing at the edge and rich cloud services, commercial products make reality the computing continuum concept nevertheless exposing its adopters to strong vendor lock-in.

According to current developments it can be the case that instead of research works feeding industry products with advanced features and ideas, it is research lagging behind industrial developments. As it happened in the area of Grid, and the successful application of Cloud utility models in the market almost a decade ago. This is to some extend corroborated by initial experimentation done in commercial offerings with rich IoT devices in connected vehicles [47, 48] which represents a clear initial step towards the realisation of Ad-hoc Edge Clouds and the Swarm computing concept defined by this work. This experimentation while exploiting the inference of ML at the edge recognises the need of edge groups of devices and its communication. Nowadays opportunities in research are apparently in scheduling, orchestration and optimisation problems instead of basic capabilities already being tackled in interesting approaches by commercial developments of major Cloud providers and open-source initiatives. These commercial offerings are advancing

Table 6.1 Edge frameworks feature comparison, research works

Works	Fog computing	ANGELS	MobileFog	Nebula	Resource provisioning
Resource management	X	X	X	X	X
Fault tolerance				X	X
Workload management	X	X			
Workload scheduling					X
Data management		X		X	
Orchestration across edge					
Edge and cloud interoperability					
Economy					
Eco-efficiency					
Security and privacy					
Connectivity and resilience					
Edge computing model	Cluster	Server	Hierarch.	Cluster	Hierarch.
Edge offering	IaaS	PaaS	PaaS	PaaS	IaaS
Prog. Model/Language				JavaScript	
Maturity	Architecture	Architecture	Architecture	Simulation	Simulation

Table 6.2 Edge frameworks feature comparison, commercial offerings

Works	AWS Greengrass	Azure IoT Edge
Resource management	X	X
Fault tolerance		
Workload management	X	X
Workload scheduling		
Data management	X	X
Orchestration across edge		
Edge and Cloud Interoperability	X	X
Economy	X	
Eco-efficiency		
Security and privacy	X	X
Connectivity and resilience	X	X
Edge computing model	Server	Server
Edge offering	PaaS	PaaS
Prog. model/language	Lambda, containers	containers

at impressive rapid pace and getting quickly into quite mature stages, research and standardisation works have yet to achieve.

6.2   Mobile Edge Computing and Networking Perspectives

The deployment of 5G sets high expectations for a diversity of technological developments such us self-driving cars and artificial intelligence that strongly depend on the availability of always-on high-speed internet connectivity. 5G establishes ambitious aspirations for the performance of network services in terms of bitrates, latency, and overall, network resilience and dependability. While 5G performance ambitions were clearly unrealistic to be offered by means of former 4G technologies, still in 5G it is generally acknowledged the existing difficulties to supply these levels of quality of service from cloud centralized data centres.

Hence, 5G's necessity to deliver efficient network services is today deriving in the requirement for 5G networks to incorporate the deployment of Edge computing infrastructures, specifically to address low latency demands. The resultant network infrastructures are constructed from the integration among network and compute technologies. These hybrid compute and network infrastructures have the purpose to enable significantly more performant access and execution of network functions, media content, and applications by means of their deployment in locations closer to where these services are consumed via frameworks such as mobile edge computing (MEC).

Table 6.3 Edge frameworks feature comparison, open source frameworks

Works	K3S	Micro k8s	Kube Edge	Starling x	ONEDge	IoFog	EdgeX Foundry
Resource management	X	X	X	X	X		
Fault tolerance	X	X	X	X	X		
Workload management	X	X	X	X	X		
Workload scheduling	X	X	X	X	X		
Data management						X	X
Orchestration across Edge				X	X		X
Edge and Cloud Interoperability				X	X		X
Economy							
Eco-efficiency							
Security and privacy				X	X		
Connectivity and resilience							
Edge computing model	Server	Server	Cluster	Cluster	Cluster	Server	Server
Edge offering	IaaS	IaaS	IaaS	IaaS	IaaS		

Overall, this is today resulting in a trend towards the cloudification of networks. At commercial level it leads to the establishment of new nexus between telecom operators and cloud providers. These two market actors are increasingly establishing strong coalitions for the experimentation of the required technological and business convergence between the cloud computing and the telecom worlds. Initial implementations for this convergence are being developed by public cloud providers with their Mobile Edge Computing services and by means of on-going efforts at standardisation bodies, such as European Telecommunications Standards Institute (ETSI)'s Multi-access Edge Computing.

Mobile Edge Computing services offerings take the view of Edge computing infrastructures based on data centres of different sizes, technologically analogous from a computing perspective to private clouds. These Mobile Edge Computing services are typically conceptualised in two different levels of Mobile Edge Computing that revolve around cloud for telecom:

Near Edge   intended to make use of Telecom operator infrastructure and being even capable of offering joint go-to-market approaches between cloud and telecom operators;
Far Edge   considering the deployment of a complete data centre in-house for telco providers in a certain user location;

Figure 6.4 represents this classification. The details on implementations of Mobile Edge Computing services offerings at public cloud providers will be presented in Sect. 6.2.2. ETSI Multi-access Edge Computing works will be developed in Sect. 6.2.1. It is important to note that initial developments at ETSI used the Mobile Edge computing terminology, while this have been updated to Multi-access Edge computing term recently.

6.2.1 ETSI Multi-Access Edge Computing Framework and Reference Architecture

ETSI Industry Specification Group defined Multi-access Edge Computing (MEC) [49]—previously known as Mobile Edge Computing—as the mechanism to offer cloud computing capabilities at the Edge of the network. Its overall ambition is to enable an environment with ultra-low latency and high bandwidth, for which applications could have access at the status of Radio Access Network (RAN) and even, serve for its deployment. The MEC approach builds on top of the Mobile Cloud Computing Cloudlet concept previously analysed in Chap. 4 [50, 51].

From a computing perspective, MEC Reference architecture and Framework [52] defines that a MEC Edge system is constituted by a set of MEC hosts and the necessary MEC Management in order to execute MEC applications into the Network operator infrastructure. The MEC Framework distinguishes among three functional elements: MEC host, MEC platform and MEC application.

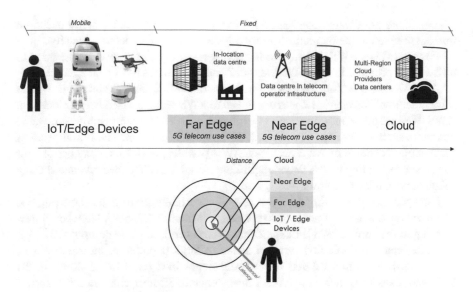

Fig. 6.4 Mobile Edge Computing classification

A MEC host contains the MEC platform and the virtualisations infrastructure that offers compute, storage and Network resources to MEC applications. MEC applications can execute as virtualised or containerised applications. The MEC platform enables to "discover, advertise, consume and offer MEC services". The core functionality of the MEC system level management is the MEC Orchestrator. It acts as infrastructure manager keeping track of available MEC hosts and executing services and Applications and their status. In addition, it is responsible for scheduling and on-boarding of application packages together with its lifecycle management. At host level, MEC platform manager handles host level application lifecycle management together with the management of the application rules and requirements. It interacts with Virtualization infrastructure manager to provide host infrastructure virtualization. OpenStack has been referenced as the Virtualisation Infrastructure Manager of choice in diverse implementations [53].

6.2.2   Existing Products in the Market

6.2.2.1   Amazon Web Services 5G telco Offerings

At level of Far Edge, AWS offers AWS Outpost [54]. As previously mentioned in Hybrid Cloud Sect. 3.5, these services offer local instantiation of AWS services in any data centre deployed in an AWS provided rack. These services have full compatibility among AWS Cloud APIs and in-house installations. At level of pricing, there are diverse configurations that define the service's pricing based on upfront pricing complemented with monthly fees based on expected capacity.

For Near Edge, AWS develops today two types of offerings: services intended to utilise telco provider in AWS Wavelength Zones [55] and AWS Local Zones [56].

AWS Wavelength Zones act as an extension of AWS Cloud in telecom providers infrastructures. Wavelength Zones are linked to AWS regions based in their location. AWS Wavelength Zones Services are offered by AWS in partnership with telco operators such as Verizon, Vodafone, KDDI, and SK Telecom. The initial services have partial coverage of AWS Services. AWS Wavelength details a pay per use for customers depending on the Wavelength Zone, in which AWS have revenue sharing schemas with telco operators.

Not specifically targeting the 5G market, but certainly sharing the same purpose of providing low latency access to services, in March 2022 AWS launched a new offering in the form of AWS Local Zones. These services place compute, storage, database, and other selected services closer to large population, industry, and IT centers [56]. AWS first offered AWS Local Zones in 6 AWS Local Zones in the U.S. and plans to launch new AWS Local Zones in 32 new cities in 26 countries worldwide [57].

6.2.2.2   Azure 5G telco Offerings

Both addressing the Far and Near Edge scopes, Azure developed a strategy to address the 5G market by means of Azure Edge Zones. Azure Edge Zones are small footprints of Azure located outside of Azure Regions which are owned and operated by Microsoft [58].

In addition, Azure offered the possibility of Azure Edge Zone private deployment in Far Edge, by means Private Edge Zones. Partnerships were established to provide E2E solutions to customers. Partners cover NFV (vEPC) vendors, Mobile Radio, SD-WAN Router vendors, Mobile operators and Global systems integrators in a network of more than 30 different companies.

Complementary, for Near Edge, Azure developed Azure Edge Zone on Carrier, located in Carrier infrastructure, for which it accounts with existing partnership with AT&T [59]. Overall, Azure offers a consistent stack in the three related offerings: Azure Edge Zones, on-carrier and private. Azure makes use of existing baseline in virtual network platform, based on open source containerized SONiC (Software for Open Networking in the Cloud) and switch operating system and SAI (Switch Abstraction Interface). These offer wide availability of Virtual Network Functions, including 5G and SD-WAN and firewalls from a network of providers.

These offerings have been recently consolidated in Azure private multi-access edge compute (MEC) [60] with the objective to "deliver ultra-low-latency networking, applications, and services at the enterprise edge". This offering agglutinates Azure Network Function Manager to be with network functions to be consumed from Microsoft marketplace solutions as well as Affirmed Private Network Service, Azure's fully managed and configurable private cellular network offering [61].

6.2.2.3   Google Cloud 5G telco Offerings

Similarly to AWS, far Edge strategy in GoogleCloud relies on its private Cloud offering Google Anthos. For which it offers a specific denomination, Anthos for Telecom [62]. The offering builds on top of Kubernetes for which Google Cloud offers a catalogue of network centric applications. The solution is tagged as "open source multi-cloud solution for telecom companies."

With regards to Near Edge strategy, Google Cloud aims to offer Vertical Telecom solutions in partnership with AT&T (retail, manufacturing and transportation). In addition, it plans to rely on partnerships with Amdocs, Netcracker SW specialist's telecom solutions. These solutions aim at using Google's Points of Presence today used for CDN. These are deployed in owned DCs and telecom operator facilities.

6.2.3   Conclusions

As previously mentioned, Mobile Edge Computing offerings today available at public Cloud providers and detailed in ETSI MEC Architecture independently of targeting Far Edge and Near Edge approaches, still rely on the consideration of a traditional data centre being available for application and network function services at the Edge.

The motivation for this approach is derived from the need for these forms of Edge deployment of re-using private cloud infrastructure management software. This is, the software toolset to be employed to manage applications and data on top of the data centres located at some network hops closer to the user than traditional cloud regions, but still not fully exploiting the Edge computing concept in terms of capability available in Edge devices and sophisticated IoT/Edge devices.

Private Cloud management toolsets were designed with the view of handling certain number of homogeneous resource-rich hardware nodes from a single location within data centre boundaries with well-established security perimeters. These tools are today uncapable to handle complexities at level of resource heterogeneity, massive number of managed devices, resilience and specific security challenges that are raised by means of the utilisation of Edge devices and sophisticated IoT/Edge devices. An observation that further reinforces the inability to handle heterogeneity in these toolsets, is the fact that some of the public Cloud Edge Telco offerings from public cloud providers previously analysed, even supply the hardware stack to be employed to ensure uniformity of all resources.

The existing approach in Mobile Edge computing of re-using private cloud management toolsets for the Edge can result still in complex to handle and suboptimal solutions. By making use of Near/Far Edge approaches, and neglecting additional compute capacity at the Edge, Mobile Edge Cloud approaches still face the risk of not yet achieving the performance improvements required by 5G to provide real-time processing in order to sustain qualitatively different applications while offering richer user experiences, faster interactions, large scale data processing, and machine to machine communications.

The very few available assessments of early 5G deployments trend to validate these concerns and demonstrate that the shorter the network links are in 5G deployments (in terms of less hops), the better performance is gained in terms of end-to-end latency [63].

Therefore, additionally in this context, there is a clear call for open approaches that permit to fully exploit in a decentralised manner, the complete compute continuum from the whole set of heterogeneous devices available at Edge to the Cloud while observing the requirements of real-time data processing.

References

1. Bonomi, F., Milito, R., Zhu, J., & Addepalli, S. (2012). Fog computing and its role in the internet of things. In *Proceedings of the First Edition of the MCC Workshop on Mobile Cloud Computing* (pp. 13–16). https://doi.org/10.1145/2342509.2342513
2. Bonomi, F., Milito, R., Natarajan, P., & Zhu, J. (2014). Fog computing: A platform for Internet of Things and analytics. In *Big Data and Internet of Things: A Roadmap For Smart Environments* (pp. 169–186). https://doi.org/10.1007/978-3-319-05029-4_7
3. Yannuzzi, M., Milito, R., Serral-Gracia, R., Montero, D., & Nemirovsky, M. (2014,12). Key ingredients in an IoT recipe: Fog computing, cloud computing, and more fog computing. In *2014 IEEE 19th International Workshop on Computer Aided Modeling and Design of Communication Links and Networks, CAMAD 2014* (pp. 325–329). http://ieeexplore.ieee.org/lpdocs/epic03/wrapper.htm?arnumber=7033259
4. Shi, W., Cao, J., Zhang, Q., Li, Y., & Xu, L. (2016). Edge computing: Vision and challenges. *IEEE Internet of Things Journal, 3*(5), 637–646. https://doi.org/10.1109/JIOT.2016.2579198
5. *Cisco systems fog computing and the Internet of Things: Extend the cloud to where the things are.* (2016). https://www.cisco.com/c/dam/en_us/solutions/trends/iot/docs/computing-overview.pdf
6. Vaquero, L., & Rodero-Merino, L. (2014). Finding your way in the fog. *ACM SIGCOMM Computer Communication Review, 44*, 27–32.
7. Garcia Lopez, P., Montresor, A., Epema, D., Datta, A., Higashino, T., Iamnitchi, A., Barcellos, M., Felber, P., & Riviere, E. (2015, 9). Edge-centric computing. *ACM SIGCOMM Computer Communication Review, 45*, 37–42. http://dl.acm.org/citation.cfm?doid=2831347.2831354
8. Satyanarayanan, M., Schuster, R., Ebling, M., Fettweis, G., Flinck, H., Joshi, K., & Sabnani, K. (2015, 3). An open ecosystem for mobile-cloud convergence. *IEEE Communications Magazine, 53*, 63–70. http://ieeexplore.ieee.org/lpdocs/epic03/wrapper.htm?arnumber=7060484
9. *AWS IoT Greengrass.* (2022). Retrieved May 26, 2022, from https://aws.amazon.com/greengrass/
10. *Azure IoT Edge.* Retrieved May 26, 2022, from https://azure.microsoft.com/en-us/services/iot-edge/
11. Bittencourt, L., Diaz-Montes, J., Buyya, R., Rana, O., & Parashar, M. (2017). Mobility-aware application scheduling in fog computing. *IEEE Cloud Computing, 4*, 26–35.
12. Pham, X., & Huh, E. (2016). Towards task scheduling in a cloud-fog computing system. In *18th Asia-Pacific Network Operations and Management Symposium, APNOMS 2016: Management of Softwarized Infrastructure - Proceedings.*
13. Deng, R., Lu, R., Lai, C., Luan, T., & Liang, H. (2016). Optimal workload allocation in fog-cloud computing toward balanced delay and power consumption. *IEEE Internet of Things Journal, 3*, 1171–1181.

14. Bitam, S., Zeadally, S., & Mellouk, A. (2018). Fog computing job scheduling optimization based on bees swarm. *Enterprise Information Systems*, *12*, 373–397 (2018). https://doi.org/10.1080/17517575.2017.1304579
15. DITAS. (2022). *Data-intensive applications improvement by moving data in mixed cloud/fog environments*. Retrieved May 26, 2022, from http://www.ditas-project.eu/
16. Zhou, Z., Chen, X., Li, E., Zeng, L., Luo, K., & Zhang, J. (2019). Edge Intelligence: Paving the last mile of artificial intelligence with edge computing. *Proceedings of the IEEE*, *107*, 1738–1762.
17. Le Duc, T., Leiva, R., Casari, P., & Östberg, P. (2019). Machine learning methods for reliable resource provisioning in edge-cloud computing: A survey. *ACM Computing Surveys*, *52*, 1.
18. Ferrer, A., Marquès, J., & Jorba, J. (2019, 1). Towards the decentralised cloud: Survey on approaches and challenges for mobile, ad hoc, and edge computing. *ACM Computing Surveys*, *51*. https://doi.org/10.1145/3243929
19. Ilager, S., Muralidhar, R., & Buyya, R. (2020). Artificial Intelligence (AI)-centric management of resources in modern distributed computing systems. http://arxiv.org/abs/2006.05075
20. Rodrigues, T., Suto, K., Nishiyama, H., Liu, J., & Kato, N. (2020). Machine learning meets computation and communication control in evolving edge and cloud: Challenges and future perspective. *IEEE Communications Surveys and Tutorials*, *22*, 38–67.
21. Wang, D., Zhang, D., Zhang, Y., Rashid, M., Shang, L., & Wei, N. (2019). Social edge intelligence: Integrating human and artificial intelligence at the edge. In *Proceedings - 2019 IEEE 1st International Conference on Cognitive Machine Intelligence, CogMI 2019* (pp. 194–201).
22. HEADS Project D3.3. (2016). *Final Framework of resource-constrained devices and networks*. http://heads-project.eu/sites/default/files/HEADS%20D3.3
23. Satyanarayanan, M. (2017). The emergence of edge computing. *Computer*, *50*, 30–39.
24. Mukherjee, A., Paul, H., Dey, S., & Banerjee, A. (2014, 3). ANGELS for distributed analytics in IoT. In *2014 IEEE World Forum on Internet of Things (WF-IoT)* (pp. 565–570). http://ieeexplore.ieee.org/lpdocs/epic03/wrapper.htm?arnumber=6803230
25. Hong, K., Lillethun, D., Ramachandran, U., Ottenwälder, B., & Koldehofe, B. (2013). Mobile fog: A programming model for large-scale applications on the Internet of Things. In *Proceedings of the Second ACM SIGCOMM Workshop on Mobile Cloud Computing* (pp. 15–20). https://doi.org/10.1145/2491266.2491270
26. Chandra, A., Weissman, J., & Heintz, B. (2013, 9). Decentralized edge clouds. *IEEE Internet Computing*. *17*, 70–73. http://ieeexplore.ieee.org/lpdocs/epic03/wrapper.htm?arnumber=6596502
27. Jonathan, A., Ryden, M., Oh, K., Chandra, A., & Weissman, J. (2017). Nebula: Distributed edge cloud for data intensive computing. *IEEE Transactions on Parallel and Distributed Systems*, *9219*, 1. http://ieeexplore.ieee.org/document/7954728/
28. Ryden, M., Oh, K., Chandra, A., & Weissman, J. (2014, 5). Nebula: Distributed edge cloud for data-intensive computing. In *2014 International Conference on Collaboration Technologies and Systems (CTS)* (pp. 491–492). http://ieeexplore.ieee.org/lpdocs/epic03/wrapper.htm?arnumber=6867613
29. Skarlat, O., Schulte, S., & Borkowski, M. (2016). Resource provisioning for IoT services in the fog resource provisioning for IoT services in the fog. In *2016 IEEE 9th International Conference on Service-Oriented Computing and Applications Resource*.
30. *Azure IoT reference architecture*. (2016). http://download.microsoft.com/download/A/4/D/A4DAD253-BC21-41D3-B9D9-87D2AE6F0719/Microsoft_Azure_IoT_Reference_Architecture.pdf
31. *Azure IoT Edge*. Retrieved May 26, 2022, from https://github.com/azure/azure-iotedge
32. *Amazon Web Services Greengrass FAQs*. Retrieved May 26, 2022, from https://aws.amazon.com/greengrass/faqs/
33. K3S. *Lightweight certified Kubernetes with Rancher*. https://rancher.com/products/k3s

34. *K3s: Lightweight Kubernetes solution sheet.* https://links.imagerelay.com/cdn/3404/ql/2e07db14c02f4b9dbd4a2805f38be28b/k3s-lightweight-kubernetes-solution-sheet.pdf
35. *K3s - Lightweight Kubernetes Github.* https://github.com/k3s-io/k3s
36. *MicroK8s - Zero-ops Kubernetes for developers, edge and IoT.* https://microk8s.io/
37. *MicroK8s documentation – home.* https://microk8s.io/docs
38. *KubeEdge-Kubernetes native edge computing framework.* https://kubeedge.io/en/
39. *Starling-X - Deploy your edge cloud now.* https://www.starlingx.io/
40. *Functional overview.* https://www.starlingx.io/
41. *ONEDge - An on-demand software-defined edge computing solution.* https://oneedge.io/
42. *OpenNebula's approach to edge computing - White Paper.* https://support.opennebula.pro/hc/en-us/articles/360050302811-Edge-Cloud-Architecture-White-Paper
43. ONEEdge.io, D2.1. *Solution Framework – A solution framework report v.1.0, OpenNebula Edge Architecture Reports.* https://support.opennebula.pro/hc/en-us/articles/360039706152-OpenNebula-Edge-Architecture-Reports
44. *IoFog – Core Concepts.* https://iofog.org/docs/2/getting-started/core-concepts.html
45. EdgeXFoundry. https://www.edgexfoundry.org/
46. Lee, S., Phan, L., Park, D., Kim, S., & Kim, T. (2022). EdgeX over Kubernetes: Enabling Container Orchestration in EdgeX. *Applied Sciences, 12.* https://www.mdpi.com/2076-3417/12/1/140
47. Barr, J. (2022). *AWS IoT, Greengrass, and machine learning for connected vehicles at CES.* Retrieved May 26, 2022, from https://aws.amazon.com/blogs/aws/aws-iot-greengrass-and-machine-learning-for-connected-vehicles-at-ces/
48. Rec, C. (2018). Building connected vehicle solutions on the AWS cloud. *The Internet of Things on AWS – Official Blog.* https://aws.amazon.com/blogs/iot/building-connected-vehicle-solutions-on-the-aws-cloud/
49. *ETSI, Multi-access Edge Computing (MEC).* https://www.etsi.org/technologies/multi-access-edge-computing/mec
50. Shahzadi, S., Iqbal, M., Dagiuklas, T., & Qayyum, Z. (2017, 12). Multi-access edge computing: Open issues, challenges and future perspectives. *J. Cloud Computing, 6.* https://doi.org/10.1186/s13677-017-0097-9
51. Mach, P., & Becvar, Z. (2017). Mobile edge computing: A survey on architecture and computation offloading. *IEEE Communications Surveys & Tutorials, 19,* 1628–1656.
52. ETSI, ETSI GS MEC 003 V3.1.1 (2022-03). *Multi-access Edge Computing (MEC); Framework and reference architecture.* https://www.etsi.org/deliver/etsi_gs/MEC/001_099/003/03.01.01_60/gs_MEC003v030101p.pdf
53. OpenStack, *OpenStack++ for cloudlet deployment.* http://reports-archive.adm.cs.cmu.edu/anon/2015/CMU-CS-15-123.pdf
54. AWS, *AWS infrastructure and services on premises – AWS Outposts.* https://aws.amazon.com/outposts/
55. AWS, *AWS wavelength.* https://aws.amazon.com/wavelength/
56. AWS, *AWS local zones.* https://aws.amazon.com/about-aws/global-infrastructure/localzones/
57. AWS, *AWS announces global expansion of AWS local zones.* https://press.aboutamazon.com/newsreleases/newsreleasedetails/awsannouncesglobalexpansionawslocalzones/
58. Khalidi, Y. *Microsoft partners with the industry to unlock new 5G scenarios with Azure Edge Zones.* https://azure.microsoft.com/nl-nl/blog/microsoft-partners-with-the-industry-to-unlock-new-5g-scenarios-with-azure-edge-zones/
59. Zander, J. *Microsoft and AT&T are accelerating the enterprise customer's journey to the edge with 5G.* https://azure.microsoft.com/enus/blog/microsoftandattareacceleratingtheenterprisecustomersjourneytotheedgewith5g/
60. *Azure private multi-access edge compute.* https://azure.microsoft.com/enus/solutions/privatemultiaccessedgecomputemec/
61. Azure. *Unlocking the enterprise opportunity with 5G, edge compute, and cloud.* https://azure.microsoft.com/enus/blog/unlocking-the-enterprise-opportunity-with-5g-edge-compute-and-cloud/

62. *Google   Cloud   for   telecommunications.*   https://cloud.google.com/solutions/ telecommunications/
63. Xu, D., Zhou, A., Zhang, X., Wang, G., Liu, X., An, C., Shi, Y., Liu, L., & Ma, H. (2020). Understanding operational 5G: A first measurement study on its coverage, performance and energy consumption. In *Proceedings of the Annual Conference of the ACM Special Interest Group on Data Communication on the Applications, Technologies, Architectures, and Protocols for Computer Communication* (pp. 479-494). https://doi.org/10.1145/3387514. 3405882

Chapter 7
Additional Technologies for Swarm Development

7.1 Security Requirements for Computing at the Edge

The enablement of trust in highly distributed computing environments — such as ad-hoc edge clouds and swarms — creates the necessity in current cybersecurity paradigms to adapt to these models, in order to progress towards more distributed and decentralised secure operation and management approaches. Environments which require the smart collaboration among multiple and heterogeneous resources across the Edge to Cloud continuum present specific characteristics, such as the fact that many of the elements to be secured are deployed outside of the well-established security controls of the data centre.

This issue poses security challenges both at the level of digital and physical security, which are of upmost importance for the adoption of Edge and Swarm technologies.

In addition, the deployment of these technologies presents security challenges from the perspective of connectivity and high heterogeneity on the devices to be protected.

These are combined with strong requirements for data security and privacy which implies the fact that Data security and privacy challenges need to be addressed appropriately, to take into consideration the specific differences among core and Edge deployments.

These challenges include the requisite for data security to consider the prevalent use devices and data sources across many locations simultaneously, as well as, specific requirements to handle scale, considering the growing number of tackled devices.

Additionally, in order to provide physical security of devices spread over these technologies, customers and providers require specific security assurances supported by tools which provide monitoring of edge nodes, access control and proper authentication with the purpose of targeting devices and data sources.

A. Juan Ferrer, *Beyond Edge Computing*, https://doi.org/10.1007/978-3-031-23344-9_7

In this sense, security and data privacy controls are required to span across all levels of the target architectures, with specific rules and policies taking into account the nature of devices and considering the complete security life cycle.

Overall, these pose a series of specific security requirements for Edge and Swarm developments which are summarised in the following non-exhaustive list:

End to End Design Principles   Edge and Swarm architectures are directed to employ trusted methodologies in order to add security and trust principles for the design of their management software systems.

Identity and access control   Incorporate identity and permissions management at the edge, with the purpose to ensure secure data management. Full access control policies are required to grant access to devices and data to third parties.

Trusted communication   Adaptation of standards, certification mechanisms and network security tools as means to validate the correctness of devices identities and capabilities.

Privacy   Privacy preserving mechanisms such as data encryption ought to ensure confidentiality and integrity of data at rest and data transmission.

Secure multi-tenancy support   To avoid integrity and confidentiality risks in sharing resources in distributed Edge and Swarm environments.

Incident Response techniques   Requirement to incorporate into the management frameworks incident response techniques that avoid relying in untrusted devices to form the infrastructures.

Automated Edge devices security updates   Demand for mechanisms to enable secure updates of operating systems, firmware and software packages over secure transmissions so as to guarantee security for device management.

Authentication mechanisms   Authentication mechanisms which take into consideration the resource limitations present in certain of the participating resources in distributed computing architectures.

Attack detection and prevention   Establish the necessary distributed security monitoring mechanisms which permit reactive and predictive reaction to attacks. Mechanisms must to be adapted to the constrained and mobile nature of certain devices as well as to cater for the application of AI for prediction features.

Decentralised and resilient security management   Security   management   in distributed Edge and Cloud environments need to avoid by means of their design, constituting a single point of failure. Besides, the design and operation mechanisms of security services in these environments have to consider the requirement of the system to continue to function in cases of communication failures.

7.2   The Role for P2P and Consensus Algorithms

Originating from file sharing applications, peer-to-peer (P2P) technologies have been prominent for many years [1]. Gnutella [2] was one of the first systems to offer distributed search capabilities. P2P systems consist of a flexible number of nodes which may join or leave the network arbitrarily, forming a highly dynamic overlay network. One of the most prominent examples is BitTorrent, which uses structured overlay networks and distributed hash tables (DHT) to allow searching for a specific resource. DHTs were also extensively studied in research of P2P networks in solutions like Chord [3] and Kademlia [4].

In a P2P overlay network, there are peers acting at the same time as servers and clients, establishing self-organised structures which are not constrained to a central management for their establishment and operation[5].

P2P overlays are logical structures or topologies of peers build on top of existing physical networks among the peers [6]. Literature distinguishes between two classes of overlay networks based on the overlay topology: structured and unstructured.

Unstructured peer-to-peer networks are formed out of the random connection of peers, not using any pre-defined structure by design. Viewed from a different perspective, structured overlay networks rely on DHT in order to deterministically determine the location of a peer in the network and its connections with the rest of network peers by utilizing consistent hashing[7]. By design, DHT form highly scalable structures and are able to manage high degree of churn rates (rate of nodes entering and leaving the system)[8].

Swarm computing and ad-hoc edge cloud architectures build on top of the p2p overlay network and DHT concepts in order to enable the dynamic formation of computing infrastructures which are fully decentralized and display a self-organised behaviour, while having inherent support for heterogeneity, are highly scalable and resilient to node failures.

For this purpose, the initial work on Swarm computing and ad-hoc edge cloud presented in this book relies in distributed storages and distributed systems consensus algorithms as the crucial mechanism for nodes coordination which enables distributed resource and service management.

Distributed storages and distributed systems consensus algorithms perform all underlying nodes coordination tasks, including cluster management, leader election and cluster membership which allow resilient resource management and distributed service handling. Distributed coordination services are essential for a practical implementation of overlay network concepts in Swarm computing.

While the specific details of the chosen implementation will be provided in the architecture in Chap. 9 and Cognitive resource management in Chap. 10, below we present a very brief introduction to the status of distributed coordination services storages and consensus algorithms.

Distributed systems such as Kubernetes or Apache Hadoop, rely in distributed coordination services such as Apache ZooKeeper [9] and etcd[10] to implement leader election processes and distributed lock mechanisms to synchronise accesses to shared resources[11].

Distributed coordination-based systems operate under the premise that the diverse components of a distributed system are inherently distributed and that the problem to address is the manner to coordinate the activities among the different components[12]. Central to a distributed coordination service is a consensus protocol. Consensus in this context is defined as "a fundamental problem in fault-tolerant distributed systems. Consensus involves multiple servers agreeing on values. Once they reach a decision on a value, that decision is final" [13].

Both etcd and ZooKeeper are distributed key-value stores and distributed coordination services which depend on variants of the Paxos Consensus algorithm[14].

The Paxos[15] protocol was defined by Lamport with the objective of defining fault tolerant consensus[14]. Paxos is known for its inherent complexity to be understood and implemented[16]. As a result, a number of variants of the Paxos consensus algorithms have been developed by the most popular distributed coordination services:

ZooKeeper ZooKeeper is an Apache project which is defined as "centralized service for maintaining configuration information, naming, providing distributed synchronization, and providing group services" [9]. ZooKeeper was initially developed by Yahoo[17] and it is nowadays the distributed coordination service of choice in multiple Apache projects such as: Apache Cassandra, Hadoop, Kafka and Mesos among many others. In addition, it is utilised in services from companies such as the mentioned Yahoo and Twitter[18]. Zookeeper relies in Zab consensus algorithm[17] based on Paxos including new features at level of atomic broadcast, allowing those messages to be received in the same order by all nodes. ZooKeeper is implemented in Java[19].

etcd etcd[10] is defined as "a strongly consistent, distributed key-value store that provides a reliable way to store data that needs to be accessed by a distributed system or cluster of machines. It gracefully handles leader elections during network partitions and can tolerate machine failure, even in the leader node.". Etcd was initially part of CoreOS and was created with the objective to manage the storage and distribution of configuration files and to handle OS upgrades in clustered systems. Etcd was designed with intention to better supporting dynamicity and on-the-fly configuration and to reduce the memory footprint of ZooKeeper [20]. Etcd is implemented in Go. Notably, Etcd is used as the underlying nodes coordination mechanism and state storage for Kubernetes. Etcd is based on the Raft consensus protocol [21, 22], citeraft-thesis which seeks to enhance the comprehensibility of the Paxos.

References

1. Barkai, D. (2001) Technologies for sharing and collaborating on the Net. In *Proceedings First International Conference On Peer-to-Peer Computing*. (pp. 13-28)
2. Lv, Q., Cao, P., Cohen, E., Li, K., & Shenker, S. (2014, 6). Search and replication in unstructured peer-to-peer networks. In *ICS 2014 - Proceedings of the 28th ACM International Conference on Supercomputing* (pp. 335–346). Publisher Copyright: © 2014 by the Association for Computing Machinery, Inc. (ACM); 25th ACM International Conference on Supercomputing, ICS 2014; Conference date: 10-06-2014 Through 13-06-2014.

3. Stoica, I., Morris, R., Karger, D., Kaashoek, M., & Balakrishnan, H. (2001). Chord: A scalable peer-to-peer lookup service for internet applications. In *SIGCOMM '01*.
4. Maymounkov, P., & Eres, D. (2002, 4). Kademlia: A peer-to-peer information system based on the XOR metric. In *Kademlia: A Peer-to-peer Information System Based on the XOR Metric* (Vol. 2429).
5. Lua, E., Crowcroft, J., Pias, M., Sharma, R., & Lim, S. (2006, 4). A survey and comparison of peer-to-peer overlay network schemes. *Communications Surveys & Tutorials, IEEE, 7*, 72–93.
6. Malatras, A. (2015). State-of-the-art survey on P2P overlay networks in pervasive computing environments. *Journal of Network and Computer Applications, 55*, 1–23. https://www.sciencedirect.com/science/article/pii/S1084804515000879
7. Jafari Navimipour, N., & Sharifi Milani, F. (2015). A comprehensive study of the resource discovery techniques in peer-to-peer networks. *Peer-to-Peer Networking and Applications, 8*, 474–492. https://doi.org/10.1007/s12083-014-0271-5
8. Rhea, S., Geels, D., Roscoe, T. & Kubiatowicz, J. (2004) Handling Churn in a DHT. In *Proceedings Of The Annual Conference On USENIX Annual Technical Conference*. (pp. 10)
9. Apache ZooKeeper. https://zookeeper.apache.org/
10. Etcd, *A distributed, reliable key-value store for the most critical data of a distributed system*. Retrieved May 26, 2022, from https://etcd.io
11. Kleppmann, M. (2017). *Designing data-intensive applications*. O'Reilly. https://www.safaribooksonline.com/library/view/designing-data-intensive-applications/9781491903063/
12. Tanenbaum, A. & Steen, (2006) M. Distributed Systems: Principles and Paradigms (2nd Edition). Prentice-Hall, Inc.
13. *The Raft consensus algorithm*. https://raft.github.io/
14. Ailijiang, A., Charapko, A., & Demirbas, M. (2016). Consensus in the cloud: Paxos systems demystified. In *2016 25th International Conference on Computer Communication and Networks (ICCCN)* (pp. 1–10).
15. Lamport, L. (1998, 5). The part-time parliament. In *ACM Transactions on Computer Systems 16, 2 (May 1998), 133–169. Also Appeared as SRC Research Report 49. This Paper was First Submitted in 1990, Setting a Personal Record for Publication Delay that has Since been Broken by [60]*. https://www.microsoft.com/en-us/research/publication/part-time-parliament/, ACM SIGOPS Hall of Fame Award in 2012.
16. Unmesh Joshi, *MartinFlower.com patterns of distributed systems Paxos*. https://martinfowler.com/articles/patterns-of-distributed-systems/paxos.html
17. Junqueira, F., Reed, B., & Serafini, M. (2011). Zab: High-performance broadcast for primary-backup systems. In *2011 IEEE/IFIP 41st International Conference on Dependable Systems & Networks (DSN)* (pp. 245–256).
18. *ZooKeeper use cases*. https://zookeeper.apache.org/doc/r3.8.0/zookeeperUseCases.html
19. Hadoop, *ZooKeeper internals*. https://zookeeper.apache.org/doc/r3.4.13/zookeeperInternals.html
20. CoreOS Blog, *The history of etcd*. https://elder.dev/archive/archive.today/fkwuc/
21. Ongaro, D., & Ousterhout, J. (2014). In search of an understandable consensus algorithm. In *Proceedings of the 2014 USENIX Conference on USENIX Annual Technical Conference* (pp. 305–320). http://dl.acm.org/citation.cfm?id=2643634.2643666
22. Ongaro, D. (2014). *Consensus: Bridging theory and practice*. Stanford University. http://purl.stanford.edu/qr033xr6097

Part II
Computing Beyond the Edge: Swarm Computing and Ad-hoc Edge Architectures

In Part I, we have partially presented the current state of the art and market developments for future Ad-hoc Edge Cloud architectures and Swarm computing models. In these systems, we observe that Mobile Cloud Computing has already developed a number of valuable tools and techniques that can significantly influence the future evolution of Cloud models, specifically, in relation to Cloudlet and Edge Computing and Mobile Ad-hoc Cloud.

Building its routes in Cloudlet concepts we remark that Edge Computing research is still in its early developmental stage. At the current state of development, multiple works have elaborated on diverse conceptual approaches for it, however, very few architectures detail the management of specific aspects and research gaps which are in research challenges such as: across Edge execution models, Economy, Connectivity and Resilience.

Interestingly enough, while part of the research community continues to debate the most appropriate term to use (Edge/Fog), major cloud providers have previously introduced significantly mature products even exploiting aspects such as ML inference at the Edge. These developments give a clear indication on how promising Edge Computing developments are and the need for future research works to take into consideration commercially developed products in order not to re-invent the wheel.

At the same time, expected gains in complexity of the connected complex IoT devices will designate specific requirements to Cloud Computing evolution towards Swarm computing, as represented in Fig. 1.

These environments are initially shaped in the evolution of Ad-hoc Edge Clouds enabling smart collaboration among mobile devices. These Ad-hoc Edge Clouds build their routes in ad-hoc networks and opportunistic computing. Further evolution of this concept is expected to enable the creation of dynamic ecosystems, meshes or swarms of complex IoT Edge devices implemented as overlay networks in fully distributed and decentralised manner in the so-called Swarm computing environments.

We are simultaneously witnessing very significant advances in AI and deep learning technologies which fuelled by the unstoppable data availability collected

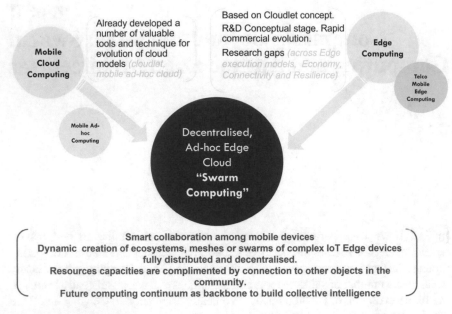

Fig. 1 Swarm Computing motivation

from complex IoT Edge devices, will soon increase computing demand by several orders of magnitude.

While the relation among these technologies is starting to be tackled by both research and commercial efforts [1–3], it further calls for development of Ad-hoc Edge Clouds and Swarm computing environments.

This part specifically addresses the given challenge by providing the Swarm computing concept definition, principles and envisaged characteristics in Chap. 8, along with the analysis of the particularities of the compute resources which participate in these infrastructures and use cases which could benefit from its implementation. Chapter 9 details the necessary building blocks to implement the Swarm computing model in a concrete architecture which exploits distributed coordination mechanisms in order to handle massive scale and fault tolerance. Subsequently, we carry out the study and evaluation of two concrete aspects essential for the development of Ad-hoc Edge Clouds architectures: Cognitive resources management is addressed in Chap. 10 presenting the mechanisms for on-the-fly swarm instantiation and resilient resource management; In Chap. 11 service placement and management mechanisms, defining admission control processes for Ad-hoc Edge Clouds are elaborated.

References

1. Morshed, A., Jayaraman, P., Sellis, T., Georgakopoulos, D., Villari, M., & Ranjan, R. (2018). Deep osmosis: Holistic distributed deep learning in osmotic computing. *IEEE Cloud Computing*, *4*, 22–32. http://ieeexplore.ieee.org/document/8260823/
2. Satyanarayanan, M. (2017). The emergence of edge computing. *Computer*, *50*, 30–39.
3. *AWS IoT Greengrass*. Retrieved May 26, 2022, from https://aws.amazon.com/greengrass/

Chapter 8
Computing Beyond Edge: The Swarm Computing Concept

8.1 Overview

As derived from the state of the art analysis presented in previous chapters, Edge Computing currently reflects one of the major IT trends, originated at the intersection among four main IT developments: Internet of Things (IoT), Cloud Computing, Networks and more recently, Artificial Intelligence (AI).

Edge computing has emerged with the objective to bring Cloud computing capacities at the "Edge" of the network so as to address latency issues present in IoT scenarios.

Edge computing serves the purpose of providing a compute environment located in the vicinity of data generation sources able to prevent latency issues detected in accessing Cloud services. Edge Computing brings together networking with distinctive cloud principles to define distributed computing platforms in charge of meeting the specific needs of IoT[1].

This union has definitively established an initial step towards the decentralisation of Cloud computing by initiating its transformation from the provision of services in dedicated datacentres for which resources were perceived as unlimited to a more decentralised approach in which these cloud services are presented in combination with stationary Edge devices [2].

The aforementioned approach is currently materialised in existing market offerings which provide initial IoT data filtering and pre-processing with integrated synchronization with cloud services by major providers such as AWS Greengrass[3] and Azure IoT Edge[4].

Today's Edge computing environments are principally considered stationary dedicated Edge computing devices and even, fully flagged data centres in the Telco conception of Mobile Edge Computing. However, Connected IoT devices are widely available while they have incorporated noteworthy compute resources. IoT environments have been gradually gathering new characteristics, they do not merely include simple sensors with 8-bit microprocessors[5], but they are increasingly composed by complex devices which are assemblies of non-negligible computing and storage

A. Juan Ferrer, *Beyond Edge Computing*, https://doi.org/10.1007/978-3-031-23344-9_8

resources aggregated together with diverse sensors and actuators. Examples of such devices include robots, drones and autonomous vehicles. Moreover, innovative compute devices are being released on the market including application specific processors for AI processing to facilitate embedding compute intelligence into all kinds of IoT devices.

The growth in the complexity of IoT devices is calling for Edge computing to profit from all compute and storage capacity available in a specific location in all kinds of stationary and IoT edge devices, evolving towards Swarm Computing [6, 7]. A compute Swarm is conceived as an ecosystem of complex IoT devices which are complemented with additional stationary Edge and Cloud resources. Within this ecosystem, each resource capacities is enhanced by connection to other participant resources in the community. Swarms are implemented by means of Ad-hoc Edge Cloud architectures. Swarms have to be designed to allow the dynamic generation of devices' ecosystems encompassing IoT devices, cyber-physical devices, edge and clouds, each of these adding to the swarm collectively their capability and insight. Swarms are expected to bring forth a future computing continuum a backbone in which to build collective intelligence.

The foreseen evolution of Cloud and Edge computing technologies towards Swarm computing is detailed in the upcoming Sect. 8.2. Apart from this aspect, the present chapter develops Swarm Computing concept, characteristics and principles in Sects. 8.3 and 8.4.

The particular attributes of the IoT devices which form this infrastructure pose special challenges to be addressed in Swarm Computing which are studied in Sect. 8.5. These challenges impact the design of the Ad-hoc Edge Cloud architecture in relation to Swarm Computing overall resource and service management practices and the foreseen lifecycle of a swarm, as presented in Sect. 8.6.

In addition, we expand on specific use cases which could benefit from the Swarm Computing concept and its development in Ad-hoc Edge Cloud architectures in Sect. 8.7.

8.2   Foreseen Evolution Towards Swarm Computing

Figure 8.1 presents the expected evolution from the baseline Cloud computing environments and its initial decentralisation by means of Edge computing, towards the materialisation of Swarm computing concept. As part of this evolution, four different development stages of Cloud and Edge computing technologies are anticipated.

Cloud computing   Has enabled the democratization of computing. It has provided the illusion of infinite computing and enabled the radical acceleration of commoditization of computing, thus opening new possibilities for enterprise users of technology to position IT as a strategic competitive weapon.

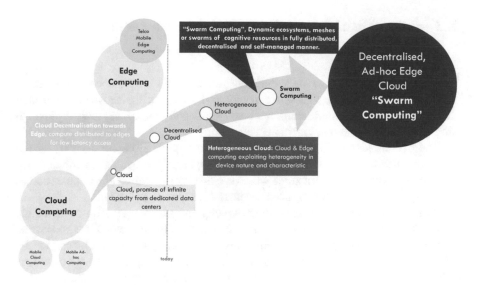

Fig. 8.1 Evolution towards Swarm Computing

Cloud Decentralisation towards Edge   Existing Cloud computing developments emerged as part of a centralised paradigm in which large and fully equipped data centres concentrate the available computing power. However, the expected growth on the number of connected things and devices requires the decentralisation of cloud computing in Edge computing in order to avoid unnecessary latencies by distributing computing to the edges of the network.

Heterogeneous Cloud   Connected things are gaining in complexity and capacities. There will be an arising need for them to go beyond rigid basic programming models to become fully networked computing systems capable of delivering advanced behaviours and interacting with their surroundings. Foreseen slowdown in Moore's law calls for progressively maximising the use of available resources by exploiting their heterogeneity and coping with the necessary balance among resources in high demand: computing and energy.

Swarm Computing   Dynamic ecosystems—swarms—of IoT, Edge and Cloud resources in fully distributed, decentralised and self-managed manner. Swarms assemble compute resources whose knowledge is enhanced by connection to other resources in the community and their information about the environment. Swarms encompass heterogeneous IoT Edge AI powered resources, cyber-physical devices, edge and clouds, each of them adding their own capacities and information in a self-management cognitive compute continuum. Swarms are temporary compute infrastructures which are generated on demand to fulfil certain needs.

8.3 Definition of Ad-hoc Edge Clouds, the Swarm Computing Concept

The extraordinary rise we are witnessing nowadays in the number of connected devices entails harnessing the idle capacity at the Edge of the network. Connected devices are not only omnipresent, but also significantly increasing their sophistication (such as robots and autonomous vehicles).

The overall idea of Swarm computing is to exploit available capacity at the Edge in order to create on-the-fly and in an opportunistic manner distributed and ephemeral compute infrastructures which are formed as swarms of resources across Edge and Clouds to address a specific demand for service execution.

Swarms are envisioned as ecosystems which jointly aggregate resources available in a specific location and point of time. In these temporary structures resources, capacity and knowledge is complimented by linking to other objects in the community and the environment. Swarm ecosystems comprehend heterogeneous IoT resources, cyber-physical devices, edge and clouds, that supply the necessary features for the swarm service provision.

As shown, Swarm Computing is conceived as a distributed, opportunistic, collaborative, heterogeneous, self-managed execution environment, bridging the Edge and Cloud, delivered in the form of Ad-hoc Edge Cloud architectures. Swarm computing and its implementation in the Ad-hoc Edge Cloud architecture aim at meeting the demand for extracting value out of the overwhelming data availability collected from IoT Edge devices and respond to the growing processing demand at the Edge based on the technological advances of AI and Deep Learning.

Swarm participant resources are not dedicated; therefore, they can reside in different domains and may have possibly conflicting interests. This approach aims at gaining full advantage of all available heterogeneous resources at the Edge to provide a service-based environment which allows for gathering and utilising these massive, diverse, and highly distributed compute capacity, by establishing dynamically service networks—swarms—which are opportunistic, and formed on-the-fly to meet the demand for service execution.

A computing Swarm will therefore become an opportunistic service network realised as an overlay network which consists of heterogeneous resources capable of coupling dynamically, flexibly and autonomously to provide assets (i.e. services and resources) to relevant applications and participants. Resources can be IoT, Edge and Cloud resources. Swarms are deployed and executed in response to requirements, which may emerge from application/user requests for services, or as response to certain events.

Thus, Swarm computing seeks to enable a service provisioning to shift from the existing predefined and fixed orientation to a pure on-demand, opportunistic, and ad-hoc approach in swarms of IoT, Edge and Cloud devices. Executing services will rely on dynamic, diverse, and distributed resources that form a dedicated overlay network.

To do so, the Ad-hoc Edge Cloud architecture and Swarm computing needs to regard the specificities of Edge devices, their characteristics and the non-dedicated inherent quality of the infrastructure by developing mechanisms to handle their expected massive number, the availability of dynamic resources (due to mobility and resources constraints) and the heterogeneous nature of IoT Edge resources.

Swarm computing aspires to create dynamic ecosystems of IoT Edge Devices, swarms, in a complete distributed and decentralised manner. Hence the Ad-hoc Edge Cloud architecture relies on decentralized management distributed among all participant resources, which avoids a single point of failure for the infrastructure and offers inherent mechanisms to scale. Likewise, this fact also ensures the autonomy of the Swarm instance, by eliminating the reliance on external management layers, for instance, located at the cloud, which can hinder its operation in case of unreliable connectivity.

The target edge devices for the Ad-hoc Edge Cloud architecture and Swarm computing constitute limited resources in terms of computational power and storage capacity. These edge devices can be increasingly regarded as non-trivial assembles of various assorted sensors with a set of storage and compute resources. The manufacturers of these kind of devices, such as drones, robots or automobiles, are submitted to constant pressure to provide more AI-enabled intelligent capabilities at commercially viable costs. The mobile nature of these devices makes them subject to restricted capacity batteries for energy supply.

Enhancing edge devices' on-board computational and storage resources, increases their cost and energy demand, therefore resulting in reduced device autonomy. Hence, any framework attempting to operate in such environment ought to consider these limitations. Thereby, Swarm computing management components will require very lightweight implementations which do not hinder the normal functioning of the target edge devices.

Distributed and decentralised management is also fundamental in order to handle the uncertainty of resource availability in the Ad-hoc Edge Cloud architecture implementing Swarm computing. As previously introduced, the dynamicity present in resource availability is commonly referred to as node churn. It refers to the volatile behaviour of resources concerning their accessibility to be part of the system. Node churn describes the dynamic behaviour of resources appearing and disappearing from the system. Node churn contemplates the "change in the set of participating nodes due to joins, graceful leaves, and failures" [8].

Node churn stresses the usefulness for the Ad-hoc Edge Computing architecture to manage uncertainty on resource availability. Edge resources, which are a component of the infrastructure, can be affected by numerous events that affect availability, including depleting the battery, changing edge device locations, and unexpectedly appearing or disappearing from the environment.

Therefore, the coordination of swarms requires the unfolding in an open and distributed self-management runtime model. This self-management model is expected to exploit cognitive techniques for their control and administration—i.e. utilising multi-objective optimisation, adaptive selection, conflict resolution—and to apply techniques for anticipating the volatility and uncertainty introduced by real-world availability of dynamic IoT Edge resources, thereby enabling an efficient and reliable service provisioning.

Consequently Swarm management scenarios will require addressing self-management and self-healing at scale and across heterogeneous IoT Edge resources and clouds types, but also consider business models and incentives which regulate the participation of different entities in swarms.

8.4 Swarm Computing Characteristics and Principles

Swarm Computing pursue the enhancement of the traditional Edge and Cloud environments by including a set of important characteristics and principles. Swarm computing concept was initially defined in [6], the upcoming sections further define its characteristics and key principles.

8.4.1 Swarm Characteristics

The central characteristics of Swarm computing are remote sensing, ad-hoc capabilities, fully decentralized operation, and self-management layers.

Sensing Swarms decipher and establish interactions with the physical world. This environmental awareness and actionability is provided by sensors and actuators of IoT edge devices.

Beyond sensors and actuators, these devices also provide cognitive capabilities which can be utilized to process sensor data streams, implementing for instance low-latency control loops at the edge. At the same time, the devices are connected to other nodes in their immediate surrounding and equally dedicated edges and clouds, allowing to dynamically activate more capabilities as needed.

Ad-hoc Character Swarms comprise a variety of resources and are by nature dynamically changing. They consist of distributed and heterogeneous IoT edge devices, Edge computing resources, as well as more centralized cloud capacity.

These resources provide significantly different capabilities and can be moderately constrained.

Resources closer to the edge are more distributed, more limited in their compute and storage capabilities, frequently also battery constrained, but at the same time closer to sensors and actuators, when compared to more centralized cloud resources. Distributed IoT and edge resources are more dynamic as well. There is usually a high degree of mobility and node churn with resources which can attach to and detach themselves from Swarms at any given time. IoT edge devices might have to leave due to potential scenarios of drained batteries, higher priority primary functions evicting Ad-hoc Edge Cloud tasks, and failures. Cloud resources on the other hand are more stable, given the high levels of availability provided by today's data center technology, yet their availability depends on working communication links, where connectivity changes dynamically as well.

Decentralised Operated Cloud Swarms contemplate at operating efficiently and reliably without a central entity for management. Instead, nodes of the continuum work in a decentralised manner, as an autonomous overlay network utilising distributed information of, and exchanging information on resources and workloads.

Such a decentralised and autonomous approach is necessary in view of the dynamic and ad-hoc nature of compute Swarms and the scale expected at levels of participant devices. Consequently, the resource management of Swarms is expected to be resilient against nodes failures and able to distribute the swarm management processes among a vast number of participants.

Self-management Swarm Computing applies autonomous computing techniques and machine learning to create adaptability in case of unforeseen situations and anticipate future circumstances. Namely, cognitive resources are self-aware, self-managed, self-protected, self-healing, and self-optimising in the realisation of an Ad-hoc Edge Cloud architecture. These features are enabled by continuous monitoring and modelling of and by all nodes of the compute continuum which take part in the infrastructure. The nodes continuously update and apply models of current and future resource availabilities, node churn and mobility, system health and anomalies, as well as of workloads and task performance. The nodes of the swarm overlay network also continuously exchange information and models among each others.

8.4.2 Key Principles

Swarms are based on three principles, placed under the term AAA—derived from IoT principles—as an acronym for the Aware, Autonomous, and Actionable characteristics [9, 10], defined as follows:

8.4.2.1 Aware

The sensing part of a Swarm must be able to perceive data or information about physical or digital nearby surroundings and has the ability to store this information to identify patterns and model changing circumstances. Such dynamically changing environments are captured in the two models of resource and context awareness in the Ad-hoc Edge Cloud architecture.

Context Awareness

A key strategy, which is needed in a Swarm instance is the ability to foresee the availabilities of participatory devices in close spatial proximity. This concept relies on the Edge computing attribute which considers physical proximity as the method facilitating latency enhancement. This complements the fact that the consideration of physical location of the IoT devices and Edge nodes which constitute an infrastructure are much of interest in certain usage scenarios. Key features to be implemented by an Ad-hoc Edge Cloud architectures are the determination of the physical areas in which are deployed the participant devices of swarm; the management of the swarm overlaps in physical locations; as well as physical node and network discovery mechanisms.

Resource Awareness

Swarms need to have knowledge of the available resources to be able to efficiently provision tasks with the required compute, communication, and storage capabilities. Some resources available in the Edge to Cloud continuum are static and, aside from failures, permanently supplied. Other resources are dynamic.

These resources can join and leave the swarm at any time, with continuous churn due to user behaviour and node mobility. Resources which are not exclusively dedicated to swarms can furthermore dynamically establish specific capabilities and the amount of resources they provide, allowing to prioritise primary device functions with fluctuating resource demands.

8.4.2.2 Autonomous

Resources in Swarm computing need to act as autonomous entities. They are responsible for their own configuration, monitoring, and management in a manner that exercises control over their own actions. The autonomous characteristic of swarms therefore apply to the resource management in the Ad-hoc Edge Cloud architecture as described in the awareness section and further extends to decentralised and independent scheduling approaches.

Furthermore, the entities in a Swarm need to be provided with autonomous mechanism in regards to fault tolerance: due to distributed and ad-hoc nature, they demand a distributed monitoring approach which can be leveraged for self-healing purposes [11]. Similar characteristics of self-management were proposed by Paul Horn as Autonomic computing [12]. This type also includes methods for self-configuration [13] as well as self-protection [14] in terms of security and can thus be summarised as general autonomous self-optimisation [15].

8.4.2.3   Actionable

Actuation is not only dependent on the environmental context, but also involves the capacities of learning from past situations, the ability to predict and simulate as well as to enable real-time automation of actions. Related actions refer to resource and service management, which are carried out within the Ad-hoc Edge Cloud architecture. Thus, the Ad-hoc Edge Cloud architecture has to intelligently schedule and foresee needs for instance in terms of infrastructure and resources adaptability, data transmission and analytics adaptability to execute services. Additionally, the Ad-hoc Edge Cloud architecture should be capable of foreseeing resource behaviour and future workloads, so that it is able to respond as a reliable infrastructure and the scalability of services is ensured.

8.5   Ad-hoc Edge Cloud Resources Characteristics

A significant factor which differentiates resource management in Swarm Computing is the high degree of heterogeneity of the edge devices likely to be involved in the Ad-hoc Edge Cloud computing infrastructure. Targeted Edge devices range from cloud resources and dedicated stationary Edge devices to rich IoT Edge devices which adjust to certain characteristics (see additional details below in this section).

In this context, diversity undoubtedly stems from the variety of capacities of the resources intended to be used, as well as from aspects such as: supported operating systems and processing architectures (i.e. CPU and GPU). It is imperative for Ad-hoc Edge Clouds to handle the diversity of edge devices engaged in the infrastructure.

In addition, the mobility of the edge devices which form this computing infrastructure leads to a significant breakdown of existing resource management practices in Cloud and data centre, as far as connectivity instabilities are concerned and their expected massive number. Furthermore, they are affected by specific factors, namely the prerequisite of energy optimization and battery lifetime, which can exert negative influence on the availability of these resources.

In view of the above, edge resource management in Swarm computing and in the Ad-hoc Edge Cloud architecture reflects the requirement to support the operation in a large number of heterogeneous constrained devices and presents the indispensable condition of being able to manage dynamic behaviour in relation to resource availability.

Therefore, the four main distinctive aspects which describe the kind of infrastructure resources Swarms rely on are: their scale in terms of constituent devices, their heterogeneity, their potential mobility and their restrictions in terms of the battery and overall capacity. These four characteristics are crucial to understanding the dynamic availability of resources considered by this Ad-hoc Edge Cloud architecture, which significantly differs from typical resource management practices in Cloud computing.

Massive scale   There is a plethora of disquisitions regarding the number of
expected devices worldwide [16]. While it seems challenging to offer a
precise estimation of the number of connected devices for the immediate
future, the reality is that all trends reflect a massive growth in the
number of connected devices in a wide diversity of scenarios [17]. This
proliferation has constituted one of the main drivers to the emergence of
Edge computing and is expected to continue. While Ad-hoc Edge Cloud
architecture is clearly not addressing all kinds of connected devices, it is
an important factor for its design and development the consideration of
scale in the number of devices able to participate in the Swarm infrastructure. The expected scale in the number of devices which punctually can be
part of the generated compute infrastructure raises the need to employ new
management styles able to cope seamlessly with situations with variable
and massive number of devices.

Heterogeneity   The cloud computing model is sustained on economies of scale
which are enabled in large public cloud providers by the capacity of
automation over standardised and homogeneous huge farms of servers
providing compute, storage and networking resources to the specific cloud
services

Homogeneity of resources which provide a specific service in these large
data centre set-ups leads to reduced operating costs with the help of
standardised management practices and automation.

Edge computing environments, on the contrary, are characterised by their
heterogeneity. The expected massive growth in connected IoT devices
together with the wide variety of use cases in which they can be
employed, creates diversity at several levels. Devices at the Edge can
range from simple sensors able to capture data (i.e. a temperature sensor)
to complex aggregations of sensors and actuators embedded together with
high performant compute and storage resources, such as an autonomous
car[18]. Edge devices can be stationary wired powered devices for which
size is not a critical design issue or constrained battery powered mobile
devices with strict requirements for optimisation of devices autonomy.

Additionally, the increasing computing demands for these devices to provide more intelligent features is prompting the emergence of innovative
sets of compute devices which can be embedded and employed into IoT
environments and devices. In recent years, the use of Raspberry Pi [19] for
this purpose has grown in enormous popularity [20]. However, nowadays
the rise of AI and its demanding compute requirements, is generating the
appearance of embeddable devices, AI accelerators, designed specifically
for the execution of AI at the edge [21] by means of providing specific
purpose hardware micro-processors and computer systems such as Intel
movidius [22], NVIDIA's Jetson systems [23] and not long ago, Google
Coral [24] to cite some noteworthy examples.

In this sense, it is crucial for the Ad-hoc Edge Cloud architecture design
to be able to cope with all diversity arising from the medley of capacities

of the edge resources which can participate in an Ad-hoc Edge Cloud including different processor architectures (CPU, GPU, TPU, FPGA) in addition to other considerations such as a variety of operating systems that target edge devices can operate (i.e. Linux, Raspbian, Robot Operating System) as well as connectivity protocols and technologies which need to be supported.

Our purpose is to adopt Edge devices categorization provided by HEADS [25] project which classifies Edge devices as: Tiny (8 and 16- bit microcontrollers), Small (between 64 and 128 kB memory) and Large ("devices running a general operating system like Linux or similar" [25]). Large classification encompass devices such as "Arduino Yun, Raspberry Pi, Android, and iOS" [25]. Devices executing general purpose operating systems (classified as Large in this categorisation) represent the specific target of Swarm Computing.

Long term feasibility of this approach is even sustained by increasing support for operating-system-level virtualisation, containerisation in typically- considered largely constrained environments. This is demonstrated through the increased availability of containerisation technologies more lightweight than Docker [26] or LXC [27], such as Unikernels [28, 29], Kata Container [30] and gVisor [31].

Resource Limitations   As previously presented, heterogeneity serves as a salient characteristic of this environment. However, generally speaking, target IoT Edge devices for this analysis are restricted in terms of computational and storage capacity. The motivation for this, is the condition for IoT Edge devices producers to achieve the appropriate trade-off among cost, energy consumption and performance in the devices being launched to the market [5].

Providers of intelligent IoT Edge devices such as smartphones, automobiles, robots or drones require the right balance among rich functionalities, appropriate energy consumption to optimise device's autonomy and overall profitable solutions' costs. In this complex environment, IoT Edge resource providers tend to choose optimal cost solutions with lower performance, reserving the option of higher performant processor architectures, as those described in the previous section, for cases from which they derive a significant competitive advantage for their devices. In this manner, a solution reliant on this kind of devices must anticipate limitations in terms of available compute and storage resources together with constraints in batteries as energy supply.

Mobility   Another source of differentiation between Resource management in the context of Ad-hoc Edge Cloud and the traditional data centre resource management in Clouds is the potential mobility of the devices participating in the infrastructure.

Mobility of resources involves using unreliable network links for the Edge device connectivity and its consequent, resource volatility and lack of reliability. These issues constitute key aspects of this study and have remained unanalysed in the present Edge and Cloud computing stationary resources environments. Node churn, the term commonly employed to describe the dynamicity in resources appearing and disappearing of the system, is instead an area widely studied in P2P [32] and to a lesser extent in Mobile Cloud Computing [33] areas.

Furthermore, mobility of devices entails battery-powered environments and an obligatory optimisation of the battery life in order not to compromise the autonomy of devices and their availability to the Swarm computing infrastructure. Hence, mobility of devices prompts two main matters to be considered as part of this study: volatility in the node availability in the infrastructure, node churn, and resource limitations.

8.6   Lifecycle of a Swarm

Swarm intelligence is defined as "the discipline that deals with natural and artificial systems composed of many individuals that coordinate using decentralized control and self-organization. The discipline particularly focuses on the collective behaviours that result from the local interactions of the individuals with each other and with their environment" [34]. The property which characterises a swarm intelligence system is its ability to act coordinately in the absence of a coordinator or an external controller. To advance a more thorough explanation, the concept refers to the combined behaviour of decentralized, massively distributed and self-organized systems.

Artificial Swarm Intelligence studies artefacts such as smart machines and robots. With the number of devices comprising the IoT foreseen to achieve unprecedented figures, and making the consideration that many of these individual devices will have very limited compute capabilities, the idea of applying artificial Swarm Intelligence-based techniques to their management, marks its emergence. Swarm Intelligence is the baseline model for Swarm computing. Compute Swarms are defined as distributed service networks formed on-the-fly with the purpose to respond to an specific and punctual need which are handled in an open and distributed self-management runtime model. Overall, Ad-hoc Edge Clouds are envisioned as dynamic ecosystems of edge resources—swarms—which are handled in a fully distributed, decentralised and self-managed manner.

In a compute swarm, it is anticipated that the resources of an IoT Edge device are complemented with resources available in other swarm members, which can be other IoT Edge devices related to the same network, or compute and storage resources which reside in dedicated Edge and Cloud environments. In this manner, compute swarms enclose heterogeneous compute resources across the IoT, Edge and Cloud compute continuum.

In addition, the nature of certain of the swarm members determine the fact that swarms are exposed to diverse degrees of resource availability instability—volatility—as a result of the probability of node churn of swarm members which stem from diverse factors such as: instability in network connectivity, battery limitations and compute and storage capacity.

Swarm orchestration is designated in the process to form and operate this decentralised and distributed runtime environments. This process will cater for the coordination of heterogenous, diverse and numerous IoT and Edge devices and resources in Cloud environments as an autonomous overlay network. The decentralised management aim at overcoming potential inefficiencies due to the potential volatility of these resources, their expected massive number and their location dispersion.

The Cognitive Resource Management in the Ad-hoc Edge Cloud architecture (see Chap. 10) will define a protocol for which IoT and Edge resources can be provided to swarms, taking into account the specific characteristics of the devices which will form the infrastructure and will formulate the mechanisms for the Ad-hoc Edge Cloud architecture for cluster instantiation and management.

For that reason, the Ad-hoc Edge Cloud architecture will define the mechanisms to harnesses available computing capacity at the Edge in order to dynamically set up ephemeral compute infrastructures—swarms—out of IoT Edge resources available in a certain physical space at a specific moment.

Figure 8.2 illustrates the lifecycle of a swarm. Initially, at formation phase, potential swarm members will be identified through mechanisms which will permit the Ad-hoc Edge Cloud architecture to discover available resources to partake in the Swarm. These resources will be later filtered as required by the purpose the swarm formation responds to, forming on the fly and on-demand an instance of the Ad-hoc Edge Cloud overlay network. The concrete model will capture information regarding the software and hardware resources, battery levels and network links, as well as the historic behaviour of the resource in terms of availability stability.

Discovery will seamlessly integrate techniques to consider the volatility and uncertainty introduced due to real-world dynamics, which affect the reliability of the resources (e.g. actual bandwidth of connections, reliability of the device, availability of resources to execute the necessary services, etc.). This process will result in several swarm network candidates to respond to a swarm instantiation request.

Based on multi-objective optimisation, adaptive selection and conflict resolution mechanisms, the final participant resources—swarm members—will be identified and reflected in the instantiation of a concrete Ad-hoc Edge Cloud cluster instance which will be used for the foundation (constitution and set up) of the swarm. Once settled, the diverse resources that form the swarm, will coordinate themselves in a fully decentralised manner, without a single source of information and command at the operation phase. This coordination will take the form of a p2p system— particularly a distributed storage and its associated consensus algorithms. This process will support the materialisation of the swarm concepts in terms of:

Autonomy and decentralization   the resources form the swarm without any exter-
          nal centralised coordination;
Fault tolerance   the formed Ad-hoc Edge Cloud cluster instance is resilient to the
          potential instability of resource availability;

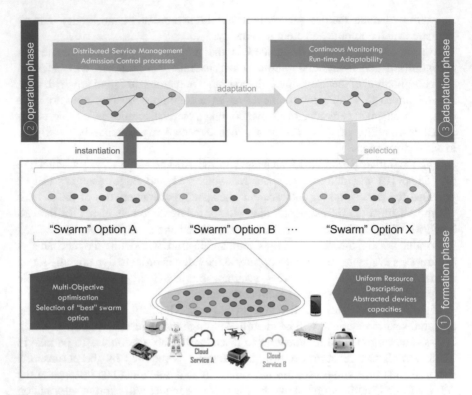

Fig. 8.2 Lifecycle of a Swarm

Scalability   the system is capable of incorporating a massive number of IoT Edge
           devices.

Therefore, the underlying distributed coordination services including distributed
key-value storages and consensus algorithms of an Ad-hoc Edge Cloud architecture
are the essential building blocks to support massive scale, reliability and decentralization.

A swarm is intended to execute services. Admission Control processes in the Ad-
hoc Cloud architecture represent the decision which determines whether to accept
a service to be executed in the infrastructure. That being the case, to identify the
set of the available IoT Edge resources which the most adequate to place service
components based on the IoT Edge devices capacity resources but also its historical
behaviour in terms of node availability.

Beyond service execution, during operation the overall behaviour of a swarm will
be placed under observation. Events will be detected and analysed in real-time based
on the collective resources status triggering actions with respect to resources (e.g.
network bandwidth) and services (e.g. frame rate transition rate) provision driving
to swarm adaptation phase, should the need arise. Runtime adaptation and swarm
repurposing mechanisms aim at analysing outcomes of real-time events to trigger

swarm evolvement according to emerging situations, service requests, context and environment characteristics.

8.7 Swarm Computing Motivational Use Cases

The following use cases aim to exemplify use cases in which Swarm Computing can demonstrate its benefits and value.

Social computing   Jordi has recently installed in his mobile phone the "ShareY-ourMobile" application. Similarly to Volunteer computing in the past [35], "ShareYourMobile" application allows sharing of mobile devices by donating computing cycles in your mobile to other users in exchange of service credits. This mobile application has been built on top of the "Ad-hoc Edge infrastructure" open source framework by exploiting its sharing model enablers which take advantage of compute capacity deployed in the location.

Jordi is today taking a high speed train from Barcelona to Madrid to attend a conference. From the moment in which the train left Barcelona central station, he is playing the "LastUltimateSuperGame" which requires the very last image rendering technology he is streaming directly from a Cloud server, as he does not have a last generation mobile. Once he is halfway his 4G internet connection starts to slow down. The image quality he is getting is poor now and cannot continue playing. It is a pity, as he was about to get a "SuperChampion badge" that unveils new features in the game. At this point in time Jordi decides to look if available capacity to execute the game in any other user of "ShareYourMobile" is around. There it is, luckily Ana is on the train. Ana is eager to get credits for getting free compute capacity for a project she is carrying out. But today she is watching the movie on the train screen, so not using her iPad at the moment. She has a "veryverylasttechnology" iPad equipped with a 8-core GPU which supports quick image rendering. When receiving a request to use her device capacity from the "ShareYourMobile" application, Ana decides to accept. Configuration of the "LastUltimateSuperGame" changes automatically to use local resources automatically discovered in Ana's iPad instead of cloud services, and continues playing. By the time they approach Madrid, Jordi realises the internet connection is good again, he already got his "SuperChampion badge", and does not want to spend all his credits in "ShareYourMobile" now. So, he indicates the application to stop using shared resources, and the configuration of the game changes to Cloud rendering and sends a thank you message to "ShareYourMobile".

Smart Home   Increasingly smart appliances such as virtual assistants and light bulbs are commonly used at home. Edge computing is expected to enable ever more interactive devices. Current market home devices typically respond to voice commands over smart devices, edge-enabled smart devices are expected to respond to conditions in the home through extensive use of sensors and controllers deployed in various areas of the house while keeping this information in close environment so respecting privacy and security.

Progressively at home we account for a series of mobile and fixed devices, including mobile phones, tablets, connected TVs and Laptops. Developments such as the ones presented in Ad-hoc Edge infrastructure context could allow the creation of "Personal" or "Home" Edge infrastructure in which our own devices could rely in order to get additional computing and storage capacities. This scenario will exploit the usage in single tenant personal context, as all available resources will belong to the same user, but will benefit from the dynamicity and churn management. The emergence of these "Personal" or "Home" Ad-hoc Edge infrastructures could even create novel opportunities in the area of Smart Home connected with Assisted Living context, by providing innovative services to patients at home depending on both home and patient health conditions.

Industrial plant   Industry 4.0 main goal is to improve efficiency, flexibility and security in Industrial Automation by means of widespread adoption of IT in the Industrial Automation operations. A fundamental component of Industry 4.0 so far has been the application of Cloud technologies to the Industrial domain. Industry 4.0 is expected to require of bringing together industrial robots to expand their capacities with computing power at the Edge and Cloud, enabling devices and production assets to become smarter. Emerging next-generation industrial robotics trends point in the direction of using small, general purpose cheap onboard processors and software defined robots as means of achieving new skills, cognitive capabilities, and greater flexibility. Edge computing contributes to the reduction on volume of data traffic from and to the robot to the resource rich computing environment, by reducing distance of transmitted data, shrinking latency, and overall improving quality of service. In this way function will cease to be solely defined by their mechanical parameters, but also by their software, processing and communication capabilities as they become IoT complex devices. In the long term, this could allow the formation of Ad-hoc Edge infrastructures among all computing elements in the industrial plant including industrial robots, specific equipment such as PLCs and dedicated Edge devices. This has the potential to bring improved flexibility on the software of industrial appliances and to take advantage of available idle capacity in the location. This case considers the single tenant aspect of the envisaged framework and exploits decentralisation approach while improving reliability though avoiding single points of failure in the industrial plant.

UAVs for inspection   Unmanned Aerial Vehicles (UAVs) provide a cost-effective solution for infrastructure inspection. Infrastructure inspection activities are relevant in diverse and heterogeneous vertical sectors such utilities, agriculture and logistics. Inspected Infrastructures can include roads, bridges, pipelines, electrical and water grids and other facilities. UAVs generate massive business opportunities enabled by their capacity of capturing valuable data. However, the challenges remain at level analysing gathered data and making UAVs' data, actionable information pieces to be ingested into the rest of IT systems. UAVs' data processing poses big data and IoT challenges by the requirement for analysis of non-standard IoT data including imagery and videos files and streams. This makes necessary specific collaboration mechanisms among UAVs fleets in order to increase flights coverage areas, combined with exploitation of hardware heterogeneity for timely data processing combining compute capacity at UAV, Edge and Cloud.

Connected vehicles   Increasingly Connected autonomous and semi-autonomous car is considered the ultimate Edge device for advanced edge computing scenarios. Autonomous cars provide the combination of enormous amounts of sensor data, critical local processing power, and the overriding need to get advanced data analysis tools in richer computing environments. Assisted or autonomous drive requires of a wide range of different computing elements and sensor data to be processed and analyse under ultra-low latency requirements. In addition to this, specific benefits can be easily observable though coordination of vehicles fleets and knowledge sharing scenarios, as well as, novel business possibilities services for car OEMs and other one tier suppliers in combination with Smart city services or even involvement of smart road infrastructures.

References

1. Bonomi, F., Milito, R., Zhu, J., & Addepalli, S. (2012). Fog computing and its role in the internet of things. In *Proceedings of the First Edition of the MCC Workshop on Mobile Cloud Computing* (pp. 13–16). https://doi.org/10.1145/2342509.2342513
2. *Cisco systems fog computing and the Internet of Things: Extend the cloud to where the things are.* (2016). https://www.cisco.com/c/dam/en_us/solutions/trends/iot/docs/computing-overview.pdf
3. *AWS IoT Greengrass.* (2022). Retrieved May 26, 2022, from https://aws.amazon.com/greengrass/
4. *Azure IoT Edge.* (2022). Retrieved May 26, 2022, from https://azure.microsoft.com/en-us/services/iot-edge/
5. Chen, D., Cong, J., Gurumani, S., Hwu, W.-m., Rupnow, K., & Zhang, Z. (2016). Platform choices and design demands for IoT platforms: Cost, power, and performance tradeoffs. *IET Cyber-Physical Systems: Theory & Applications, 1*(1), 70–77. https://doi.org/10.1049/iet-cps.2016.0020
6. Juan Ferrer, A., Iorizzo, C., Gruber, M., Pichler, W., Kurstjens, P. P., & Janeczko, J. (2018). *Swarm Computing: Concepts, technologies and architecture.* https://atos.net/wp-content/uploads/2018/12/atos-swarm-computing-white-paper.pdf

7. Ferrer, A., Becker, S., Schmidt, F., Thamsen, L., & Kao, O. (2021, 5). Towards a cognitive compute continuum: An architecture for ad-hoc self-managed swarms. In *2021 IEEE/ACM 21st International Symposium on Cluster, Cloud and Internet Computing (CCGrid)* (pp. 634–641). https://doi.ieeecomputersociety.org/10.1109/CCGrid51090.2021.00076

8. Godfrey, P., Shenker, S., & Stoica, I. (2006, 8). Minimizing churn in distributed systems. *ACM SIGCOMM Computer Communication Review, 36*, 147–158. https://doi.org/10.1145/1151659.1159931

9. Oriwoh, E., Sant, P., & Epiphaniou, G. (2013). Guidelines for internet of things deployment approaches–the thing commandments. *Procedia Computer Science, 21*, 122–131.

10. Sun, X., & Ansari, N. (2016). EdgeIoT: Mobile edge computing for the Internet of Things. *IEEE Communications Magazine, 54*, 22–29.

11. Dai, Y., Xiang, Y., & Zhang, G. (2009). Self-healing and hybrid diagnosis in cloud computing. In *Cloud Computing* (pp. 45–56).

12. Horn, P. (2001) Autonomic Computing: IBM's Perspective on the State of the Information Technology. http://www.research.ibm.com/autonomic/manifesto

13. Athreya, A., DeBruhl, B., & Tague, P. (2013). Designing for self-configuration and self-adaptation in the Internet of Things. In *9th IEEE International Conference on Collaborative Computing: Networking, Applications and Worksharing* (pp. 585–592).

14. Wailly, A., Lacoste, M., & Debar, H. (2012). Vespa: Multi-layered self-protection for cloud resources. In *Proceedings of the 9th International Conference on Autonomic Computing* (pp. 155–160).

15. Nallur, V., Bahsoon, R., & Yao, X. (2009). Self-optimizing architecture for ensuring quality attributes in the cloud. In *2009 Joint Working IEEE/IFIP Conference on Software Architecture & European Conference on Software Architecture* (pp. 281–284).

16. Nordrum, A. (2016). *The Internet of fewer things - IEEE Spectrum.* https://spectrum.ieee.org/telecom/internet/the-internet-of-fewer-things

17. Petrov, C. (2022). *40 Internet of Things statistics from 2019 to justify the rise of IoT.* Retrieved May 26, 2022, from https://techjury.net/stats-about/internet-of-things-statistics/#gref

18. Taivalsaari, A., & Mikkonen, T. (2018). A taxonomy of IoT client architectures. *IEEE Software, 35*, 83–88.

19. Raspberry Pi. (2022). Retrieved May 26, 2022, from https://www.raspberrypi.org/

20. Johnston, S., & Cox, S. (2017, 7). The Raspberry Pi: A technology disrupter, and the enabler of dreams. *Electronics, 6*, 51. https://doi.org/10.3390/electronics6030051

21. Tang, S. (2022). *A list of chip/IP for deep learning.* Retrieved May 26, 2022, from https://medium.com/@shan.tang.g/a-list-of-chip-ip-for-deep-learning-48d05f1759ae

22. Intel Movidious. (2019). Retrieved August 15, 2019, from https://www.movidius.com/

23. NVIDIA Jetson. (2019). Retrieved August 15, 2019, from https://www.nvidia.com/en-us/autonomous-machines/embedded-systems/

24. Google Coral (beta). Retrieved May 26, 2022, from https://coral.withgoogle.com/

25. HEADS Project D3.3. (2016). *Final Framework of resource-constrained devices and networks.* http://heads-project.eu/sites/default/files/HEADS%20D3.3

26. *Docker: Enterprise container platform for high-velocity innovation.* (2022). Retrieved May 26, 2022, from https://www.docker.com/

27. Linux Containers. Retrieved May 26, 2022, from https://linuxcontainers.org/

28. Unikernels, *Rethinking cloud infrastructure.* Retrieved May 26, 2022, from http://unikernel.org/

29. Madhavapeddy, A., Mortier, R., Rotsos, C., Scott, D., Singh, B., Gazagnaire, T., Smith, S., Hand, S., & Crowcroft, J. (2013). Unikernels: Library operating systems for the cloud. In *Proceedings of the Eighteenth International Conference on Architectural Support for Programming Languages and Operating Systems* (pp. 461–472). https://doi.org/10.1145/2451116.2451167

30. Kata Containers. Retrieved May 26, 2022, from https://katacontainers.io/

31. gVisor. (2022). *Container runtime sandbox.* Retrieved May 26, 2022, from https://github.com/google/gvisor

32. Stutzbach, D., & Rejaie, R. (2006). Understanding churn in peer-to-peer networks. In *Proceedings of the 6th ACM SIGCOMM Conference on Internet Measurement* (pp. 189–202). http://doi.acm.org/10.1145/1177080.1177105

33. Juan Ferrer, A., Marquès, J. M., & Jorba, J. (2019). Towards the decentralised cloud: Survey on approaches and challenges for mobile, ad hoc, and edge computing. *ACM Computing Surveys*, *51*(6). https://doi.org/10.1145/3243929

34. Bonabeau, E., Dorigo, M., & Theraulaz, G. (1999). *Swarm Intelligence: From natural to artificial systems*. Oxford University Press.

35. SETI@home. (2022). Retrieved May 26, 2022, from https://setiathome.berkeley.edu/

Chapter 9
Building Blocks for Ad-hoc Edge Clouds

9.1 Introduction

The aim of Ad-hoc Edge Cloud is to define a Swarm management system which
harnesses the increasingly available computing capacity at the Edge of the network
so as to form ephemeral compute infrastructures out of resources available in a
certain physical space at a specific point in time.

The Ad-hoc Edge Cloud Architecture presents a novel Edge computing infrastructure management system with the purpose to respond to the rising demands
for processing at the Edge driven by the advances of AI via exploiting the
existing capacity. Its overall ambition is to enable the on-demand and opportunistic
formation of fully decentralised and distributed compute infrastructures by making
use of the ever-increasing resources already available on IoT Edge devices.

The Ad-hoc Edge Cloud architecture materialises the idea of Swarm computing
[1] to avoid unnecessary latencies and exploit accessible complex compute capacity
at the edge of the network. At present, IoT Edge devices are solely deemed as objects
from which to extract data in Edge computing environments.

However, over the last years and thanks to Moore's law, these devices have
progressively increased their complexity and many of them today are equipped with
substantial compute capacity. Ad-hoc Edge Cloud extends existing Edge computing
concept by considering as valid execution environments the vast amount of IoT
devices enabled with compute features which is progressively available in all kind
of static and mobile devices at the Edge.

The particular characteristics of the IoT Edge devices which can partake in this
compute infrastructure pose special challenges to its overall resource management
practices, including its Admission control processes and Service management.

These challenges relate to the dynamicity of the resources availability. The
dynamicity of resources availability is motivated on the one hand by the yet
constrained nature in terms of battery and compute capacities of the heterogeneous
IoT devices. But more importantly, it is determined by the mobile nature of some of
these IoT devices due to their associated connectivity instability.

A. Juan Ferrer, *Beyond Edge Computing*, https://doi.org/10.1007/978-3-031-23344-9_9

   These underline the pressing need for Ad-hoc Edge Cloud to handle scale, heterogeneity, dynamicity, and volatility of resources, resulting into a probability of node churn. In this context, node churn is characterised by the dynamic and volatile behaviour of IoT Edge resources being intermittently available and unavailable to the system.

9.2   Ad-hoc Edge Cloud Framework

Figure 9.1 presents the proposed architecture for Ad-hoc Edge Infrastructure. The architecture is structured in two main contexts which are present in all participant devices in the Ad-hoc Edge Infrastructure. Contexts represent separations of concerns:

Edge Device Context   entails tools and mechanisms for the management of a particular node of the infrastructure. It enables IoT Edge resources to execute services or parts of them. Node Manager allows handling a node as part of the infrastructure. It allows for the unified description of the specific resource static characteristics, and with support of Node monitor, of its dynamic characteristics. Finally, the component executor can manage the life-cycle of services components to be executed in the

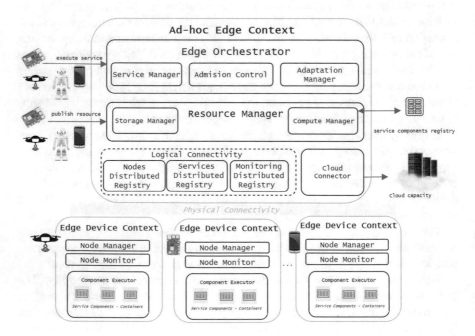

Fig. 9.1   Ad-hoc Edge Cloud architecture

Edge node with support of OS workload virtualisation tools such as
Docker.

Ad-hoc Edge Cloud Context   designates the components devoted to the manage-
    ment of the overall infrastructure cluster distributed among all participant
    resources. The core component in this layer is the Logical connectivity
    layer, that represents the overlay network that forms a swarm which is
    based on etcd [2]. The Logical connectivity layer handles the distributed
    indexes to manage nodes in the infrastructure, services and monitoring
    information as a distributed system with no central management. Etcd
    distributed storage allows Resource management, Admission control,
    and Service management to have a unified view of the status of the
    infrastructure utilising its distributed nodes coordination features, such as
    out-of-the-box replica and data distribution mechanisms.

It is noteworthy to highlight that contexts do not represent layers. This is
performed with the objective of evidencing that the architecture is not built in a
stack-like manner, but rather that modules and contexts can be executed in any of
the Edge Device nodes. Contexts define the separation of concerns with regard to
the management of the particular Edge node, Edge Device Context; and Ad-hoc
Edge Cloud Context, denoting the overall infrastructure cluster formed out of all
participant Edge devices.

It is also worth to remark that a crucial element of this architecture are the
features for distributed nodes coordination offered by Etcd [3] in the Logical
connectivity layer. As presented previously during the study of the state of the art in
Chap. 7 Sect. 7.2, P2P baseline technologies based on distributed systems theory and
existing tools for distributed nodes coordination systems are indispensable elements
for the construction of Ad-hoc Edge Clouds.

Distributed nodes coordination systems enable dynamic construction of the
overlay network that forms the swarm, among the selected set of IoT Edge
devices and Cloud resources. In addition, by means of its underlying distributed
key-value storage state and coordination, information can be shared among the
swarm participants. More importantly, its underlying consensus algorithms allow
to seamless handle the dynamicity on node availability and manage node churn,
empowering a critical feature for Ad-hoc Edge Clouds implementation.

As it will be presented in more detail in Chap. 10, the choice of Etcd to perform
these operations in Ad-hoc Edge Clouds is driven by three main factors:

– First, by the necessity in our context to handle dynamicity in nodes availability
  efficiently;
– Due to the demand to handle massive scale at level of number of participants in
  the compute swarm;
– And last by not least, because of the requirement to limit the nodes resources
  utilised by Ad-hoc Edge Swarm management processes in the targeted devices,
  due to the inherent IoT Edge resources limitations, specifically in memory.

The comparative analysis performed in Chap. 10 among the Zookeeper [4] based tool, Apache Cassandra [5] and Etcd demonstrates at current state of technology developments, the credibility of the choice for Etcd.

9.2.1 Edge Device Context

The Edge Device context modules enable the Edge resources to execute services or parts of them (services' components).

Node Manager   The Node manager component oversees the interface in order to manage a node, handling the resources at the Edge device. The main aim of this component is to deliver a unified description for the Edge resource characteristics and capabilities, and their offered capacity to the rest of the infrastructure. The Node manager develops an abstraction layer for all types of resources in the infrastructure which permits heterogeneous resources to be handled uniformly in the Ad-hoc Edge infrastructure.

Component Executor   This component provides the means to perform actions related to the life-cycle of application components. The workload virtualisation is based on containers, which facilitate the unified execution in heterogeneous execution environments in a variety of Edge devices. The most popular containerisation system, Docker [6] is now present in diverse constrained environments such as Raspbian Raspberry Pi Operating System [7, 8], or Robot Operating System [9] as well as specific network devices [10]. Docker is increasingly being complemented with even more lightweight implementations of the containerisation technologies among which are included Unikernels [11, 12], Kata Container [13] and gVisor [14]. This permits us to predict the feasibility of our approach in even more constrained execution environments to those able to support Docker at this point in time.

Node Monitor   It collects monitoring information about the status of the Edge node. The compiled parameters include the following aspects: physical infrastructure (memory, CPU usage and available storage) bandwidth (connection type and transmission rate), as well as, battery level status. While bandwidth parameters provide a clear understanding of the quality offered by the node to the rest of the Ad-hoc infrastructure, the battery level is particularly important as a factor indicating probability of churn, therefore with the potential of affecting the availability of the node in the infrastructure.

9.2.2 Ad-hoc Edge Context

Modules in the Ad-hoc Edge Context offer the functionalities which enable the overall infrastructure management. They warrant the handling of all participant IoT Edge resources as a cluster. A crucial module in this context is the Logical Connectivity Layer. It creates and maintains a distributed registry among all participant Edge nodes, allowing for building distributed indexes. The Logical Connectivity layer offers the mechanisms to handle two of the main challenges in the Ad-hoc Edge Infrastructure: distributed management over all available nodes, in order to manage scale; and resource volatility, owing to the probability of node churn. Three distributed indexes are illustrated in this work: Nodes Distributed Registry, which supports the storage of the information about the physical resources of Edge nodes added to the system; Services Distributed Registry, granting access to information of services in the system; and Monitoring and Accounting Distributed Storage, which collects information of node and service execution status and resources consumption.

The enabling mechanism for these modules are distributed key stores. These store the correspondence between a key and a value, similarly to traditional hash tables, running in a distributed system in which look up and storage are scattered among nodes with no central management. Instead, each node maintains a portion of the information along with pointers to the ranges of keys available in other nodes of the distributed storage. Any read, write or look-up operation has to handle, by dint of distributed storage mechanisms, the operation at node level. In Ad-hoc Edge Cloud infrastructure, each Edge node is responsible for a certain part of the overall information system. Each node stores information about resources, services components in execution and monitoring information, therefore without a centralised management as a single point of failure. Distributed key stores offer data distribution and replica mechanisms that supports across node synchronisation and information recovery in the case of a node abandoning the system, and permit the Ad-hoc Edge Infrastructure to manage node churn at information level.

Resource Manager   Resource manager component allows resources to be published into the Ad-hoc Edge Infrastructure. It provides the resource specification in terms of device characteristics and capacity. The registration of the node is obtained by means of its incorporation to the Nodes Distributed Registry. The publication of a resource adds it to the set of resources to be used in the Ad-hoc Edge Infrastructure. This requires the new node to be bootstrapped into the distributed storage and the generation and management of a cluster among the participant resources, making use of distributed storage capabilities. The Resource Manager also plays an essential role at service deployment time. Resource Manager offers the interface to the Edge Orchestrator to locate nodes selected as part of Admission control process. Within the Resource Manager, the Compute Manager component is responsible for controlling Compute resources in the Edge infrastructure; while Storage Manager handles

Block storage resources. As previously introduced, the complete Resource management process together with technology choices and evaluation of distributed nodes coordination mechanisms and storages as the enabling mechanisms for Resource Manager and Nodes Distributed Registry are provided in Chap. 10.

Admission Control   Admission control supplies the necessary mechanisms which allow the decision making regarding the acceptance or rejection of a service to be executed into the Ad-hoc Edge infrastructure. The challenge of the Admission control component is to select the set of resources that offer sufficient capacity to execute the service, but also to favour those which offer a more stable execution environment in order to handle the environment dynamicity due to node churn. The Admission Control receives the requirements of the service to be executed from the Edge Orchestration in terms of CPU, memory and storage of its components. The Admission Control obtains up- to -date information about available nodes in the Edge infrastructure. Admission Control later performs a filtering and prioritisation process among the available Edge nodes in order to select the candidates able to host a service. Filters represent the set of parameters connected with the capacity of the node. These help to determine whether the Edge device host is able or not to host the workload for a minimum period of time. The filter parameters cover: Capacity, as function of (Memory, CPU and Storage) and available percentage of battery. Once the initial filtering process is performed, the remaining nodes are prioritised according to Ranker parameters. Rankers are viewed as the parameters which measure the quality of the node and its stability. They aim to determine or estimate the QoS provided by the edge device host. Among them, we intend to select Edge devices endowed with longer connection times and better battery levels with the aim of minimising node churn. The result of the admission control process is the assignment of each Service Component to one or a set of Edge Nodes.

Service Manager   This module empowers the management of service execution in remote nodes via the Node Manager interfaces interacting with Services Distributed Registry and Monitoring Distributed Storage. Thus, it obtains information regarding the status of nodes and services controlling their availability and performance. The Service Manager is in charge of performing the operational actions in the operational lifecycle for the complete service. The Service Manager locates, via the Resource Manager, the node(s) responsible for the execution of a certain service component. Once located, it interacts with the correspondent Node Manager to implement the required operational action on each node. In case of remote node failure (i.e. due to node churn), it handles, together with the Adaptation Engine, the service re-collocation in another available node. In addition to this, the continuous monitoring process can entail other adaptation actions as a result of the necessity to scale-up or down the number of instances of a component of a service.

Adaptation Engine   This module works in close cooperation with the Service
  Manager which performs the necessary adaptation actions suggested by
  it. In the event of adding a new Service Component instance to the
  execution of a service, it relies on the Admission Control which performs
  the placement decision for this new component.
Edge Orchestrator   This component constitutes the entry point to execute a service
  in the Ad-hoc Edge infrastructure. It receives the Service template which
  provides a deployment specification of a service to be executed in the
  Ad-hoc Edge infrastructure. The Edge Orchestrator coordinates via the
  Service Manager and Node Manager the deployment of the different Service components, interacting with Admission Control to obtain placement
  alternatives. The Service Manager observes service execution interacting
  with Adaptation engine for ensuring proper service execution.

9.2.3   Ad-hoc Edge Cloud Architecture Flow of Events

A request to execute a service raises the Ad-hoc Edge cluster instantiation forming
dynamically an overlay network among the participants, which represents a swarm.
The initiating device utilizes nodes distributed registry reliant on etcd[2] in order
to dynamically discover other available nodes in the specific location. Chap. 10
provides full details of this process.

It is important to note that the Ad-hoc Edge Cloud architecture does not consider
at this stage the physical location of the nodes that constitute the infrastructure.
Overall, location is regarded in this work as conceptual mechanism that permits
that a set of compute resources are gathered together to form a cluster under a pre-
defined networking set-up which make them accessible to each other. While the
consideration of physical location of the IoT Edge nodes that constitute an Ad-
hoc Edge infrastructure can be of upmost interest in certain usage scenarios, it also
brings a number of research questions such as the determination of the physical
areas in which an Ad-hoc Edge cluster operates, the management of Ad-hoc Edge
Cluster overlaps in physical locations and physical node discovery mechanisms
which mainly operate at the networking level and that are considered beyond the
scope of this work.

The Admission Control mechanism determine the acceptance or rejection of
the initiating service considering the placement options it can detect from the
characteristics of the service to be executed and the current status of resources
currently available to the infrastructure. This process is presented in Chap. 11. In
case a feasible placement option has been identified by the Admission Control
process, the different service components are instantiated into the correspondent
Edge resources using Service management and Edge Device Context Components
in each node.

Having reached that point, Service Management processes take responsibility
for monitoring the availability and performance of both resources and executing

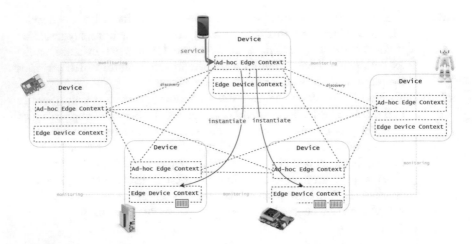

Fig. 9.2 Ad-hoc Edge Cloud architecture flow of events

services thanks to the node coordination features empowered by Etcd[3] and its
associated consensus algorithms. In the event of remote node failure for instance,
due to node churn, the Service Manager manages the reallocation of the service
component to a different available node by executing the Admission control process
for the specific part of the service. What is more, it can handle additional deployment
adaptations such as carrying out the addition or removal of services' components
instances raised by performance observation and elasticity monitoring. This process
is illustrated in Fig. 9.2.

9.2.4 Conclusions

Over the last decade the growth of connected devices has undergone an extraordinary surge. At present time, connected devices aside from being massively
available ubiquitously, have also acquired high levels of sophistication which
warrant significant compute and storage resources. Therefore, computing ceases
to be available on determined dedicated stationary compute devices, to become
widespread and permeating a substantial amount of devices. At the same time, the
popularity of AI is rapidly evidencing the necessity of performant data analysis at
the Edge. The aforementioned aspects uncover the growing demand for employing
all processing capable resources at the Edge of the network.

In this chapter, we have presented the envisaged Ad-hoc Edge Cloud Architecture
developing a framework in which increasing compute capacity at the Edge can
be exploited in a distributed manner by enabling ad-hoc formation of Edge
infrastructures created out of participant edge devices. This architecture serves as
guiding principle for the rest of this book in which we elaborate on the Resource
management and Admission Control processes and mechanisms.

References

1. Juan Ferrer, A., Marquès, J. M., & Jorba, J. (2019). Towards the decentralised cloud: Survey on approaches and challenges for mobile, ad hoc, and edge computing. *ACM Computing Surveys*, *51*(6). https://doi.org/10.1145/3243929
2. *Etcd Discovery service protocol* (2022). Retrieved May 26, 2022, from https://etcd.io/docs/v3.4/dev/internal/discovery_protocol/
3. Etcd. (2022). *A distributed, reliable key-value store for the most critical data of a distributed system.* Retrieved May 26, 2022, from https://etcd.io
4. Apache ZooKeeper. https://zookeeper.apache.org/
5. Apache Cassandra. Retrieved May 26, 2022, from http://cassandra.apache.org/
6. *Docker: Enterprise container platform for high-velocity innovation.* (2022). Retrieved May 26, 2022, from https://www.docker.com/
7. Raspberry Pi. (2022). Retrieved May 26, 2022, from https://www.raspberrypi.org/
8. *Docker comes to Raspberry Pi.* https://www.raspberrypi.org/blog/dockercomestoraspberrypi/
9. *Powering the world's robots.* (2022). Retrieved May 26, 2022, from https://www.ros.org/
10. Vizard Mike. (2022). *Cisco to run containers at the network edge.* Retrieved May 26, 2022, from https://containerjournal.com/features/ciscoruncontainersnetworkedge/
11. Unikernels. http://unikernel.org/
12. Madhavapeddy, A., & Scott, D. (2013, 11). Unikernels: Rise of the virtual library operating system. *Queue*, *11*, 30.
13. Kata Containers. Retrieved May 26, 2022, from https://katacontainers.io/
14. gVisor. (2022). *Container runtime sandbox.* Retrieved May 26, 2022, from https://github.com/google/gvisor

Chapter 10
Cognitive Resource Management in Ad-hoc Edge Clouds

10.1 Overview

The overarching goal of the Ad-hoc Edge Cloud is to dynamically form ephemeral compute infrastructures by harnessing heterogeneous non-dedicated resources accessible at a certain location at a specific point in time.

As previously introduced in Chap. 9, IoT Edge resources form Ad-hoc Edge Clouds. These IoT Edge resources are characterised by four particular factors which distinguish Resource management in this context from existing studies in Edge and Cloud computing: Massive scale, Heterogeneity, Resource Limitations and Mobility (see Sect. 8.5 for complete details). All these factors lead to a high degree of volatility of resources owing to probability of node churn. Node churn is the term used to describe the volatile and dynamic availability of IoT Edge resources which constitute the Ad-hoc Edge infrastructure. Node churn particularly affects Resource management processes in Ad-hoc Edge Cloud.

The study of the consequences of node churn is crucial to the developments put forward in this chapter. Node churn determines the mechanisms defined for handling the participation of IoT Edge devices in Ad-hoc Edge Cloud infrastructures, but more importantly it calls for using, distributed nodes coordination services, fault tolerant distributed storage systems and distributed consensus algorithms, as the key building block for Resource management in our work.

This chapter starts by presenting the defined protocol for which IoT Edge resources will be provided to the Ad-hoc Edge infrastructure, enabling available IoT devices to take part in Ad-hoc Edge Cluster infrastructure and through its entire lifecycle. Afterwards, it details the mechanisms defined in Ad-hoc Edge Cloud for cluster instantiation and management. Finally, it presents the evaluation of two main aspects in terms of handling resources in this context: measurement of the ability to scale in terms of the number of nodes which take part in the cluster, as well as, the reliability to support certain degrees of node churn. The experimentation focuses on the ability to support these features as required for Ad-hoc Edge Cloud architecture and Swarm computing for two candidate distributed nodes coordination

A. Juan Ferrer, *Beyond Edge Computing*, https://doi.org/10.1007/978-3-031-23344-9_10

tools: Etcd [1] and the distributed storage Cassandra [2] which is based in Zookeeper [3].

10.2   IoT Device Availability Protocol

The protocol for IoT Device availability as a service host in the Ad-hoc Edge infrastructure entails the complete resource availability life-cycle. It is depicted in Fig. 10.1 and described in the subsections below. This protocol describes a particularisation of the general protocol for resource collaboration in P2P described in [4].

10.2.1   Publication

In this phase an IoT Edge Device renders itself available to the Ad-hoc Edge infrastructure. Devices are described by means of resorting to a defined resource specification language able to support heterogeneity on the typologies of resources to engage in the infrastructure. A minimal resource description provides information regarding the characteristics and resources of the host in the following terms:

Static device characteristics: These are device physical characteristics which remain unchangeable over time. It includes elements such as the description of the architecture of the processors, their overall amount and characteristics, the complete memory capacity of the device, its installed operating system and supported application middleware, such as container execution support.

Dynamic device characteristics: These are device characteristics related to the device capacity and its load, which will change over the operation time of the resource. They describe the resource in terms of available different processors usage, memory and internal storage, active network protocol, upload, and download network transmission rate, as well as, battery levels at a certain point of time.

Fig. 10.1 Resource availability phases in Ad-hoc Edge Cloud infrastructure

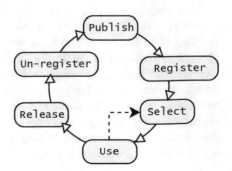

In this way in the Ad-hoc Edge Cloud infrastructure an IoT Edge Device host is described as two collections of attributes, static and dynamic attributes, which constitute an available node in the infrastructure. The static characteristics of the devices are determined at publication phase while dynamic device characteristics are fed by means of the collected information on Node Monitor architecture component.

Device Characteristics specification

$h =$

$\{static_{characteristics} = (s_1 = vs_1, s_2 = vs_2, \ldots s_i = vs_i),$

$dynamic_{characteristics} = (d_1 = vd_1, d_2 = vd_2, \ldots d_i = vd_i)\}$

In addition to these, depending on the specific usage scenario other attributes linked with location could be of specific interest such as indoor or GPS coordinates.

The description of a Node permits the Edge Device Context of the Ad-hoc Edge Cloud framework (see Sect. 9.2.1) to uniformly describe all participant IoT Edge resources detailing their offered capacities and features by means of the Node Manager component. This information is used at operational time by the Admission Control in order to determine the best placement of a service to be executed in Ad-hoc Edge Cloud from all available IoT Edge resources. A diversity of resource description languages has been put forward over time in Grid and Cloud computing environments. Examples of these are the following: Kubernetes Node capacity description [5], Cloud Infrastructure Management Interface (CIMI) Machine Definition [6] or GLUE Schema in Grid Computing [7]. The suggested format for IoT Edge device description is adapted to the Ad-hoc Edge Cloud needs by offering information on processor heterogeneity and node connections. It is described in the code listing below and represents a minimal description easily adaptable to future needs.

Proposed JSON format for IoT Edge device description

"IoTEdgeDevice":

"id": "number",

"IP": "string",

"discoveryURL": "string",

"labels":

"name": "string"

"static":

"architecture": "string",

"os": "string",

(continued)

"totalMemory": "number",
"totalDisk": "number",
"totalCPU": "number",
"totalGPU": "number",
"connections": ["string",]

"dynamic":
"memory": "number",
"disk": "number",
"cpu": "number",
"gpu": "number",
"uploadSpeed": "number",
"downloadSpeed": "number",
"batteryLevel": "number"

10.2.2   Registration

This phase requires keeping track of all available resources to a certain Ad-hoc Edge infrastructure. Given the suggested architecture for Ad-hoc Edge Cloud, this process involves the registration of the published node into the Logical connectivity layer Nodes' Distributed Registry. The selected mechanism for this module is to use a distributed nodes coordination mechanism which offers a distributed key-storage together with all necessary processes for cluster membership management. In the Ad-hoc Edge Clod architecture the tool of choice is etcd [1]. Etcd [1]. relies in the Raft consensus algorithm [8–10] in order to provide reliable distributed nodes management, fault tolerant automated replication process among all swarm nodes and high availability, even in situations of high rates of node churn. The process of Node registration and cluster formation in an Ad-hoc Edge Cluster is detailed in Sect. 10.3.

At the stage in which a Node is registered, it begins to be monitored, gathering information about its dynamic characteristics and also connection and disconnections to the Ad-hoc Edge Cloud infrastructure in different periods. This information is the keystone on which to develop the resources availability prediction model which will be presented in Chap. 11 Sect. 11.3 Resource Availability prediction model.

10.2.3   Select

Selection occurs at the time a user makes a service execution request to the Ad-hoc Edge infrastructure. It consists of the Admission control process of identifying from the available host resources those which are in charge of executing the requested service. This phase involves the process of the resource appearing in the list of candidates to execute a service (or a part of it), given provided service requirements. Ad-hoc Edge Cloud provides an innovative mechanism in order to assess the quality of a resource in the infrastructure. This is formulated as a resource availability prediction model. These processes are presented in detail in upcoming Chap. 11 Sect. 11.3.

10.2.4   Use

Once the resource is selected as a potential executor of a service (or a part of it) the corresponding service components have to be instantiated on the target device. When components are deployed, this phase also considers their operational lifecycle management, including start, stop and resume of corresponding components. Owing to the nature of devices considered, diverse factors, as previously exposed, affect its availability to be part of the Edge infrastructure. Node churn and resource failures must be considered in order to address resource volatility. Therefore, the use phase has to implement continuous monitoring of the operation and put in place mechanisms for effective workload migration in case of node failure. At the same time, continuous monitoring will also allow the continuous adaptation of the size of the set-up to the defined application needs and user resource contribution constraints by triggering elasticity events. All operational adaptations of the service execution in a given resource will require repetition of phase Selection in favour of replacing or acquiring new resources.

10.2.5   Release

The Release of service resources will be associated with the finalisation of a service a resource executes once this has been terminated. This phase will consider the clean-up of all occupied resources due to the service deployment with a view to ensure its used capacity is released and remains available to other services.

10.2.6 Un-register

Resources registered in the Ad-hoc Edge infrastructure will be continuously monitored. An unreachable resource for a certain period will be considered no longer available to participate in the Ad-hoc Edge infrastructure and therefore un-registered after a certain period.

10.3 Ad-hoc Edge Cluster Instantiation and Management

Two inherent characteristics of Ad-hoc Edge Cloud are: the requirement for lightweight implementation, considering the nature of IoT Edge devices it aims to operate in; and the requisite to support high degrees of dynamicity, which stems from the high degrees of node churn in this context. While the first characteristic is specifically related to the framework implementation, reliability to node volatility directly influences the design of the Ad-hoc Edge Cloud.

As opposed to traditional centralised cloud resource management systems, Ad-hoc Edge Cloud aims at building a decentralised resource management system able to cope with instabilities in resource availability previously analysed. In order to do so, it observes previous research in distributed and P2P systems and its applicability to the build distributed storages which are vital for supporting dynamicity and decentralisation in Ad-hoc Edge Cloud distributed Resource and Service management.

A widely employed mechanism in distributed systems such Ad-hoc Edge Cloud for handling unreliability in network nodes are distributed nodes coordination services and their fundamental distributed storages and associated consensus algorithms. As previously mentioned in this book, Ad-hoc Edge Cloud does not intend to build these from scratch but instead it targets at developing these features by employing widely spread technologies, such as Etcd [1]. In the upcoming subsections the intended mechanisms in Resource management of Ad-hoc Edge Cloud for cluster initialisation and management are presented. These rely on built-in capacities in the selected distributed nodes coordination system, etcd [1] and its associated Raft consensus algorithm [8, 10].

In Sect. 10.4, we will pinpoint the differences among the distributed storage systems, etcd [1] and Apache Cassandra [2], and their nodes coordination performance in order to provide the evaluation for Resource management and Nodes distributed registry, performed as part of this work. These results have driven our choice for the Ad-hoc Edge Cloud architecture nodes coordination mechanism.

10.3.1   Ad-hoc Edge Cluster Instantiation

The capability of being able to participate in Ad-hoc Edge Clusters is granted by downloading and installing on the device the Ad-hoc Edge Cloud framework software described in Sect. 9.2. The framework is intended to be packaged as a Docker container, and therefore available, at the time of writing, natively in Linux and derivatives in x86-64, ARM and other diverse CPU architectures, as well as on Windows (x86-64). This process is described as Step 0 in Fig. 10.2. Source code generated for initial validation of this approach is publicly available in GitHub Ad-hoc Cloud Software repository [11]. This repository currently contains code from validation of Etcd [1] and Apache Cassandra [2] which will be introduced in Sect. 10.4.

By obtaining the container image from existing repositories and executing the image in the device, the administrator will provide all Ad-hoc Edge Cloud framework software services to the node. In addition, this process will also generate the empty data structures for Nodes and Services Distributed registry and Monitoring distributed storage by instantiating an etcd Node as part of Ad-hoc Edge Cloud node instantiation.

During the execution of this Docker image, the administrator will be able to provide the URL for a discovery service as an environment variable. Depending on the desired configuration, this discovery service will be a public discovery service available in a Cloud or an existing local node external to the Ad-hoc Edge

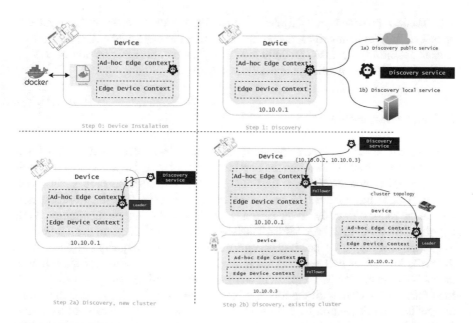

Fig. 10.2 Ad-hoc Edge Cluster instantiation steps

infrastructure. This variable will be fed into the discovery configuration of the etcd node.

To finalise the bootstrapping of the new Ad-hoc Edge Cloud node, the node will make a request to the configured discovery service to register itself into the discovery service supported natively by etcd [12]. The process is profiled in Fig. 10.2 Step 1.

In the case that the discovery service returns an empty set of IP addresses (Fig. 10.2 Step 2a), the node will know it is the first node in the Ad-hoc Edge Cloud and associated distributed storage cluster, therefore it will become the Leader of the etcd cluster and register itself into the Nodes distributed registry including its static and dynamic information.

On the contrary, in the case the etcd discovery service returns information about other available nodes in the cluster (Fig. 10.2 Step 2b), the etcd node of the device will connect to the fist of returned IP addresses getting all cluster topology and synchronising data on the rest of existing nodes in addition to itself. By definition of the Raft consensus algorithm [10] the new added node will only be available to the rest of etcd cluster with full rights, including possibility of becoming cluster leader, once all synchronisation processes are finalised and the node is stabilised and in a consistent state as part of the distributed storage cluster.

10.3.2 Ad-hoc Edge Cluster Management

This section provides an analysis of the Ad-hoc Edge Resource Management operation. It is constituted by the analysis of three distinguished cases: the normal cluster operation, the case of addition of a new node and the situation of a node failure. These three situations are detailed in the next sections.

10.3.2.1 Cluster Operation

During Ad-hoc Edge Cluster operation, the node which receives a request for a service execution registers it into the Services distributed registry. The way in which the Etcd distributed storage and Raft consensus algorithm handles it is illustrated in Fig. 10.3. If the node which has received the request is a cluster leader, it will handle the request directly. In the case it is a follower, it redirects the request to the appointed distributed storage leader. The leader will initiate a request to all followers to add the new registry. Once it gets confirmation from the majority of followers on the write the leader will respond to the request. In the case some of the follower nodes fail to respond, the Leader will continue to try until the write is confirmed in the failing follower or until the follower is removed from the cluster. It is important to note that in this section we are merely approaching the functioning of a Service Request in terms of cluster operation, all the rest of related operations in Ad-hoc

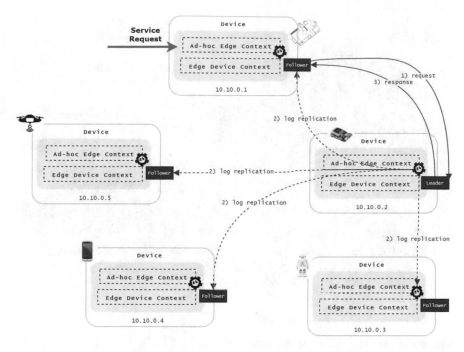

Fig. 10.3 Ad-hoc Edge Cluster operation

Edge Cloud have already been presented in Chap. 9 Sect. 9.2 describing the Ad-hoc Edge Cloud architecture and upcoming Chap. 11.

10.3.2.2 Node Addition

The process of addition of a node has already been presented in Sect. 10.3.1. It is worth to mention that once a new node has completed the discovery process the Node will add itself to the Nodes Distributed Registry. In this sense the new node will be known to the rest of the cluster at the level of Ad-hoc Edge Cloud Architecture. At the level of the distributed storage layer, the new Node is acknowledged by the existing distributed storage cluster leader by means of the discovery process previously introduced. It is interesting to note that by definition of the Raft consensus algorithm the new Node will never initiate its operation as a leader, if there is an existing cluster, instead all leader election procedures will be activated strictly in the case the existing leader fails.

Typically, a new Node added to the infrastructure will not include pre-existing data. Depending on the amount of data available in distributed storage, data synchronisation process can require some time, and to some extend compromise the performance of the overall distributed storage cluster mechanism. The procedure distributed storage and consensus algorithm [13] proposes for managing this

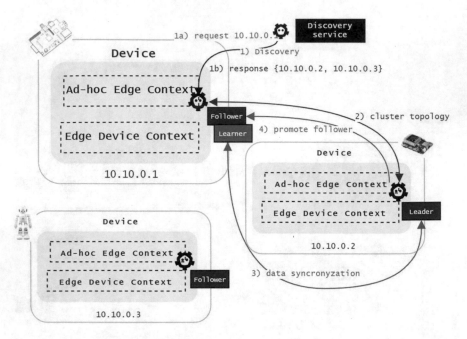

Fig. 10.4 Ad-hoc Edge Cluster Node Addition process

situation is to add the new member as Learner during the data synchronisation process. Learner nodes synchronise data but they do not participate in several management processes, such as leader election and they do not answer to client requests [14]. Once the Learner node determines that is in a healthy state, it accepts Leader's request to be promoted as Follower in the cluster. This mechanism is depicted in Fig. 10.4.

10.3.2.3 Node Failure

The case of the Node failure is divided into two situations: the situation in which the failing node is a follower at level of the distributed storage or the failure of a node which is acting as a leader.

Node Failure as Follower   The failure to of a Node as a follower is the simplest case to manage from a cluster management perspective. At distributed storage level, the leader has a continuous heartbeat process to its followers which sustain its authority. Fault tolerance methods in etcd and Raft are able to lend support until the failure of the majority of the cluster. At Ad-hoc Edge Resource management level, a Node not being able to be contacted during a certain period will trigger the removal of the Node in the Nodes distributed storage. In order not to compromise quorum in the distributed storage, it will also trigger a cluster reconfiguration operation

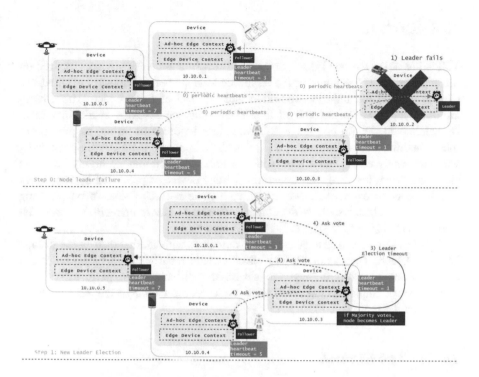

Fig. 10.5 Ad-hoc Edge Cluster Node failure as Leader process

to remove the failing node from the list of distributed storage cluster nodes.

Node Failure as Leader The failure of a Node which is a distributed storage leader will follow a similar approach as the previously described from an Ad-hoc Edge Resource management perspective. In other words, it will involve significant changes in terms of the distributed storage and consensus algorithm. In the case of the distributed storage leader failure, followers will cease to receive heartbeats of the leader for a certain period (see Fig. 10.5 Step 0). By Raft definition, all nodes are configured with a certain time out to activate a leader election process which is a random value. The first follower node to get the timeout will raise a new leader election process. If it gets the majority of the rest of available nodes votes, it will become the new cluster leader (see Fig. 10.5 Step 1). Afterwards, the new leader will begin to send heartbeats to the rest of nodes, preventing the rest of available nodes to initiate the process or terminate it in the case it has been already initiated.

10.4   Evaluation

Validation of the Ad-hoc Edge Computing Infrastructure work has been centred on the analysis of the behaviour of the Resource Management component in situations of massive and dynamic incorporation and removal of Edge nodes. The driving ambition has been to understand how dynamicity on resource availability must be handled in the Ad-hoc Edge Infrastructure. In order to do so, as previously mentioned, we have relied on Etcd [1] distributed nodes coordination. Specifically, we have analysed its behaviour and resource consumption in highly dynamic situations when installed over constrained Edge devices represented by Raspberry Pis. In order to extrapolate our results to a scale not achievable in our existing physical Edge cluster, we have developed a simulation environment in Amazon Web Services [15] using EC2 [16] and A1 [17] services.

This has also served us to compare the outcomes with another distributed storage system, Apache Cassandra [2, 18] based on the distributed nodes coordination system Zookeeper [3] in order to assess the differences in performance and feasibility for implementing distributed nodes coordination in the Ad-hoc Edge Cloud architecture.

10.4.1   Lab Evaluation

Our available physical testbed is depicted in Fig. 10.6 and it is composed of hardware of the following characteristics:

Fig. 10.6 Raspberry Pi set-up Ethernet and WLAN connectivity

- 3 x Raspberry Pi 3 Model B [19]).
- 5 x Raspberry Pi 3 Model B + [20]).

The initial step has consisted of flashing all Raspberry Pis micro-sd memory cards with Raspbian Stretch Lite Kernel version 4.1.4 [21]. Afterwards, in each Raspberry, Docker was installed. In the interest of respecting the constrained nature of Edge devices when executing Nodes Distributed Registry and Resource Manager functionalities, Docker containers in this the Edge environment have been limited to use a maximum of 32 Mb. This parametrisation is an extremely constrained execution environment for Ad-hoc Edge infrastructure management processes. Our aim when setting up this outstanding resource limited environment has been to validate our approach in an environment which is lightweight in resources occupied by our runtime, leaving capacity for the execution of external workloads. However, we are fully cognisant of the fact that such constrained runtime parametrisation is likely to affect the resultant response times of our results.

The focal points of the evaluation of this environment have been the ability of Nodes Distributed Registry layer to support scale in a timely manner, as well as, analysis of the behaviour and response time in dynamic resource volatility scenarios, considering diverse rates of nodes churn for the Resource Manager. For both of the considered aspects we have drawn a comparison between the results obtained by utilising the Ethernet connectivity versus the usage of a Wireless LAN (WLAN) for the same operations. This has enabled us to establish a baseline in order to assess the impact of using WLAN connectivity. It is important to note, that in both cases, experimentation has relied on best effort from network perspective, as any of the developments of this work or the Ad-hoc Edge framework addresses networking aspects associated to this research area.

10.4.1.1   Scalability Experimentation

Experimentation concerning scalability aspects has targeted the evaluation of the behaviour of Nodes Distributed Registry and Resource Manager to support the relevant addition of Edge nodes and the response times obtained. As previously presented in Sect. 10.3.2, the process of adding a new node consists of instantiating the Docker container in the Raspberry Pi out of the customised Docker image which contains the distributed storage and Node Resource management code. The new node is registering itself both in the Ad-hoc Edge Computing Infrastructure and Nodes Distributed Registry. By doing so, added resources on the infrastructure become an intrinsic part of it, by means of storing part of the information dedicated to its management. As previously mentioned, Source code responsible for implementing this behaviour for Cassandra and Etcd distributed registries is available on GitHub [11].

Scalability experimentation in the physical Raspberry Pi environment has involved all available Raspberry Pis supported by the subsequent creation of clusters of 2, 4, 6 and 8 nodes. In order to do so, the measured aspects have

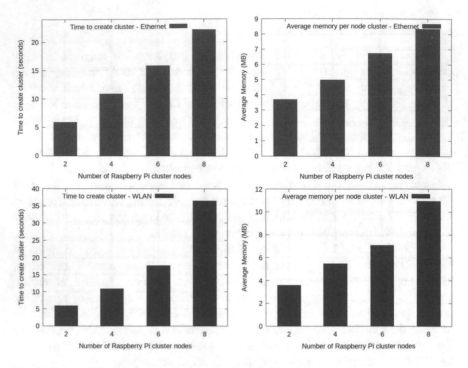

Fig. 10.7 Scalability experimentation over Raspberry Pi testbed

been the necessary time to have an operative Ad-hoc Edge cluster distributed over the selected Raspberry nodes and the resources (memory) these processes consume from the physical nodes. In the execution of these tests we have observed a high degree of variability in response times, due to variable network conditions, therefore this experimentation presents average results obtained by 10 executions of the experiment.

Figure 10.7 exhibits tests performed using both Ethernet and WLAN connectivity. In these tests we can detect that on average the use of WLAN connectivity increases the time to create a cluster. The percentage of increment grows in relation with the size of the cluster. For a two-node cluster the difference of creation time is of 1% reaching 64% for an 8 Nodes cluster. The explanation encountered for this fact is the additional requisite for data synchronisation processes among distributed nodes given that both Ethernet and WLAN experimentation have used the same devices in the same order (with diverse hardware configurations, see Sect. 10.4.1). This observation imposes the requirement to keep clusters to the minimal possible granularity at level of constituent number of nodes to consider in a single cluster, or at least to take into account the performance overhead produced by larger clusters. It is significant to note that differences detected in memory usage of the nodes in the cluster present on average less than 10% variability.

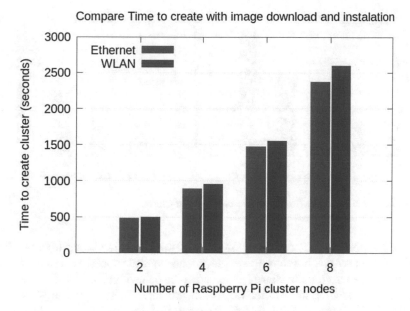

Fig. 10.8 Cluster creation times considering Docker image installation

Figure 10.8 presents another important aspect for cluster creation, the initial installation of the docker images on the target devices. Previous experiments were performed using a pre-installation of the docker image in the Raspberry Pis as a preliminary configuration step. This has proven to be necessary, as resultant cluster creation times considering image download and installation in the Raspberry Pi reach orders of magnitude of minutes per each aggregated node.

10.4.1.2 Availability/Churn Rates Experimentation

The experimentation on node availability explores the behaviour of the Ad-hoc Edge Cloud under diverse churn rates. Namely, once the cluster is set up and a certain number of nodes become suddenly unavailable to the system. The overall intention of this experimentation is to comprehend how a highly dynamic environment with regard to nodes abandoning the system and therefore, in failure state from distributed storage perspective, affects the overall performance of Ad-hoc Edge Computing Infrastructure.

In this set of experiments, we measure the time required for the Ad-hoc Edge Computing Infrastructure Nodes Distributed Registry to get to a consistent and healthy state once a given number of previously available nodes disappear. We define as consistent state the fact that all remaining nodes are in a healthy state concerning the cluster and the available data in the Nodes distributed registry is replicated among remaining nodes. It is paramount to underline that at this stage

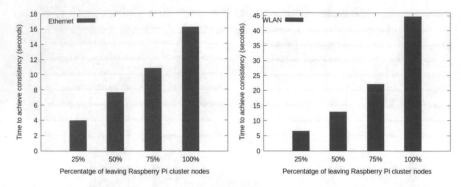

Fig. 10.9   Time to recover from % node churn in 8 RPI Cluster

we are not considering migration processes of workloads in execution in this Edge
node, instead we solely focus on the Node management processes. The analysis of
recovery times from node churn has included the behaviour for 2, 4, 6 and 8 nodes
suddenly abandoning the Ad-hoc Edge Infrastructure. These represent percentages
of 25%, 50%, 75% and 100% (the disappearance of the cluster).

Figure 10.9 shows the obtained results for Ethernet and WLAN connectivity, we
view this recovery time as the time necessary for the cluster to be in a consistent
state once certain percentage of the nodes of the cluster leave the system. Following
a logical correspondence with the rest of results gathered in this evaluation, recovery
times increment as the number of nodes disappearing from the system increase.
Both from Ethernet and WLAN (Fig. 10.9) tests it is apparent that the larger the
number of abandoning members of the cluster, the longer times to recover. This
is determined in the extreme cases which possess more that 75% of node churn,
obtaining substantially long recovery times for the two last members remaining in
the system.

10.4.2   Large Scale Evaluation in AWS EC2

10.4.2.1   Scalability Experimentation

Experimentation in the AWS simulated environment focused on studying the
behaviour of two distributed storage systems Apache Cassandra and Etcd in
dynamic environments and at scale. The purpose of this validation has been to
examine our initial technology choice based on Etcd and Raft consensus protocol.
It is important to acknowledge that although both Apache Cassandra and Etcd are
distributed storage systems, there are significant differences between them. Some
examples of these are: Apache Cassandra is a fully-flagged database developed in
Java to cover multipurpose application, whereas Etcd is a key-value distributed stor-

age implemented in Go with the purpose of supporting multi-server configuration replication.

The first experiment examines scalability by reproducing the process of creating from scratch a complete Ad-hoc Edge Computing Infrastructure cluster composed by 10, 20, 30, 40, 50 and 100 nodes, and response times obtained in seconds for this operation. Hence, it is immediately noticeable that creation times of Etcd clusters enhance results obtained by Apache Cassandra both in terms of time and necessary resources. In Etcd we obtain orders of magnitude of less than 1.4 minutes (87 seconds) to set-up a 100 nodes cluster, while necessary time in the same environment for a 10 nodes cluster for Apache Cassandra is 8.5 minutes. When checking resource consumption of the created nodes, the results are aligned: the average memory consumption of an Apache Cassandra node in a 10 nodes cluster is 328 Mb while results obtained for Etcd are 14 Mb. Growth on cluster size follows a similar trend obtaining average memory usage of 100 nodes Etcd clusters inferior to 10 nodes cluster for Apache Cassandra. It has to be mentioned that tests for Apache Cassandra were ceased after the creation of 40 nodes, as the cluster state remained unstable. Figure 10.10 illustrates this information.

It is essential to establish the fact that while the memory consumption for Apache Cassandra is above 280 Mb for a 10-node cluster, it remains steady on similar orders of magnitude as the cluster grows. Conversely, Etcd average memory usage per

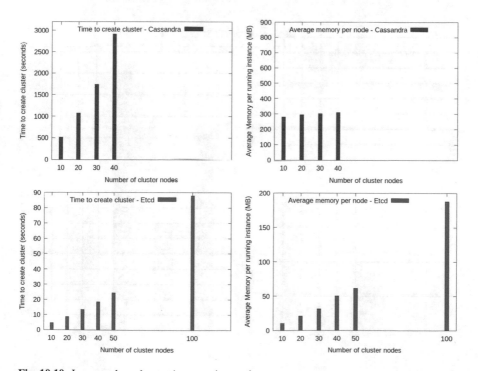

Fig. 10.10 Large scale node creation experimentation

node increases with the size of the cluster. Average memory employed per node ranged from 10 Mb for a cluster of 10 nodes to 188 Mb in a 100 nodes cluster (see Fig. 10.10). This is, by all means, explained considering the node synchronisation processes among data storage cluster nodes, however it raises an important aspect to take into account in future developments for our Ad-hoc Edge Cloud framework scalability. It is significant to remark that in Etcd the limit on memory consumption of our resource management tools stated in 32 Mb to be usable in constrained Edge devices such as Raspberry Pis is in this environment achieved at a cluster size of 30 nodes.

Availability/Churn rates Experimentation

This experiment employs a 10-nodes cluster and checks the time required to achieve the consistency state under diverse node churn rates: 20% churn rate representing 2 nodes becoming abruptly not available; 40% churn rate with 4 nodes abandoning; 60% with 6 nodes; and 80% corresponding to 8 nodes. The data obtained is illustrated in Fig. 10.11. It shows that the time to recover, due to the data synchronisation processes, is linearly related with the number of nodes withdrawing from the system. As exemplary value, for Cassandra it takes 1.4 min for a 10 nodes cluster to recover from 20% nodes churn rate. Suffice it to say that this process is significantly more performant in Etcd, for which we have experimented 20%, 40%, 60% and 80% churn rates over 10 and 100 nodes cluster obtaining recovery times of

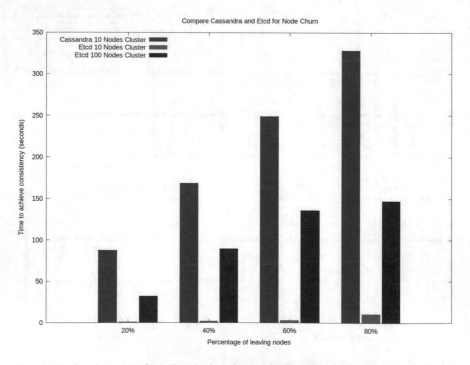

Fig. 10.11 Time to recover from % node churn in 10 and 100 nodes cluster

1 second for 20% churn rate in with cluster size of 10 nodes and 15 seconds for 100 nodes cluster. It is remarkable that Etcd is showing notably better recovery times for 80% churn rates than Cassandra for a 10 nodes cluster.

10.4.2.2 Large Scale Evaluation via AWS A1

In November 2018 Amazon Web Services announced the availability of its new EC2 A1 instances which offer for the first time ARM processor via the AWS EC2 Computing platform [17]. AWS EC2 A1 instances were presented in diverse flavors ranging 1–16 vCPUs and 2–32 Gb memory. With the aim of simulating the constrained nature of devices desired to used by this study, we have employed the more constrained image offered, the a1.medium, equipped with 2 Gb memory, 1vCPU and 8 Gb Disk for our validation. The aim of these tests has been to understand the behaviour of Etcd in Cloud resources which are more similar in hardware architecture and available resources to the ARM physical nodes to be used. Due to existing user quotas related to the recent launch of this service, maximum number of simultaneous instances allowed to be created in AWS Ireland region used, was 5. It is important to note, that this limitation was applied by AWS while having A1 service in Beta, and it is not related to any specific constraint in ARM architecture. In this constrained environment (accounting with a maximum of 4 nodes), we have performed initial tests over Etcd to validate the results obtained in our Lab environment with Raspberry Pis. Figure 10.12 shows that creation times in A1 for same size cluster are in very similar orders of magnitude only accounting with differences of milliseconds for seconds and similar values in terms of used memory. The observable time difference in churn rates experimentation are due to the limited size of the cluster which minimise synchronisation processes among cluster members.

10.5 Conclusions

This chapter has presented the defined protocols for resource availability in the Ad-hoc Edge Cloud. It has also analysed the defined mechanism for Ad-hoc Edge Cluster instantiation and management relying on native capabilities offered by distributed storage systems.

The performed experimentation allows us to validate our initial technology choice of leveraging in Etcd for a key component of the Ad-hoc Edge Architecture for Resource management, the Distributed nodes coordination mechanism which enables the formation of an overlay network among all swarm participants.

Etcd has demonstrated outstanding performance in comparison to Apache Cassandra for this purpose. Etcd's baseline consensus algorithm enables Ad-hoc Edge Architecture to become fully decentralised and distributed, permitting the overall ambition to profit from the growing compute capacity at the Edge of the network

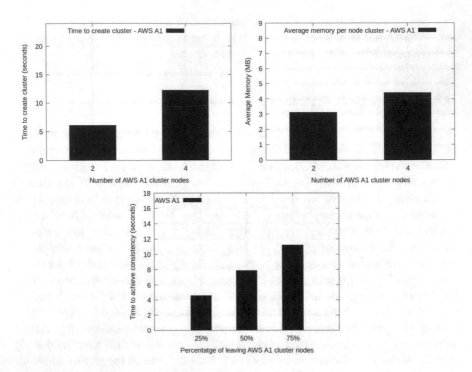

Fig. 10.12 Experimentation over ARM-powered cluster in AWS

in complex IoT devices, by dynamically forming out clusters of these devices in a decentralised and distributed manner.

The experimentation has also demonstrated that fault tolerance features of Etcd in terms of resource volatility are capable of coping with certain degrees of resource volatility when these are kept in volumes below to 75% of Nodes suddenly abandoning the system. This is a key lesson drawn from the applicability of this framework to use cases with situations of elevated levels of node churn can be expected. At current state of affairs, in scenarios which can account for volatility levels around 75% implications of the learned behaviour may imply the need of keeping a determined number of fixed nodes in order to achieve certain levels of quality in the services provided by the Ad-hoc Edge infrastructure.

In addition, this experimentation has reinforced the necessity of an initial registration phase in which the framework components are installed and registered into the target devices due to the performance overhead that installation of Docker component adds to this process, which get orders of magnitude of minutes, depending on network configuration.

Moreover, experimentation evidenced the relevance of scale both in terms of having the ability to support churn rates along with the management performance overheads it brings. These are directly related to the observed fact the Etcd clusters memory consumption is directly associated with the number of Nodes that participate in the cluster. In order to address this in future deployments of this technology, this is an essential consideration given that the larger the cluster is expected to be in terms of participating resources, the bigger these have to be dimensioned in order to address the observed scale overhead.

References

1. Etcd. (2022). *A distributed, reliable key-value store for the most critical data of a distributed system*. Retrieved May 26, 2022, from https://etcd.io
2. Apache Cassandra. Retrieved May 26, 2022, from http://cassandra.apache.org/
3. Apache ZooKeeper. https://zookeeper.apache.org/
4. Bandara, H., & Jayasumana, A. (2013). Collaborative applications over peer-to-peer systems-challenges and solutions. *Peer-to-Peer Networking and Applications*, 6, 257–276.
5. *Nodes Kubernetes by Example*. https://kubernetesbyexample.com/nodes/
6. DMTF. (2022). *DSP0263 Cloud Infrastructure Management Interface (CIMI) model and RESTful HTTP-based protocol*. Retrieved May 26, 2022, from https://www.dmtf.org/sites/default/files/standards/documents/DSP0263_2.0.0.pdf
7. Andreozzi Sergio. (2022). *GLUE specification v. 2.0*. Retrieved May 26, 2022, from https://www.ogf.org/documents/GFD.147.pdf
8. Ongaro, D., & Ousterhout, J. (2014). In search of an understandable consensus algorithm. In *Proceedings of the 2014 USENIX Conference on USENIX Annual Technical Conference* (pp. 305–320). http://dl.acm.org/citation.cfm?id=2643634.2643666
9. *The Raft consensus algorithm*. https://raft.github.io/
10. Ongaro, D. (2014). *Consensus: Bridging theory and practice*. Stanford University. http://purl.stanford.edu/qr033xr6097
11. Juan Ferrer, A. *adhoc-edge-cloud*. Retrieved May 26, 2022, from https://github.com/anajuan/adhocedgecloud
12. *Etcd Discovery service protocol*. Retrieved May 26, 2022, from https://etcd.io/docs/v3.4/dev/internal/discovery_protocol/
13. *Etcd Runtime reconfiguration*. Retrieved May 26, 2022, from https://etcd.io/docs/v3.3/op-guide/runtimeconfiguration/
14. *Etcd Learner design*. Retrieved May 26, 2022, from https://etcd.io/docs/v3.4/learning/designlearner/
15. Amazon Web Services, Cloud Computing Services - Amazon Web Services (AWS). https://aws.amazon.com/
16. Amazon Web Services EC2. https://aws.amazon.com/ec2/
17. Amazon Web Services EC2 A1 Instances. https://aws.amazon.com/ec2/instance-types/a1/
18. Lakshman, A., & Malik, P. (2010, 4). Cassandra – A decentralized structured storage system. *Operating Systems Review*, 44, 35–40.
19. RaspberryPi.org, *Raspberry Pi 3 Model B*. https://www.raspberrypi.org/products/raspberry-pi-3-model-b/
20. RaspberryPi.org, *Raspberry Pi 3 Model B+*. https://www.raspberrypi.org/products/raspberry-pi-3-model-b-plus/
21. Raspberrypi.org, *Raspbian*. https://downloads.raspberrypi.org/raspbian_lite_latest

Chapter 11
Service Placement and Management

11.1 Overview

Admission Control processes represent the decision which determines whether to accept a service to be executed in the infrastructure and if that is the case, its most suitable service placement. It is the mechanism to identify the set of the available IoT Edge resources which are most appropriate in order to place the different service components. The proper considerations regarding the level of Admission control mechanisms in Ad-hoc Edge Cloud are defined taking into account resources past behaviour in terms of connections and disconnections, representing the source on which we base the resource availability prediction model for infrastructure which is the main research area of this chapter.

Konstanteli et al. [1] describes the admission control problem for Cloud computing as "the mechanism for deciding whether or not it is worth to admit a service into a Cloud, and in case of acceptance, obtain the optimum allocation for each of the components that comprise the service". Admission control and resource scheduling in loosely-coupled distributed systems such as Grid and Cloud computing systems have represented an extensively researched area [2, 3].

Especially in Ad-hoc Edge computing Infrastructure, difficulties in the scope of Admission control for the Edge infrastructure of non-dedicated resources are not anticipated stemming from the characteristics of services to execute but due to volatility of resources which affects their availability, as described by Park [4]. In this work it is acknowledged that unpredictability of Edge resources (such as mobile devices) increments due to the following problems: unstable wireless connection, limitation of power capacity, low communication bandwidth and frequent location changes. These issues significantly increase levels of node churn—a continuous process of resource enrolment and un-enrolment—that Ad-hoc Edge computing Infrastructure must handle.

To be more precise, two factors are considered to significantly influence service placement decisions in the context of Ad-hoc Edge Cloud:

A. Juan Ferrer, *Beyond Edge Computing*, https://doi.org/10.1007/978-3-031-23344-9_11

Stability in the resource availability: Placement decisions in Ad-hoc Edge Cloud
         has to take into account the analysis of historical information on resource
         availability so as to determine if a service can be accepted, and which is be
         the most adequate assignment among available resources for this service
         by considering its requirements and the available resource' characteristics.
         Both Admission control and Service management are designed to support
         churn and subsequent resource volatility with the aim of ensuring as much
         as possible reliability of the overall infrastructure. With this aim, in this
         work we employ the Node quality concept defined in [5]. The Node
         Quality concept defines the predicted probability of a node be available
         in a certain time slot based on its historical behaviour of connections and
         disconnections to the Ad-hoc Edge Infrastructure.
Available battery levels in the contributed resources: Intrinsically   related   to
         Node's stability, energy scarcity in IoT Edge devices is an issue largely
         studied in the context of IoT [6, 7] and Mobile Cloud computing [8].
         Especially, as introduced in Chap. 4, energy optimisation of devices
         has been often used as motivation for off-loading computational loads
         to external clouds resulting in the production of energy savings in the
         context of Mobile Cloud Computing. Although this is not the main focus
         approach in this dissertation, it is clear that the available level of energy in
         the resource is a factor that cannot be neglected in the services placement
         decision to engage in the admission control, therefore this is a specific
         parameter Admission Control mechanism contemplates.

   It is beneficial with a view to fully grasping the admission control issue to analyse
the Service life-cycle in the Ad-hoc Edge infrastructure to introduce the phases of
this lifecycle in which allocation decisions take place. Besides, we will introduce
the Service Model we consider for Ad-hoc Edge Cloud. Afterwards we will present
Ad-hoc Edge Cloud admission control and its associated mechanism to assess Node
Quality based on the defined resource availability prediction model.

11.1.1   Admission Control in Service Lifecycle of Ad-hoc Edge Infrastructure

Figure 11.1 describes the proposed Service Life-cycle in the Ad-hoc Edge infrastructure. This life-cycle provides an adaptation of the Life-cycle of a job inside a
IaaS cloud defined by Ghosh in [9] extending it to the concept of Edge service as
appliance considering multiple inter-related components.

   This lifecycle describes the flow of actions from the time a specific IoT Edge
device requests for service deployment until this service is up-and-running in the
Ad-hoc Edge infrastructure. Actions in the operational lifecycle of services being
executed respond to user requests.

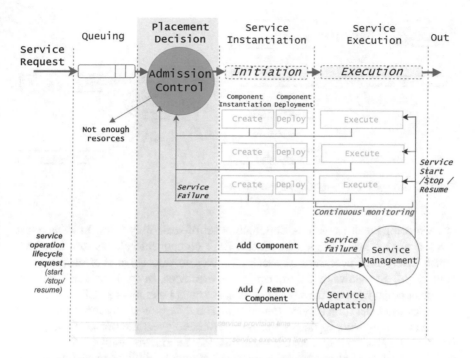

Fig. 11.1   Ad-hoc Edge service life-cycle, Admission control role

In this context, it is observable that Admission control placement decisions crop up in two specific phases of this flow: at initial placement decision for the complete service and as a consequence of an adaptation decision, to allocate one or more service parts.

11.2   Ad-hoc Edge Service Model

So as to ensure sufficient interoperability of the Ad-hoc Edge Computing infras-tructure with existing Edge and Cloud offerings the resource model is illustrated in a generic manner which could be implemented using available service descriptors in standards and commercial offerings. Diverse examples exist of such service descriptors: in the Kubernetes architecture, these are represented by means of deployments and pods [10] while Cloud vendors, such as AWS implement their own descriptors in AWS CloudFormation [11] template and specific technologies like Terraform [12] make use of service templates for this task. Independently of the language selected to express the workload execution characteristics, existing languages offer a similar structure which is represented in Fig. 11.2.

More precisely, a service is composed of a series of components. The definition of a service is provided based on these set of components, the number of instances

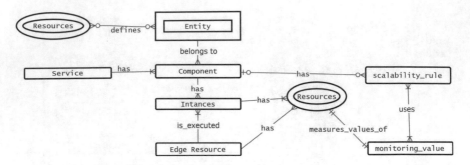

Fig. 11.2 Ad-hoc Edge Computing service model

of each component, as well as, optionally a set of scalability rules. In its simplest form, a service has a single component. Each component belongs to a template, which determines necessary physical resources to allocate it. For each service component, its hardware requirements are expressed in its template. Common resources considered are the amount of disk, amount of memory and CPUs. Multiple instances can exist for a service component. The definition of the service indicates how many component instances will be instantiated when the service is deployed (minimum value of instances), as well as the maximum number of instances which can be created overall (as a result of the application of scalability rules). Each instance is deployed in the resource which has enough capacity to host its hardware requirements defined by its template. We name component creation to the instantiation of a significant component on an available resource. A deployment determines the necessary steps to have a service component up and running in a concrete infrastructure resource.

Typically, a service will be deployed as a set of containers described as service components. The use of virtualisation (i.e. OS or hypervisor based virtualisation) techniques provides isolation mechanisms among the user data and execution in hosting resources. It also allows transparent allocation of each component of the distributed service inside the Ad-hoc Edge Infrastructure. Moreover, it facilitates the process of horizontal elasticity, by adding or removing extra capacity for each component during runtime to maintain a certain level of performance for the overall service when variations occur in the workload.

11.3   Admission Control Mechanism Formulation

The Admission Control mechanism sorts out the problem of responding if a service s can be executed in an Ad-hoc Edge computing infrastructure E, and if so identifies the set of resources that can host it, R.

1. If in the certain point of time in which the service execution request is done there are no hosts whose available capacity is sufficient to fulfil the execution requirements of the service, $R = \emptyset$.
2. Otherwise, R is an ordered list of hosts h.

The Admission Control mechanisms considers that an Ad-hoc Edge computing infrastructure E is constituted by a set of computing nodes, hosts $H = \{1, ..., N_h\}$.

As introduced in 10.2, each participating resource in the Ad-hoc Edge computing infrastructure, a host h is characterised by two kinds of attributes: static and dynamic attributes. Among others, these attributes include: Computing Capacity by quantifying the number of available processors, their architecture and characteristics C_h; Available Memory M_h; Available Disk D_h; Available Battery level B_h and Quality of a node, Q_h. Q_h is based on the assessed node quality of a node based on its historical behaviour with regards to connections and disconnections to the Ad-hoc Edge infrastructure.

The Admission control considers that a service instance s to be executed in the Ad-hoc Edge Infrastructure belongs to a Service template which poses a set of requirements to the host to execute the service (see more details in Sect. 11.2). In its minimal form, these will include: Minimum computing capacity C_t; Minimum available memory M_t; Minimum available disk D_t; Processor Architecture Requirement $Arch_t$ and Operating System Requirement OS_t.

In order to admit a service to be executed in the Ad-hoc Edge Cloud, the Admission Control process executes two main steps: Filter and Ranking. Filter initial step is quantitative. It filters from all available resources those offering the sufficient device capacity in terms of dynamic characteristics (namely CPU, memory and storage) for the different parts that compose a service. The second step, Ranking, focuses on Qualitative characteristics. It prioritizes requirements according to critical aspects in resource management in Ad-hoc Edge Cloud infrastructure: node stability and node's current battery level. Node's stability is estimated employing the Node Quality value taking into account the time the device has been part of the infrastructure.

Table 11.1 presents the parameters considered in each IoT Device which takes part in the Ad-hoc Edge infrastructure and its role in Admission control mechanism while upcoming sections itemise the above mentioned two-step process.

Filter

The filter process determines from all available hosts $H = \{1, ..., N_h\}$, the set of host H' which available resources and characteristics meet the requirements of the service. These are set in terms of computing capacity, memory and disk which are sufficient to host the service, as well as, the host conforms to the execution environment characteristics determined by the processor's architecture and operating system, according to the requirements exposed by the service template T. Therefore H' is the subset of H hosts which:

1. Computing Capacity is greater than service s minimum computing capacity, $C_h \geq C_t$

Table 11.1 IoT edge device parameters classification

Parameter	Category	Type	Threshold	Rationale
% of connected time	Dynamic	Ranker, Quality	Maximize	Priories connection stability
# of disconnections	Dynamic	Ranker, Quality	Minimize	Penalize host with a higher number of disconnections
Computing capacity, Memory and Disk	Dynamic	Filter, Capacity	Available values	If the host does not hold enough capacity to host the service, it is discarded
Processor architecture	Static	Filter, Capacity	Defined host value	If the host does not posses the required value, it is discarded
Upload/Download speed	Dynamic	Filter, Capacity	Maximize	If the host does not include a certain value of upload/download network capacity, it is discarded
Battery level	Dynamic	Filter, Capacity	Maximize	If the host does not have a minimum level of battery, it is discarded
Battery level	Dynamic	Ranker, Quality	Maximize	Devices with higher battery level available are considered better

2. Available Memory is greater than service s minimum available memory, $M_h \geq M_t$
3. Available Disk is greater than service s minimum available disk, $D_h \geq D_t$
4. Processor Architecture corresponds to s requirement, $Arch_h = Arch_t$
5. Operating System matches to s requirement, $OS_h = OS_t$
6. And the available battery level is above a certain battery level threshold B_E established for the Ad-hoc Edge computing infrastructure E, $B_h \geq B_E$

If there are not hosts fulfilling the above-mentioned capacities and characteristics the $H' = \emptyset$. Therefore $R = \emptyset$ and the admission control process for service s resolves that the service cannot be hosted in the Ad-hoc Edge Cloud infrastructure at this point.

Ranker
If $H' \neq \emptyset$ the Ranker node returns the list of hosts $R = \{1, ..., N_R\}$ in H' ordered according to the assessed quality of the node, Q_h. As will be presented in detail in the upcoming section, Q_h value is calculated making use of historical values on resource availability to the infrastructure: percentage of connected time and number of disconnections since the initial registration of the host. In addition to this, in order to determine the overall Node Quality, the percentage of available battery of the host can be used with the purpose of balancing from all available hosts above a certain battery level, those with closest values to 100% battery levels and adequate historical behaviour, so as to give the current status of the device a prominent role in device selection.

11.3.1   Resource Availability Prediction

As it has been previously mentioned, the Resource Availability prediction in this chapter extends the concept of Node Quality presented in [5]. This builds on top of two parameters:

Percentage of connected time: which represents the percentage of time the node has been available to the infrastructure from its initial registration to the Ad-hoc Edge Cluster. This value is expressed as a value between 0 and 1, where higher percentages of connected time result in better node stability and reliability to the overall infrastructure.

Number of disconnections: Reflects the number of disconnections this specific node has had, normalised to the higher number of disconnections from all nodes currently available in the Ad-hoc Edge infrastructure. This parameter provides the sense of balance of the quality of the specific node behaviour for the rest of the available nodes in the infrastructure.

In more accurate terms, the Quality of a Node represents the probability of an IoT Edge Device to remain connected to the Ad-hoc Edge Infrastructure for a certain period. A significant difference among this work and [5] as well as existing literature on Node availability prediction reported in Sect. 11.5, is the area of application which has been commonly present in Volunteer Computing environment. These utilise mechanisms to calculate availability prediction to forecast the behaviour of available peers in a matter of weeks, based on the behaviour on the different week days over the last month. The latter is motivated by the roots of volunteer computing on using spare capacity of desktop computers in enterprise and home environments. This resulted in resource usage patterns in Volunteer Computing which outlines the distinction among working days for determining the time these resources have more probability of remaining idle.

Instead in Ad-hoc Edge Cloud environment we aim to interpret the behaviour of complex IoT devices located at the Edge of the network for determining periods in which these edge nodes exhibit more probability of having resources available for the Ad-hoc Edge infrastructure. In the interest of understanding this behaviour, there are significant difficulties at the current state of affairs: lack of real deployments of these specific scenarios for which we could gather data permitting us to discern the behaviour on the use patterns of the devices, and without leaving aside, the fact that this behaviour can significantly differ from specific usage scenarios we aim to address.

As far as IoT devices are concerned, usage patterns available literature in this field is particularly scarce [6, 7, 13]. We have not been able to identify any references to specific time usage patterns. The entirety of the analysed literature mainly focuses on the use of energy of devices and is strongly oriented to a specific type of IoT device. By way of example, the closest device to the kind of IoT Edge device we aim to employ is in [13]. This work focuses on analysing the behaviour of SmartWatches' users while observing usage patterns of 32 users in

70 days of continuous use. This analysis concludes with the general statement that SmartWatches devices are in an idle state 89% of the time.

Smartphone usage patterns have been studied in depth, however, the number of analyses on mobile phone usage patterns which include references to idle time and time use patterns is also limited [14–16]. Findings of the available studies have reached the conclusion that a phone is largely in an idle state 89% of the time [14] (note that percentage is the same range as the assessed for smartwatches in [13]). Shye et al. [14] has analysed the activity of users on smartphones logs of 25 users over 6 months. When focusing on weekday behaviour, overall differences between week and weekend days do not appear as significantly different. Bhih et al. [15] examines patterns for mobile data traffic. It studies 3.3 terabytes of data gathered by the University of Cambridge using Device Analyzer. This information contains over 100 billion records of 17,000 android devices worldwide and extends from December 2010 to January 2014. These do not reveal any significant difference in Mobile data traffic between the weekend and working days. Otherwise, Van Canneyt et al. [16] collects information from 230K mobile apps and 600M daily unique users in 221 countries. Van Canneyt et al. [16] focuses on application sessions, concluding that during the weekend, application sessions seem to start and finish later, with a margin of 1 hour.

A striking aspect to be considered is the fact that these studies also examine mobile phone day hour patterns from different perspectives: [16] shows that mobile users are more active on the mobile device throughout the day, having the maximum activity during evenings locating the activity peak at 9pm. Bhih et al. [15] shows a similar pattern, stating that although the data traffic is quite stable during the day hours, it significantly increments and peaks around 22:00 hours. Finally [17] studies the temporal distribution of the traffic of apps focusing on more specific temporal patterns. It also reveals diurnal patterns concerning traffic volume and network access time. In contrast to previous papers, it locates the minimum use around 1AM and 2AM. This study shows that traffic volume starts increasing around 4AM and hits its peak around noon. After 3PM it decreases, to arrive at its minimal value after 8PM.

Intending to overcome the above-mentioned difficulties related to the availability of data to establish resource IoT Edge resource usage data, we have decided to centre our prediction model on the usage patterns of mobile phones, whose patterns on usage data are at this stage much more stable. Mobile phones are the most widespread devices available at the Edge the network. Figures on Edge devices penetration also present analogies in terms of scale with the expected distribution of IoT Edge devices.

Resting on the patterns that we could extract on mobile phone usage patterns from the data available in the previously identified works [15–17], we have determined the appropriate period to study in the context of Ad-hoc Edge Cloud. In our case, the time period to analyse is the behaviour of the IoT Edge device during the previous week. In addition, it is necessary that we consider four different time-slots along the day to inspect connection and disconnection patterns.

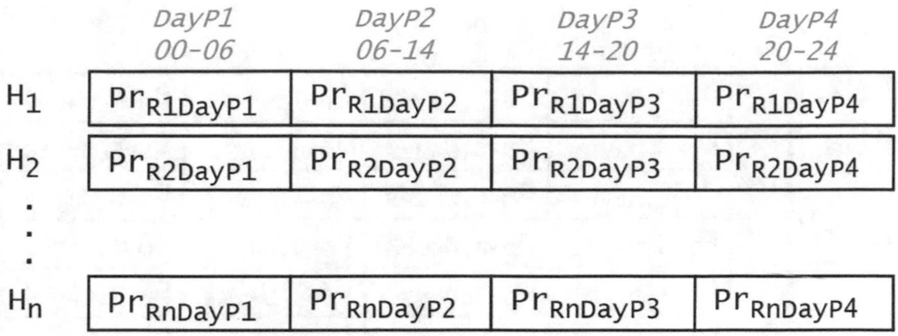

	DayP1 00-06	DayP2 06-14	DayP3 14-20	DayP4 20-24
H_1	$Pr_{R1DayP1}$	$Pr_{R1DayP2}$	$Pr_{R1DayP3}$	$Pr_{R1DayP4}$
H_2	$Pr_{R2DayP1}$	$Pr_{R2DayP2}$	$Pr_{R2DayP3}$	$Pr_{R2DayP4}$
.				
.				
.				
H_n	$Pr_{RnDayP1}$	$Pr_{RnDayP2}$	$Pr_{RnDayP3}$	$Pr_{RnDayP4}$

Fig. 11.3 Representation of data structure for disconnection probabilities

The timeslots we have taken into consideration comprise the following intervals:

1. Day period 1 (DayP1): From 0:00:00 to 5:59:59
2. Day period 2 (DayP2): From 6:00:00 to 13:59:59
3. Day period 3 (DayP3): From 14:00:00 to 19:59:59
4. Day period 4 (DayP4) From 20:00:00 to 23:59:59

Hence, in order to predict the probability of an IoT Edge Device to continue to be part of the Ad-hoc Edge Infrastructure we will employ the data on its behaviour during the previous week, gathering the data according to the four intervals in which we have divided each of the days, and obtaining a probability of a node to remain connected for a given period.

Therefore, for each host h we keep a data structure of disconnection probabilities as an array of 4 positions which stores host's probability of disconnection of each day period (host $h \in \{1, 2, ...N\}$, $Pr_{hDayPeriodp}$ day period $p \in \{1, ..4\}$) calculated by the prediction model using the information of the last 7 days. See representation in Fig. 11.3.

In addition to this, we keep data structure to collect disconnection patterns during the previous week of execution for every node. This maintains the disconnection patterns of all nodes in the last 7 days. The data structure used is represented in Fig. 11.4. It is a matrix of 7×4, which will store for a period of 1 week, the number of times a node has changed the state (disconnections and connections) per each of 4 day periods.

In detail per each host there is a matrix M_h which represents the seven position matrix corresponding to the node h. D is the Day number $d \in \{1, ..7\}$) and day period is $p \in \{1, ..4\}$). $D_{d,p}$ is the number of disconnections experienced by host h in day d period p. This matrix is kept updated by a daily process that each day analyses the performance of all nodes, updating the number of disconnections that each host experienced in the previous day aggregated by each of the four periods of the day. This process resorts to the monitoring information kept by each node.

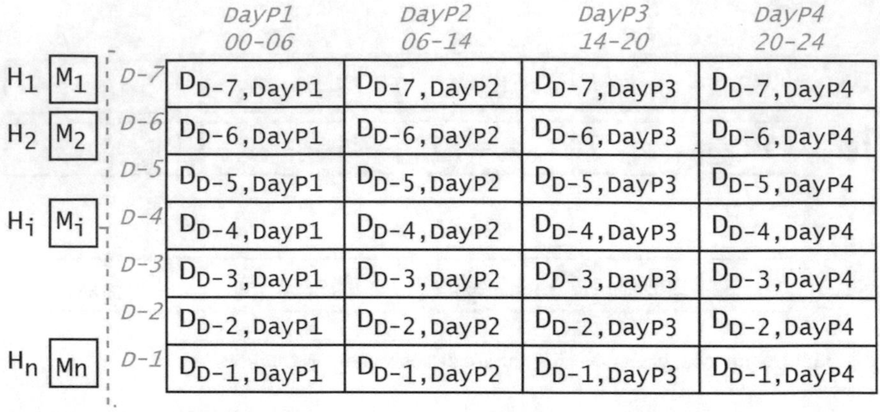

			DayP1 00-06	DayP2 06-14	DayP3 14-20	DayP4 20-24
H_1 $\boxed{M_1}$	$D-7$		$D_{D-7,DayP1}$	$D_{D-7,DayP2}$	$D_{D-7,DayP3}$	$D_{D-7,DayP4}$
H_2 $\boxed{M_2}$	$D-6$		$D_{D-6,DayP1}$	$D_{D-6,DayP2}$	$D_{D-6,DayP3}$	$D_{D-6,DayP4}$
	$D-5$		$D_{D-5,DayP1}$	$D_{D-5,DayP2}$	$D_{D-5,DayP3}$	$D_{D-5,DayP4}$
H_i $\boxed{M_i}$	$D-4$		$D_{D-4,DayP1}$	$D_{D-4,DayP2}$	$D_{D-4,DayP3}$	$D_{D-4,DayP4}$
	$D-3$		$D_{D-3,DayP1}$	$D_{D-3,DayP2}$	$D_{D-3,DayP3}$	$D_{D-3,DayP4}$
	$D-2$		$D_{D-2,DayP1}$	$D_{D-2,DayP2}$	$D_{D-2,DayP3}$	$D_{D-2,DayP4}$
H_n $\boxed{Mn}$	$D-1$		$D_{D-1,DayP1}$	$D_{D-1,DayP2}$	$D_{D-1,DayP3}$	$D_{D-1,DayP4}$

Fig. 11.4 Representation of data structure for storing the disconnection patterns per day period of the last 7 days

Therefore, we define the probability of disconnection of a host h in a given day period as:

$$Pr_{h,p} = normalise(\frac{\sum_{d=D-7}^{D} D_{d,p}}{7})$$

By using this probability we can calculate, employing the algorithm depicted in Fig. 11.5, the connection probability of a certain host in a given period as the inverse probability of disconnection of a node from its initial registration, represented by $t_{registration}$ and the next t_{units} as:

$$Pr_{h,t_{units}} = 1 - (DiscProb(h, t_{units}) * DiscProb(h, -t_{registration}))$$

Disconnection probability results into the estimated Node Quality. This value allows us to have a measurement of the node's stability as part of the Ad-hoc Edge infrastructure for a given time period based on its past behaviour.

11.4   Evaluation

Evaluation has focused on the assessment of the resource availability prediction model previously presented in Sect. 11.3.1 as part of the Admission control mechanism. This validation assesses the ability to predict node behaviour as the probability of a node to stay connected to the Ad-hoc Edge infrastructure in a certain period of the day. This is an essential building block for the defined Ad-hoc Edge Admission control mechanism as the procedure that determines Node

---

Algorithm 1 Disconnection Probability

```
 1: procedure DISCPROB(h, x)
 2:     nPeriods ← numTimePeriods(x)    ▷ Number of time periods within x
 3:     sum ← 0
 4:     if x > 0 then
 5:         for i ← 1 to i = nPeriods do
 6:             p ← period(now() + i)
 7:             sum ← sum + Pr_{h,p}
 8:     else
 9:         for i ← 1 to i = nPeriods do
10:             p ← period(now() − i)
11:             sum ← sum + Pr_{h,p}
        return sum/nPeriods
```

Fig. 11.5 Disconnection probability algorithm

Quality. The overall aim is to evaluate separately this key mechanism that allows us to ensure service placement in more reliable and stable nodes in the dynamic churn-prone environments expected in the Ad-hoc Edge infrastructure. With this purpose we have developed a set of experiments utilising a distributed large-scale resource allocation simulator [5].

This simulator allows us to represent large-scale and high dynamic and heterogeneous environments with diverse rates of node churn and diverse nodes configurations by means of the definition of different kinds of nodes that determine certain quality level (High, Medium and Low) for each node. Nodes of quality High have high probability of re-connection and low probability of disconnection. Nodes defined as Low quality show the opposite behaviour. The distributed large-scale resource allocation simulator is implemented in Java (SE 7).

For all the experiments we have represented three different experimentation scenarios which correspond to three different distributions of kinds of nodes for the experiment, namely the three scenarios used for experimentation are: Most_Nodes_High, Most_Nodes_Medium and Most_Nodes_Low. In each of these three scenarios we assign a certain percentage of nodes of each quality over the total experiment number of nodes. These percentages determine the number of nodes of each node quality (*High, Medium, Low*) that will be present during the execution of the experiment. The configured node type determines the node quality, therefore defines its behaviour during experimentation with regards to number of disconnections and probability of re-connection.

The three defined experimentation scenarios are represented in Table 11.2. To be more precise, in the scenario Most_Nodes_High for each experiment a 60% of nodes are configured of type High, while a 20% of generated nodes correspond to Low and Medium quality nodes. Scenario Most_Nodes_Medium represents an execution environment in which 60% of nodes are of Medium quality and 20% to

Table 11.2 Scenarios: Percentage of nodes of *High*, *Medium* and *Low* quality per scenario

Scenario	Percentage of nodes with *High* quality	Percentage of nodes with *Medium* quality	Percentage of nodes with *Low* quality
Most_Nodes_High	60%	20%	20%
Most_Nodes_Medium	20%	60%	20%
Most_Nodes_Low	20%	20%	60%

are of High and Low quality. Similarly, Most_Nodes_Low account of a 60% of Low quality nodes and 20% of High and Medium nodes quality.

Attempting to fully assess the impact of scale both in terms of nodes and services we have performed the experimentation the execution of up to 200, 400, 600, 800 and 1000 services over 100, 200, 300, 400 and 500 nodes of the three different experimentation scenarios described before. The number of nodes present in each experiment of each node type is determined by the percentages over the total number of nodes defined in each execution scenario (Most_Nodes_High, Most_Nodes_Medium and Most_Nodes_Low). All executed services have been constructed with the same configuration, with two replicated components. Overall, the execution of these different service and node combinations have resulted in the execution of 75 experiments. The findings of this experimentation have been summarised in the following subsections.

11.4.1   Node Quality

Figures 11.6, 11.7, and 11.8 exhibit per each of the three experimentation scenarios (Most_Nodes_High, Most_Nodes_Medium and Most_Nodes_Low) the total number of nodes created by the experiment of nodes of each node quality (Number of nodes per Quality), the number of disconnections of each node quality (Disconnections per Quality) and the time each type of node has been connected during for the execution of 600 concurrent services (Connection Time per Quality).

More specifically each figure represents per each scenario (Most_Nodes_High, Most_Nodes_Medium and Most_Nodes_Low) in the first row Number of Nodes, the actual number of nodes of each quality type generated by the simulator in each of the three defined nodes qualities (High, Medium and Low) when creating environments of 100–500 nodes. For instance, in the experiment which corresponds to scenario Most_Nodes_High with 500 nodes, 300 nodes are created of quality High, this means these nodes have low probability of disconnection and high probability of re-connection. At the same time, additional 20% of total experiment nodes (100 nodes) are created with qualities Low and Medium, exposing their corresponding connection and re-connection patterns. This behaviour is observable in the number of disconnections of nodes per quality (Disconnections per Quality, second row) and evidenced the overall connection time (Connection Time, third row) this node quality presents in the experiment.

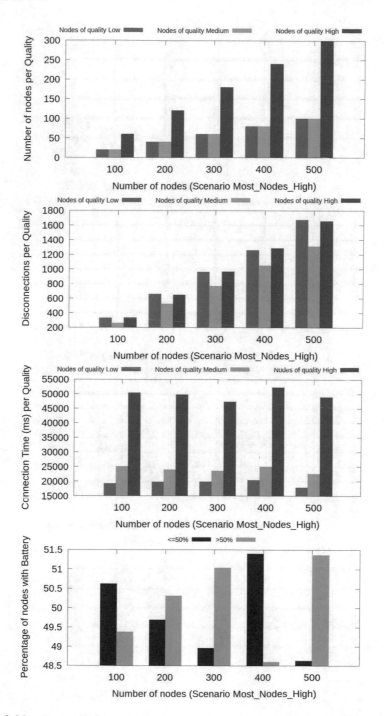

Fig. 11.6 Most_Nodes_High experimentation scenario

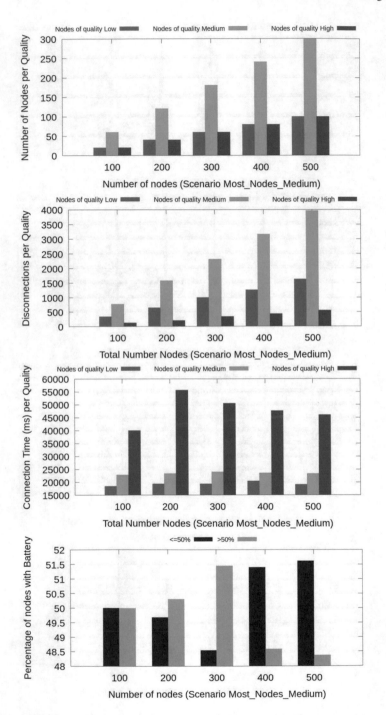

Fig. 11.7 Most_Nodes_Medium experimentation scenario

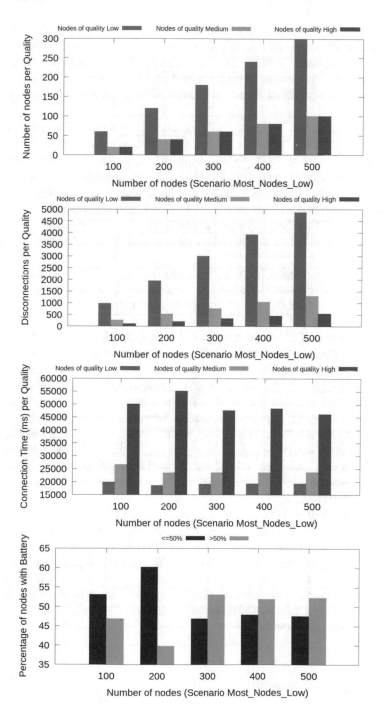

Fig. 11.8 Most_Nodes_Low experimentation scenario

Additionally, Figs. 11.6, 11.7, and 11.8 display in the bottom row the values of battery level, a dynamic node characteristic defined in our IoT Edge Device parameters presented in Table 11.1 and Sect. 10.2 classification used in these experiments. As "Percentage of Nodes with Battery" we represent number of nodes with average battery level below and above 50% created in the corresponding scenario.

Overall, Figs. 11.6, 11.7, and 11.8 are meant for representing the execution environment generated for each of the three defined experimentation scenarios which was used for the Node Quality experiments, as the measure that allows us to assess the stability of a node. In this execution environment, we aim to represent the different nodes behaviours in each scenario, as well as, the heterogeneity on the characteristics of nodes taking part in the Ad-hoc Edge infrastructure.

Relying on the previously presented scenarios, tests performed with the execution of 600 services over 100–500 nodes obtain nodes qualities aligned to the defined nodes behaviours.

Node quality represent the value between 0 and 1 which is obtained by the resource availability prediction model as calculation of its disconnection probability considering node behaviour with regards to connections and disconnections, as introduced in Sect. 11.3.1.

Results obtained in these tests are depicted in Fig. 11.9. In the scenario Most_Nodes_High, nodes obtain Node Qualities values between 0.86 and 0.90 while these qualities descend to values that range among 0.80 and 0.88 in for the scenario Most_Nodes_Medium (with 60% presence of medium quality nodes), and among 0.77 and 0.82 for the high presence of low-quality nodes in scenario Most_Nodes_Low. It is important to note that the performed experimentation shows for 600 services execution increments of Node Quality of percentages among 3 and 5 for scenarios Most_Nodes_High, Most_Nodes_Medium and Most_Nodes_Low, however keeping coherent values for probabilities of disconnection and its associated Node Quality independently of the number of nodes being employed in the experiment.

This assessment is further demonstrated in the analysis of the performance of obtained average Node Quality values by generalising services' execution figures from 600 services to the execution of 200–1000 services over 100–500 nodes (Fig. 11.10) for the three defined scenarios. We can observe once more that both node scale and services scale do not influence the obtained values of Node Quality. Consequently, we conclude that Node Quality is solely determined by the specific node characteristics and its historical behaviour concerning connection and disconnection to the system.

11.4.2   Service Quality

The quality of a Service is assessed by the employed large scale simulation environment as the sum of the Node Quality values of the different nodes that

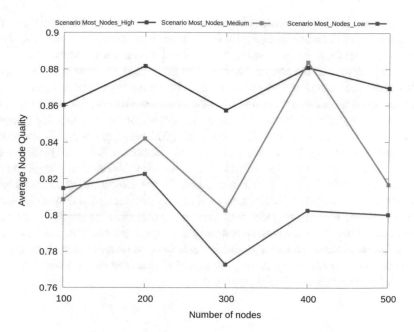

Fig. 11.9 Nodes Quality per scenario

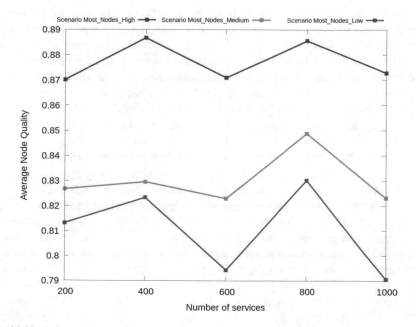

Fig. 11.10 Average Nodes Quality in 100–500 Nodes executing 200–1000 services

execute a service together with normalised values for nodes characteristics. The configuration of Ad-hoc Edge experimentation has considered the execution of two replicas of each service representing two identical service components.

In addition to this, the assessed Service Quality takes into account the characteristics of the normalised values per each node for computing capacity, memory, and available disk, available upload and download connectivity speed and battery level.

The values gathered during this experimentation for Service Quality obtained on the execution of 200, 400, 600, 800 and 1000 services over 100–500 nodes are illustrated in Fig. 11.11. We observe that maximum Service Quality value is collected on the execution of 1000 services over 500 nodes accounting for 4.5 and minimum values of 2.2 are found in the execution of services with execution scenario Most_Nodes_Low, with more presence of low quality nodes. This behaviour is again aligned with previous conclusions on Node Quality and allows us to infer that based on the results of our experimentation the presented Ad-hoc Edge Resource management and its associated mechanism for Node Quality prediction is adequate for managing the expected scale and heterogeneity expected in such dynamic and distributed environment.

11.5   Related Works

Resource Availability prediction has been an area previously studied in Contributory communities and Volunteer Computing. These computing systems have the objective of taking advantage of spare compute capacity of desktop computers at home or offices for individual resources or for groups of them. In order to do so, they take into account desktop computers, hosts, usage patterns in terms of connections and disconnections. Differently, devices tackled in the context of Ad-hoc Edge Cloud are IoT Edge devices. IoT Edge devices probability of node churn require that the mechanisms to predict IoT device node availability evolve in order to cope with higher dynamicity rates on resource availability, as well as, to define mechanism that permit us to discern usage patterns in IoT Edge devices environment.

To elaborate on this topic, in the context of volunteer computing [5] provides a multi-criteria optimisation strategy for selection of reliable nodes in large scale systems based on a Multi Criteria Biased Randomized method. Panadero et al. [5] prediction of node availability capitalises on the behaviour of nodes regarding the connections and disconnections over the past 4 weeks to calculate the probability of disconnection of a node in a given weekday. Along these lines nonetheless using a different granularity level for representing the availability of a host [18, 19] employs the availability of the hosts per hour for the previous week to represent resource availability. These two papers had available existing traces of 11,000 hosts in SETI@HOME collected by means of the instrumentation of BOINC server during 7 months period [19]. This aspect has allowed for the understanding of the devices' usage patterns, determining day of week and hour of week hosts connection patterns for the constituent hosts in these Contributed Desktop Grids environments.

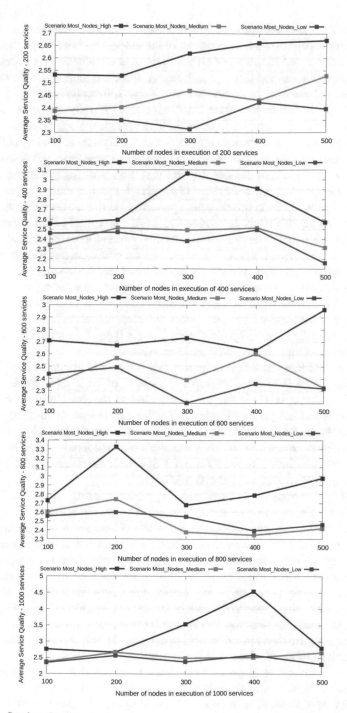

Fig. 11.11 Services Quality per scenario

Our work in Ad-hoc Edge Cloud environment advances these previous works in Desktop Grids and Volunteer computing in the time granularity employed to build the model, elaborated in matter of weeks in these environments and being evolved to day periods for Ad-hoc Edge Clouds, as we foresee a more dynamic behaviour of complex IoT devices. In addition, a significant differentiation among resource availability prediction in Volunteer Computing and IoT Edge environments is the availability of data that permits to understand the resource usage patterns.

The fact that IoT Edge devices are not yet so widely spread hinders at this stage the availability of data to be analysed to determine connection and disconnection patterns for these kinds of devices. In the interest of overcoming these difficulties, we have extrapolated the behaviour of available specific edge devices, mobile phones, and draw on its common usage patterns in order to describe our resource availability model. This has determined us to define a mechanism which instead of focusing on connection and disconnection patterns over weekdays we have employed the resource historical behaviour over four different day periods in a week therefore being capable of providing probability of node disconnection for certain day hours instead of week days in volunteer computing. Moreover, we understand that in the long term, as IoT and Edge deployments become more widely available and data on devices usage patterns is accessible, this model could be further refined in order to consider even the specific behaviour per type of complex IoT Device and could be tailored for particular IoT usage scenarios.

In the area of Fog and Edge computing scheduling and placement, only recently some works have started to envelop the aspects of edge node availability and churn. We understand this is due to the fact that so far typically Edge computing environments are not yet considering IoT Edge devices as appropriate execution environments for Edge service execution. Therefore, their dynamic behaviour in which this book focuses on is yet generally not considered. Some examples of papers which take into consideration IoT Edge device resource availability issues and heterogeneity aspects are presented below.

Broggi [20] recognises that IoT and Fog nodes mobility and dynamicity have not yet been addressed to a greater extent and acknowledges the emerging need of addressing application placement adapted to the phenomenon of node instabilities at the Edge, as elaborated by Ad-hoc Edge Cloud admission control mechanism. Ad-hoc Edge Cloud Admission Control processes selects from the existing pool of resources in a determined point in time, those assessed to be the existing set of resources which better serve the service execution request. This mechanism establishes a two step process in which resources are first filtered according to their dynamic and static features considering the service execution needs. Results of the filtering process are then ranked according to assessed Node Quality which assesses the probability of an IoT Edge Device to continue to be part of the Ad-hoc Edge Infrastructure for a certain period time. Therefore, Admission control in Ad-hoc Edge Cloud addresses existing challenges in relation to resource instability, dynamic availability and probability of node churn identified by Broggi as application placement challenges.

Bittencourt et al. [21] introduces the concept of mobility in the Edge infrastructure formulating it as User mobility. It studies how user mobility affects the demand that has to be served from Edge infrastructures, to optimise user application provision bringing it closer to the user. In this context, [21] still considers Edge infrastructures as stationary environments, therefore not yet taking into account the challenges that instability on Edge resource availability can bring to scheduling in Edge infrastructures.

Differently, [22] is one of the few examples that at this stage contemplates uncertainty of Edge node availability in fog infrastructure management in a similar approach than Ad-hoc Edge Cloud. It constructs a centralised environment that the users contact in order to execute services in the fog infrastructure comprised of several fog nodes for which a predefined availability rate has been calculated. It formulates an Integer Program to indicate if a user has to send a service to one of the Edge nodes and the probability of failure of the service execution is used as QoS measurement. Two main aspects differentiate the Ad-hoc Edge Cloud approach and this paper: first of all, the consideration of a central decision system; and secondly, our view on the need of formulating resource availability based on the Edge devices' current status, given all dynamic aspects which influence it.

Mouradian et al. [23] develops on the placement of Virtual Network Functions in Edge infrastructure nodes for scenarios in which fog nodes are mobile. It models the location of a fog node as Random Waypoint Model formulating among others movement velocity and probabilities for nodes to be static and paused. While the problem approach in this paper is different and complementary to Ad-hoc Edge Cloud, it assesses that higher mobility probabilities drive to lower qualities of service similarly to our conclusions.

Lera [24] elaborates in a Service placement policy that takes into account the availability for complex services composed by multiple service components as addressed by Ad-hoc Edge Cloud. This study tackles the node availability system following a completely different approach to Ad-hoc Edge computing. It creates the concept of a community of nodes, as a set of mutually- interconnected devices. By deploying services to devices in communities it aims to avoid service failure generated by the failure of a specific node, however adding the need for an additional management layer at a community level. In this way, it avoids directly taking the issues raised by probability of node churn addressed in Ad-hoc Edge Clouds by relying on node redundancy to ensure service availability.

The consideration of Edge node heterogeneity in combination to user mobility is addressed in [25] which presents a scheduling mechanism for privacy constrained real-time jobs in Edge micro data centres. Heterogeneity in this work is considered at the level of the different compute capacities available on each node, however no concrete formulation on how to define these characteristics is provided permitting the comparison to the approach based on device characteristics and processor architectures (CPU, GPU, TPU, FPGA) developed in this Ad-hoc Edge Cloud.

11.6   Conclusions

This chapter has elaborated on a Service Placement and Admission control mechanism which takes into consideration the specifics in terms of dynamic availability present in Ad-hoc Edge Clouds. As part of this work we have defined and validated a cognitive mechanism for prediction of resource availability based on past behaviour.

This evaluation reveals that node behaviour concerning connection and disconnection is crucial for the overall performance of services provisioned by the infrastructure, as we intuitively understood.

Also, at this stage, the data we could use to develop our availability prediction model relates to the behaviour of mobile devices. This fact results from the absence of reports on usage patterns of a diversity of complex IoT devices, such as drones, robots and connected cars. We understand that the diversity of IoT devices and different usage contexts of these devices will facilitate the future definitions of more specific prediction models adjusted to the diversities of the common behaviour of additional IoT devices in concrete usage scenarios.

Furthermore, it is important to notice, that in this chapter we have focused on the analysis of the computational part of decentralised cloud management however we acknowledge that a multitude of concerns remains to be explored both at network, security, and data storage levels.

References

1. Konstanteli, K., Cucinotta, T., Psychas, K., & Varvarigou, T. (2012). Admission control for elastic cloud services. In *Proceedings of the 2012 IEEE Fifth International Conference on Cloud Computing* (pp. 41–48). https://doi.org/10.1109/CLOUD.2012.63
2. Bagchi, S. (2014, 7). Admission control and scheduling of remote processes in loosely-coupled distributed systems. *Computers and Electrical Engineering, 40*, 1666–1682.
3. Chang, D., Xu, G., Hu, L., & Yang, K. (2013). A network-aware virtual machine placement algorithm in mobile cloud computing environment. In *2013 IEEE Wireless Communications and Networking Conference Workshops, WCNCW 2013* (pp. 117–121).
4. Park, J., Yu, H., Chung, K., & Lee, E. (2011, 3). Markov chain based monitoring service for fault tolerance in mobile cloud computing. In *2011 IEEE Workshops of International Conference on Advanced Information Networking and Applications* (pp. 520–525). http://ieeexplore.ieee.org/lpdocs/epic03/wrapper.htm?arnumber=5763554
5. Panadero, J., de Armas, J., Serra, X., & Marquès, J. M. (2018). Multi criteria biased randomized method for resource allocation in distributed systems: Application in a volunteer computing system. *Future Generation Computer Systems, 82*, 29–40. https://doi.org/10.1016/j.future.2017.11.039
6. Reinfurt, L., Breitenbücher, U., Falkenthal, M., Leymann, F., & Riegg, A. (2016). Internet of Things patterns. In *Proceedings of the 21st European Conference on Pattern Languages of Programs*. https://doi.org/10.1145/3011784.3011789
7. Mousavi, N., Aksanli, B., Akyurek, A., & Rosing, T. (2017). Accuracy-resource tradeoff for edge devices in Internet of Things. In *2017 IEEE International Conference on Pervasive Computing and Communications Workshops, PerCom Workshops 2017* (pp. 581–586).

8. Juan Ferrer, A., Marquès, J. M., & Jorba, J. (2019). Towards the decentralised cloud: Survey on approaches and challenges for mobile, ad hoc, and edge computing. *ACM Computing Surveys*, *51*(6). https://doi.org/10.1145/3243929

9. Ghosh, R., Trivedi, K. S., Naik, V. K., & Kim, D. S. (2010, 12). End-to-end performability analysis for infrastructure-as-a-service cloud: An interacting stochastic models approach. In *2010 IEEE 16th Pacific Rim International Symposium on Dependable Computing* (pp. 125–132). http://ieeexplore.ieee.org/lpdocs/epic03/wrapper.htm?arnumber=5703236

10. *Kubernetes pod overview*. (2022). Retrieved May 26, 2022, from https://kubernetes.io/docs/concepts/workloads/pods/pod-overview/

11. *Amazon web services CloudFormation*. (2022). Retrieved May 26, 2022, from https://aws.amazon.com/cloudformation/

12. Terraform.org. (2022). *Terraform*. Retrieved May 26, 2022, from https://www.terraform.io/

13. Poyraz, E., & Memik, G. (2016). Analyzing power consumption and characterizing user activities on smartwatches: Summary. In *Proceedings of the 2016 IEEE International Symposium on Workload Characterization, IISWC 2016* (pp. 219–220).

14. Shye, A., Scholbrock, B., Memik, G., & Dinda, P. (2010, 6). Characterizing and modeling user activity on smartphones: Summary. *ACM SIGMETRICS Performance Evaluation Review*, *38*, 375–376. https://doi.org/10.1145/1811099.1811094

15. Bhih, A., Johnson, P., & Randles, M. (2016). Diversity in smartphone usage. In *Proceedings of the 17th International Conference on Computer Systems and Technologies 2016* (pp. 81–88). https://doi.org/10.1145/2983468.2983496

16. Van Canneyt, S., Bron, M., Lalmas, M., & Haines, A. (2019). Describing patterns and disruptions in large scale mobile app usage data. In *26th International World Wide Web Conference 2017, WWW 2017 Companion* (pp. 1579–1584). http://dl.acm.org/citation.cfm?doid=3041021.3051113

17. Xu, Q., Erman, J., Gerber, A., Mao, Z., Pang, J., & Venkataraman, S. (2011). Identifying diverse usage behaviors of smartphone apps. In *Proceedings of the 2011 ACM SIGCOMM Conference on Internet Measurement Conference* (pp. 329–344). https://doi.org/10.1145/2068816.2068847

18. Lázaro, D., Kondo, D., & Marquès, J. (2012). Long-term availability prediction for groups of volunteer resources. *Journal of Parallel and Distributed Computing*, *72*, 281–296. https://doi.org/10.1016/j.jpdc.2011.10.007

19. Kondo, D., Andrzejak, A., & Anderson, D. (2008). On correlated availability in internet-distributed systems. In *Proceedings of the 2008 9th IEEE/ACM International Conference on Grid Computing* (pp. 276–283). https://doi.org/10.1109/GRID.2008.4662809

20. Brogi, A., Forti, S., Guerrero, C., & Lera, I. (2020). How to place your apps in the fog: State of the art and open challenges. *Software: Practice and Experience*, *50*, 719–740. https://onlinelibrary.wiley.com/doi/abs/10.1002/spe.2766

21. Bittencourt, L., Diaz-Montes, J., Buyya, R., Rana, O., & Parashar, M. (2017). Mobility-aware application scheduling in fog computing. *IEEE Cloud Computing*, *4*, 26–35.

22. Daneshfar, N., Pappas, N., Polishchuk, V., & Angelakis, V. (2019). Service allocation in a mobile fog infrastructure under availability and QoS constraints. In *2018 IEEE Global Communications Conference, GLOBECOM 2018 - Proceedings* (pp. 1–6).

23. Mouradian, C., Kianpisheh, S., Abu-Lebdeh, M., Ebrahimnezhad, F., Jahromi, N., & Glitho, R. (2019). Application component placement in NFV-based hybrid cloud/fog systems with mobile fog nodes. *IEEE Journal on Selected Areas in Communications*, *37*, 1130–1143 (2019)

24. Lera, I., Guerrero, C., & Juiz, C. (2019). Availability-aware service placement policy in fog computing based on graph partitions. *IEEE Internet of Things Journal*, *6*, 3641–3651.

25. Fizza, K., Auluck, N., Rana, O., & Bittencourt, L. (2018). PASHE: Privacy aware scheduling in a heterogeneous fog environment. In *Proceedings - 2018 IEEE 6th International Conference on Future Internet of Things and Cloud, FiCloud 2018* (pp. 333–340).

Part III
Looking Ahead, Next Steps for Ad-hoc Edge Clouds and Swarm Computing Realization

The main idea which has driven the development of this book is the perception that computing is now commonly spread outside the Data Centres boundaries.

Initially driven by the popularisation of smartphones, computing is now available everywhere in a myriad of connected devices, and accessible at the palm of our hands in our last generation phones, in our speakers, fridges, in our TV, to cite some examples. Considering the increasing compute demands we observe in multitude of situations in our daily life today, it is presumed as an unjustifiable wastage to only use compute capacity in all kinds of devices as gateway to access services offered from data centre clouds.

This initial reflection has been increasingly conceded by the rapid development of IoT, Cloud and AI technologies. First by observing how Internet of Things development is expanding at a significant rapid pace, making the figures on the expected number of connected devices increment year after year. In addition, Internet of Things proliferation now complements growth of smartphones, and is facilitating to further distribute computing elements at the Edge of the network in large number of locations in environments counting on dedicated Edge compute units to serve nearby IoT technology deployments.

More recently, we can witness how increasingly IoT devices are surpassing initial capabilities focused on just sensing, to gain significant sophistication in the computational power they are today able to carry. This is making that the limits initially established in Edge computing among the IoT and Edge devices are today blurring, making it possible to pack in a single device sensing and compute capacities, thanks to the development of micro-processor technologies owing to Moore's law.

These complex IoT Edge devices, such as robots and autonomous vehicles, can be viewed as mobile devices which provide complex aggregations of computing and storage resources together with diverse and heterogeneous sensors and actuators which all together implement a cognitive loop.

According to predictions these devices will need to become better, faster and cheaper. Producers will soon be under pressure to provide complex behaviours, cognitive capabilities and skills at competitive costs, while increasing on-board computation and storage of IoT Edge Compute devices will raise their costs, increase energy demand and reduce their autonomy.

The self-contained and self-sustaining nature of these novel IoT Edge resources combined with their size and energy harvesting constrains will require of novel computing and communication architectures beyond state of the art today.

A caveat has to be made in relation to Moore's law development. For the last few decades, overcoming similar challenges has always relied on the application of Moore's law.

This has allowed producing ever better and capable hardware. Hardware manufacturers are increasingly encountering more difficulties in producing ever miniaturised low-power computing units which are cheaper and faster. This does not probably mean that computing progress will suddenly stall, but rather it can affect the nature of that progress. The computing progress could be progressively changing to approaches which take better advantage of available resources while coping with the necessary balance among resources in high demand: computing and energy.

In this book we have addressed some of the challenges these expected changes will bring to the development of Edge computing technologies by developing the concept of Ad-hoc Edge Clouds and advancing an architecture model for its implementation. This architectural approach represents a significant breakthrough to initial Edge computing developments concentrated in providing low latency compute environments for which IoT devices are solely considered as data sources. Ad-hoc Edge Cloud is a distributed and decentralised Edge computing system dynamically formed out of IoT Edge computing resources, which aims to exploit increasingly available compute capacity at the Edge.

In addition, we have deeply analysed the particularities of IoT Edge devices which constitute this infrastructure. IoT Edge devices pose explicit challenges to resource and service management in this context especially due to heterogeneity, dynamicity, and volatility of resources, resulting in the probability of node churn. We have analysed these specific issues in two main contexts: At the level of Resource management, elaborating on the mechanisms for Ad-hoc Edge Cluster formation and management; in relation to Admission control and Service placement processes, presenting an Admission Control mechanism and an associated resource availability prediction model driven by the needs exposed by dynamic behaviour of participant IoT Edge devices.

Beyond the proposed work in this book, the chapter in this part aims at elaborating in future research areas and challenges in the context of Ad-hoc Edge Cloud architectures and Swarm computing.

Chapter 12
Next Steps for Ad-hoc Edge Cloud and Swarm Computing Realization

12.1 Edge Computing Research Areas

12.1.1 Heterogeneity Exploitation and New Hardware Architectures: Neuromorphic Edge Computing

OpenAI reveals that "the amount of compute used in the largest AI training runs has been increasing exponentially with a 3.4-month doubling time since 2012" [1]. Together with the emergence of Edge computing, there is the identified requirement to execute an increasing number of these processes at the Edge. With this purpose, a number of specialised devices and chipsets have been released to the market bringing to the Edge the power of accelerators. Some notable examples are Intel Movidius, NVIDIA's Jetson systems and Google TPUs. In this context, providing appropriated Edge virtualisation and management tools which support the proper exploitation of GPUs and other accelerators is of paramount importance, moreover due to the constrained nature of Edge resources. However, this might be insufficient in the long term to cope with all AI and other compute demands which are expected to require tremendous computational power at a stringent power budget at the Edge. The emergence of novel compute architectures specialised in AI execution, such as neuromorphic architectures, are nowadays seen as the mechanism to cope with these demands. Developments in this area are required to range from specific secure and low-power hardware micro-processors to software tools which permit to fully benefit from these novel hardware features.

12.1.2 Energy Efficiency Optimisation

Sustainability and Energy efficiency are increasingly becoming critical aspects to analyse in each and every technology. Studies such as Lean ICT estimate that

© The Author(s), under exclusive license to Springer Nature Switzerland AG 2023
A. Juan Ferrer, *Beyond Edge Computing*, https://doi.org/10.1007/978-3-031-23344-9_12

"Watching a video online on the Cloud for 10 minutes results in the electricity consumption equivalent to the consumption of a smartphone over 10 days" [2]. The optimisation of energy consumption in large Data Centres, has been a large area of development in the last decade and has achieved important advances like the definition of PUE and DCiE metrics [3]. However, the majority of these extensions are concentrated only on the data centre optimisation. The heterogeneity of devices capable of offering Edge services raises the need to reconsider the applicability of consolidated energy efficiency metrics in data centres, due to the existence of Edge devices which do not require of i.e. cooling systems. Moreover, the battery limitations of other of these devices, together with the demonstrated impact of network transmission in energy consumption calls for focused energy efficiency and sustainability focused research in the Edge. Additional research which analyses the potential energy efficiency and sustainability gains derived from the use of optimised novel hardware architectures together with the use of energy-aware compute, network and memory resource management systems as end-to-end frameworks are critical for future progress across the Edge to Cloud compute continuum.

12.1.3 Multi-Level Edge

Edge Server approaches are the ones which consider the Edge environment a device, labelled as server which delivers computing and storage capacities to a series of Edge sensors and other resource poorer devices that are connected to it in a locally close environment. These Edge servers can be represented by devices ranging from servers to low-cost compute boards, likewise for devices such as connected cars, network equipment, or other rich smart IoT devices, on condition they provide a minimum computing and storage capacity. Edge Server approaches are the ones we encounter today in commercial products such as Amazon Greengrass, and Azure IoT Edge. The individual management of Edge servers is foreseen as cumbersome, as Edge computing deployments go beyond piloting stages and are widely deployed. As Multi-level Edge, we name approaches which consider sets of jointly coordinated Edge server devices. This clustered approach could be evaluated at diverse granularity levels in view of the nature of the proposed scenario and the compute/storage requirements. An exemplification of the concept could be performed in a smart home scenario considering that all complex enough devices, servers, aggregate their capacity to provide compute/storage capacities to other more resource constrained home appliances. Beyond that, we anticipate the demand for even more complex compute structures in Hierarchical Edge organisations which consider layered configurations of Edge clusters. The layered approach could be construed according to diverse criteria which focus on increasingly resources capabilities or location (aggregating at diverse levels, i.e., resources at home, neighbourhood, and smart city).

12.1.4   Edge Intelligence

As previously mentioned, Edge computing is presently valued as an essential element for AI democratisation, employed as an enabler for embedding AI into a wide diversity of objects and application scenarios while providing the advantages of affordability and proximity to the user. In this context, Edge intelligence refers to the ability of exploiting all computing continuum from the Edge to the Cloud for benefit of AI workloads. While execution of AI workloads at the Edge is the driver for the growing hardware heterogeneity at the Edge, there are a number of research challenges still to be explored in relation to AI execution and training at the Edge. These include among others, mechanisms and tools to enable near real-time and real-time execution, specific QoS management as well as enhanced tools and mechanisms for Edge to Cloud federated learning.

12.1.5   Data Management

Data intensive applications have been the key motivation spreading Edge computing need. Novel systems able to manage data scattered on an Edge heterogeneous and distributed environment needs to deal with the intricacies of the underlying complex infrastructure composed by sophisticated IoT Edge devices, sensors, as well as dedicated Edge computing nodes. Conversely, developers must focus on establishing the relevant data to keep, their format and quality, and how to process it in a fully defined data lifecycle. This process should avoid details concerning the method to gather data and include the location to store or process it. In addition to these, attention has to be paid to security, privacy and legal data movement constraints. Key research areas in this context are the definition of strategies and tools which cover the complete data lifecycle (including historian, archiving, QoS on data loss), to maximise the data utility associated with the managed data, considering aspects related to the data privacy, constraints on data formats and storage capacity and reliability, applicable regulations and legislation.

12.1.6   Edge Management

Resource heterogeneity, scalability, fault tolerance, reliability and performance are service management aspects still pending in Edge computing. These are of specific interest due to the nature of devices and their volatility in addition to this need of including supplementary aspects for QoS management, scalability and management of heterogeneity in processors. Resiliency is also a core characteristic required for Edge computing set-ups, notably for mission critical IoT applications which present near and real time execution constraints. There is an overall need for these applications to continue providing their services from the Edge even when network links to Cloud are inoperative or seriously overloaded. Diverse techniques are being studied to provide lack of connectivity resilience capability, among them fault tolerance systems across diverse Edge installations in a close location and techniques for unconnected Edge limited operation. At the same time workload or task scheduling in Edge computing has to take into account specificities of the Edge devices, such as energy constraints and QoS (usually in terms of latency optimisation). Similarly, encapsulation of edge workloads on top of Edge systems will have to take an Infrastructure as Code approach and accommodate diverse workload typologies as well as the different processors types where these workloads can be computed, for which the final encapsulation solution may vary. Many of today's approaches to workload management in Edge computing are based on Docker. This technological approach offers the advantage of having a common technology context with existing Cloud computing developments; however, it limits its applicability devices equipped with general purpose OS capable of supporting this technology. At the same time, several more lightweight virtualisation technologies have recently been released, such as Unikernels and micro-containers. In this context, advanced lightweight compute containers can be the enabler technology which will allow the execution of self-contained, purpose-specific services which specifically target only certain functions needed at the edge in more resource constrained devices.

12.1.7 Computing Continuum Exploration

Current status of Edge computing developments in commercial cloud providers relies on specific vendor solutions which directly connect Edge devices with their specific Cloud offerings. These developments bring closed Edge to Cloud solutions which motivate vendor lock-in concerns. In order to facilitate general interoperability among Edge computing technologies and cloud technologies, new standards and tools have to emerge to manage the expected scale of edge set-ups and facilitate the interoperability with diverse clouds, as well as Edge devices. In addition, the notion of a compute continuum which embraces Edge deployments with a variety of Cloud offerings—denominated Swarm computing—requires mechanisms to help optimise resource utilisation and find the best location to execute a workload, enabled by intelligent off-loading schemes as well as simple and transparent potability among Edge and Cloud resource types and models. Movement towards hyper distribution of computing will have to enable edge and cloud computing continuum scenarios to consider interoperability, portability, elasticity, self-organisation, self-management and self-healing across many and heterogeneous resources in edge clouds, private enterprise clouds, aggregated cloud models and large Cloud set-ups. Orchestration and placement problems in this context require considering heterogeneity and trade-offs among consistency, reliability, availability, cost and performance. These challenges are explored in the upcoming Swarm Computing section.

12.2 Swarm Computing Research Areas

12.2.1 Swarm Management Techniques

Swarm intelligence refers to the combined behaviour of decentralised, massively distributed and self-organised systems. With the number of IoT/Edge devices foreseen to achieve unprecedented figures and making the consideration that many of these individual devices will have very limited compute capabilities, the idea of Swarm management arises. In compute Swarms, each limited devices (resources) will be complimented by connection to other objects in a community, therefore creating dynamic eco-systems which encompass cyber-physical devices, edge and clouds, each of these adding to the collective capability and insight. Swarm computing aims at enabling service provisioning to shift from the existing pre-defined and fixed orientation to a pure collaborative, on-demand and opportunistic approach. In this approach, applications need to rely on dynamic, limited, distributed resources, which are governed under different domains and may potentially have conflicting interests. This approach aims to exploit all available highly heterogeneous resources (i.e. edge, clouds, communicating objects, sensors and smart devices) procurable at the Edge in order to provide a decentralised service-based environment. It is developed with the purpose of collecting, dynamically creating and managing these massive, diverse, unconnected and highly distributed resources. Swarm distributed service networks are envisaged as opportunistic (created on-the-fly) in order to respond to a specific need, coordinated in an open and distributed self-* runtime model. In this context, business models which regulate the collaboration of different entities in the swam networks will be considered jointly with the definition of the required mechanisms that incentivise participation. Other aspects part of the equation include reservation, adaptive selection, conflict resolution. Techniques to handle reliability and fault tolerance to resource volatility introduced by real-world dynamics should be developed to enable efficient and reliable service provision. To this end, mechanisms based on Distributed Ledgers and P2P systems will require further exploration.

12.2.2 Resource Discovery

Overall, location is typically seen in Edge computing works as the one of the method which facilitates latency enhancement and considers pre-defined discovered resources. However, only a few works so far have explored the potential origin of the mechanisms which will permit the determination of the physical location of resources. These mechanisms are the networking techniques which could allow the discovery of the resources available in a certain location. In addition, these mechanisms could include protection techniques to ensure protected access, as well as tools to determine how execution zones and associate clusters of diverse granularities in swarm computing could be created in an automated manner.

12.2.3   Self-management and Autonomic Systems

Autonomic computing advocates for computing systems which can implement self-management automatically. In order to do so, compute resources need to: self-configure, be able to understand their configuration with minimal human intervention; develop self-awareness by recognising environment changes; perform self-healing, take the adequate remedial actions automatically and by configuration; and self-protect, reacting automatedly to performance and security risks. The use of cognitive and machine learning techniques for autonomic resource and overall swarm infrastructure management in Swarm computing shows great potential for reliable resource provisioning in the areas such as workload prediction, scheduling, elasticity and predictive QoS. This aspect together with swarms' decentralised deployments will require evolving existing mechanisms for edge, cloud and multi-cloud management towards autonomic management systems which consider self-management and self-healing across this diversity of environments and copes with requirements on reliability and extreme scalability. As a peer-to-peer approach, blockchains have gained a lot of interest in the recent years and have shown to be highly available, tamper-proof and provide non-repudiation. Current research has shown that blockchain is a suitable approach for value transfer between IoT devices in untrusted, open environments. Specific research is paramount for studying the use blockchains for registry and smart contracts in Swarms. In current blockchains, all involved endpoints have to be known for broadcasts and confirmations. In Swarm Computing it would be needed to extend this notion and rely on efforts which create highly scalable blockchains, clustered approaches and replication mechanisms.

12.2.4   Bio Inspired Optimisation Techniques

Bio-inspired optimisation algorithms, known also as Swarm Intelligence, are recognised as a machine learning tool which help find optimal solutions to complex problems in engineering, scientific, medical and space contexts. Our intention is to explore the use of Swarm Intelligence techniques in relation to the previously presented Swarm computing research areas. Swarm intelligence is developed as a tactic to control and optimise many types of distributed systems. The idea is to use resilient, decentralised, self-organised methods which are derived from the mechanisms a diversity of animals employ for their social interactions. These techniques have been successfully employed for the coordination of robotic swarms and handling of production system. A diversity of these bio-inspired optimisation techniques can be found in the existing literature. Among them we highlight

Genetic Algorithms, Ant Colony Optimisation, Particle Swarm Optimisation and Artificial Bee Colony optimisation. It is important to note that swarm computing instances are conceived as fully decentralised environments guided by the principle of subsidiarity of intelligence, meaning that optimal decision-making is intended to be taken at lowest suitable level. Intelligence and knowledge about the overall status of the swarm is decentralised and spread across diverse cooperating instances, which act as autonomous entities and can result in conflicting decision-making. Developing the swarm computing concept in a successful way necessitates of a deep analysis and validation how these diverse techniques can be applied to swarm computing lifecycle phases (from how swarm computing instances are created, purposed, operated, reformulated and decommissioned) and taking into account cooperation principles among participating instances as well as mechanisms for knowledge acquisition and transfer.

References

1. *OpenAI, AI and Compute.* https://openai.com/blog/aiandcompute/
2. *The Shift project, Lean ICT: Towards digital sobriety.* https://theshiftproject.org/wpcontent/uploads/2019/03/LeanICTReport_The-Shift-Project_2019.pdf
3. *DCIM Support, About PUE and DCiE.* https://dcimsupport.ecostruxureit.com/hc/enus/articles/360039292493AboutPUEandDCiE

Printed in the United States
by Baker & Taylor Publisher Services